Date Loaned

The Belles-Lettres Series

SECTION IV
LITERARY CRITICISM AND CRITICAL THEORY

GENERAL EDITOR
CHARLES HAROLD HERFORD, Litt.D.
PROFESSOR OF THE ENGLISH LANGUAGE AND LITERATURE
UNIVERSITY OF MANCHESTER

ESSAYS
AND CRITICISMS

BY

THOMAS GRAY

EDITED WITH INTRODUCTION AND NOTES

BY

CLARK SUTHERLAND NORTHUP, Ph.D.

ASSISTANT PROFESSOR OF THE ENGLISH LANGUAGE AND
LITERATURE IN CORNELL UNIVERSITY

BOSTON, U.S.A., AND LONDON
D. C. HEATH & CO., PUBLISHERS

COPYRIGHT, 1911, BY D. C. HEATH & CO.

ALL RIGHTS RESERVED

To
JAMES MORGAN HART
TEACHER AND FRIEND

Preface

THE present volume is, I believe, the first entirely devoted to Gray's critical prose. Editions of his poetry are numerous; and it has been generally assumed that he was chiefly a poet. The slender collection of poems, however, was not the only product, possibly not the chief product, of Gray's intellectual life. It is idle, of course, to discuss the comparative worth of creative and critical effort; it is worth while, however, in this age, to emphasize the necessity of sound criticism and to insist on the high value of Gray's contribution, slight as it was in quantity, to the critical thought of his time.

I have endeavored to present an accurate text; but as the volume is intended for general as well as scholarly use, I have modernized the spelling and punctuation, indicating in the notes Gray's few peculiar spellings, when the peculiarity seemed worthy of attention. Little is gained by retaining, in a text like this, the outworn spellings of a bygone age; while much may be said in favor of uniformity, even though that involves the use of some forms that we do not like. All the footnotes are Gray's own. My notes are gathered at the end of the text.

It remains to express my obligations to Professor Herford for his courtesies in connection with the preparation of the book. To Professor Martin W. Sampson I am indebted for his kindness in reading the introduction in manuscript. My debt to my predecessors, especially Professor Duncan C. Tovey, for the substance of many of the notes, will be obvious and is gratefully acknowledged.

C. S. N.

CORNELL UNIVERSITY, ITHACA, N. Y.,
July, 1909.

Contents

	PAGE
PREFACE	vii
INTRODUCTION	xi
I. The Life of Gray	xi
II. Gray's Productivity	xxii
III. His Position in the Development of Criticism	xxvii
IV. His Qualifications as a Critic	xxxv
V. His Critical Works	xxxix
VI. Summary	li
VII. Bibliographical Note	lii
PHÆDO (309)	3
ESSAY ON THE PHILOSOPHY OF LORD BOLINGBROKE (309)	7
ESSAY ON NORMAN ARCHITECTURE (310)	13
OBSERVATIONS ON ENGLISH METRE (312)	21
THE MEASURES OF VERSE (314)	39
OBSERVATIONS ON THE PSEUDO-RHYTHMUS (317)	57
SOME OBSERVATIONS ON THE USE OF RHYME (320)	73
ADDITIONAL OBSERVATIONS AND CONJECTURES ON RHYME (322)	80
SOME REMARKS ON THE POEMS OF JOHN LYDGATE (323)	87
SAMUEL DANIEL (325)	118
SELECTIONS FROM THE LETTERS (326)	122
NOTES	309
INDEX	367

Introduction

I. THE LIFE OF GRAY

THOMAS GRAY, one of the most eminent men of letters of his time, was born in Cornhill, London, on December 26, 1716, the son of Philip and Dorothy Antrobus Gray. He was the fifth of twelve children; all the others died in infancy. His father, a well-to-do merchant, was extremely eccentric, not to say brutal, and was probably insane. He refused to educate the lad, and the expense of his education was borne by his mother, who with her sister Mary "kept a kind of India warehouse." About 1727 Thomas Gray was sent to Eton College, where his uncle Robert Antrobus was assistant to Dr. George, the principal. At Eton Gray formed lasting friendships with Horace Walpole, son of the Prime Minister; Richard West, son of the Lord Chancellor of Ireland; and Thomas Ashton, nicknamed "Plato." The four formed what they called "the Quadruple Alliance,"[1] which produced at least the interesting letters collected by Mr. Tovey in *Gray and His Friends*.

After seven years of Eton, Gray was ready for the university. Robert Antrobus was a fellow of Peterhouse, Cambridge, and his younger brother Thomas was a fellow of King's College. It was natural, therefore, that their nephew should proceed to Cambridge; thither

[1] H. Walpole, *Letters*, ed. Mrs. Toynbee, i. 10, 20.

Thomas Gray went in 1734, and after a short stay at Pembroke Hall, he became on July 3 a pensioner of Peterhouse. The curriculum, especially the mathematical part, did not appeal to him, and he soon decided (*Letters*, ed. Tovey, i. 3) not to take a degree. He was not athletic; he had no exercise; and he was by some considered effeminate, partly because he drank tea for breakfast while others for the most part drank beer. Melancholy early "marked him for her own"; and the dulness of life never ceased to weigh on his spirits.[1] But he was constantly — doubtless too constantly — busy, with his reading of the Latin, Greek, and Italian authors. He became familiar with Ovid, Horace, and Livy. He wrote Richard West (May 8, 1736) that he had been having a game at quoits with Statius. He read Virgil under a venerable beech on his uncle's estate at Burnham; in a Latin letter to West he quotes Lucretius, Poseidippus, and Homer. He was an ardent Greek scholar at a time when interest in Greek studies at Cambridge was at a low ebb.

Gray left Cambridge in September, 1738, and after staying for a time at his father's house, accepted Horace Walpole's invitation[2] to join him in a tour of the Continent. Leaving Dover on March 29, 1739, the two men spent two months in Paris, three in Rheims, and two at Lyons. Gray's letters to his father and mother reveal a mind alert, sensitive, and unconventional. At a time when men were only repelled by the "horrors"

[1] See his *Letters*, ed. Tovey, i. 1, 3, 6, 9, 95, 103, 196, 281, 301, 334, 345, ii. 2, 14, 23, 24, 26, 36, 48, 54, 165; *Works*, ed. Gosse, iii. 167, 181, 240, 261, etc.

[2] Cf. Walpole, *Letters*, ed. Mrs. Toynbee, viii. 259.

of Alpine travel, he writes to West of his journey up to the Grande Chartreuse: "There are certain scenes that would awe an atheist into belief." Crossing the Alps, Gray and Walpole visited Turin, Genoa, which Gray thought "a charming place," and Bologna, arriving at Florence about the middle of December. Here Gray began his *De Principiis Cogitandi*. In the spring they visited Siena, Rome, and Naples, returning to Florence in July. At Reggio a quarrel occurred between the two travelers, occasioned probably by Walpole's somewhat supercilious treatment of his sensitive companion;[1] and the two parted. Gray returned home by way of Padua, Verona, Milan, Turin, and Lyons, visiting a second time the Grande Chartreuse and writing in the album his ode *O tu severi relligio loci*. Two months after his return, on November 6, 1741, his father died of gout. About a year later his mother and aunt went to West End, Stoke Pogis, to live with their recently widowed sister Mrs. Rogers.

The year 1742 is memorable in Gray's life for his prolific composition of English verse. He began with a tragedy, *Agrippina*, inspired by Racine; but receiving frankly hostile criticism from his friend West, he abandoned it. At Stoke Pogis, in June, 1742, he wrote his *Ode to Spring*. In August he wrote his touching sonnet on the death of West; his *Ode on a Distant Prospect of Eton College;* and his *Hymn to Adversity*. In the autumn, too, he began the *Elegy*, which was to lie un-

---

[1] See Tovey, *Gray and His Friends*, pp. 5-12, and Walpole's letter to Mason, March 2, 1773, in his *Letters*, ed. Mrs. Toynbee, viii. 245 f.

finished for seven years. Truly, had physical energy and ambition combined to spur on the young poet, this year had been an auspicious beginning of a great poetical career.

The next six years of Gray's life, however, were to be devoted not to composition but to study. After his father's death, supposing his means to be ample, Gray had begun to read law in London; but the condition of the family finances after the death of his uncle Jonathan Rogers (in October, 1742) made it impossible to go on with the study of law. So he returned in the winter of 1742 to Peterhouse, and taking his degree of LL.B. in 1744,[1] settled down as a permanent resident of the college. The Greek authors claimed his attention, and he read widely and carefully, making notes on Plato, Aristotle, Strabo, Aristophanes, the *Anthology*, etc., and projecting editions of some of these writers. During these years he saw little of Cambridge society, for which he had a certain contempt;[2] but he made occasional journeys to London. Through the mediation of "a Lady who wished well to both parties," in November, 1745,[3] he became reconciled to Walpole, and thereafter saw him frequently. He seems also to have known Pope (this is implied in his letter to Walpole, February 3, 1746); and he is said to have met Hogarth at a dinner given by Walpole. In 1748 he began a philosophical poem on *The Alliance of Education and Government*. He explained to Wharton that he intended to

[1] Cf. *Letters*, ed. Tovey, i. 113, n. 1.
[2] See his *Hymn to Ignorance*, written in 1742 or 1743.
[3] Cf. *Letters*, ed. Tovey, i. 124, and n. 2.

show that education and government "must necessarily concur to produce great and useful Men."[1] But when Montesquieu's *L'esprit des lois* appeared in 1749, Gray found that the French author had anticipated some of his best thoughts, and losing interest in his poem, soon ceased work upon it.

The death of his aunt Mary Antrobus, on November 5, 1749, seems to have induced Gray to take up his *Elegy* again; and at length, on June 12, 1750, he finished it and sent it to Walpole. In this place criticism of the now classic poem is entirely superfluous. It is interesting, to those who love dates, to note that the *Elegy in a Country Churchyard* was finished exactly a century before the publication of *In Memoriam*, and that even Tennyson himself, though he strove to express universal feeling about death, did not succeed in coming so near the heart of mankind and in saying so exquisitely what the living ever think in regard to the dead. Recluse though he might be, the man who could write the *Elegy* had not lost his humanity. On February 16, 1751, the *Elegy* was published in a large quarto pamphlet and was immediately and prodigiously successful.

While still in manuscript the *Elegy* had been read by Lady Cobham, Gray's neighbor at Stoke, who sent her guest Lady Schaub and her niece Miss Harriet Speed[2] to call on the poet. The incidents of this call and the one Gray made in return form the material of the amusing *jeu d'esprit* entitled *A Long Story*, which Gray wrote in the autumn.

[1] *Letters*, ed. Tovey, i. 192.
[2] Cf. *Letters*, ed. Tovey, i. 351, n. 3.

Probably at Horace Walpole's suggestion, Richard Bentley, son of the Master of Trinity, made several illustrations for the poems of Gray, which Dodsley published in February, 1753, under the title of *Designs by Mr. R. Bentley for Six Poems by Mr. T. Gray*. The engraving, which was of a high order, was done by John Sebastian Müller and Charles Grignion.

On March 15, 1753, Gray's mother died at Stoke, at the age of sixty-seven. In the inscription which he placed on her tomb, Gray speaks of her as "the careful tender mother of many children, one of whom alone had the misfortune to survive her." This tribute, beautiful in itself, well indicates the depth of Gray's devotion to his mother; and read in the light of other remarks of his, it may be regarded as more than a merely conventional expression of his deep-seated despondency.

At the death of his mother, Gray came into possession of the remainder of the small fortune left by his father, part of which had already fallen to him; and his income now sufficed to meet the needs of his simple habits of life. Though he was not rich, the poet never had to work for his living, and even scorned to receive pay for his writing.

To the following year, 1754, belongs the incomplete *Ode on Vicissitude*, which was found after Gray's death in a diary of that year; and to the same year Mr. Gosse assigns the *Essay on Norman Architecture*. More certain is it that at the end of this year Gray began the Pindaric odes. *The Progress of Poesy* was sent on December 26 to Wharton. *The Bard* occupied much of his time in the following year, but in the autumn was laid aside, and was not completed till three years later.

An important event of 1756 in Gray's quiet life was his removal to Pembroke College, to which he was admitted as a resident on March 6. The cause of his leaving Peterhouse was apparently some rudeness on the part of the younger inmates of the college; there is no good authority, however, for the story that he was induced to descend his rope-ladder into a tub of water.[1]

The publication of the two Pindaric odes by Dodsley in the summer of 1757 gave Gray a wide reputation as the greatest living poet of England. On the death of Colley Cibber (December 12, 1757), he was offered the laureateship by the Duke of Devonshire, then Lord Chamberlain, but declined the honor. "The office itself," he wrote to Mason, "has always humbled the professor hitherto (even in an age when kings were somebody), if he were a poor writer by making him more conspicuous, and if he were a good one by setting him at war with the little fry of his own profession."

In the early part of 1758 Gray made an antiquarian and architectural tour in the Fen country, visiting Ely, Peterborough, Croyland Abbey, Thorney, Fotheringay, etc. After this he staid for a time with Lord and Lady Cobham, and spent the month of July with Walpole at Strawberry Hill. Toward the end of the year his aunt, Mrs. Rogers, died, and after settling her estate he closed the house at Stoke Pogis and went to

---

[1] See *Letters*, ed. Tovey, i. 292, n. 3, ii. 304; G. L. Kittredge, "Gray's Ladder of Ropes," *The Nation*, Sept. 27, 1900, lxxi. 251; Walpole, *Letters*, ed. Mrs. Toynbee, viii. 444 f.

live in London, in order to read at the recently opened British Museum. Here he spent four hours a day, engaged especially in studies preparatory to writing his *History of English Poetry*. His friend Lady Cobham died in April, 1760, leaving her fortune of £30,000 to Miss Speed. It was rumored [1] that a match had been planned by her between her niece and Gray; but whether or not the rumor was well founded, the plan came to nothing; Gray "knew his own mind." [2]

In June, 1760, he writes to Wharton that he is gone mad over Macpherson's translations from the Erse. In the celebrated Ossianic controversy we find Gray strongly inclined to believe in the genuineness of the fragments, but frankly admitting the difficulties that opposed this belief. He corresponded on the subject with Hume and Adam Smith. He began to take interest not only in Celtic (at least Gaelic and Welsh) but also in Norse literature; and all of his own later poetry reflects the romantic impulse to which he now readily yielded. Evans's *Specimens of Welsh Poetry* (1764) is said to have supplied him with suggestions for his own fragments in verse that date from this period.

Returning to Cambridge in November, 1761, Gray made his home at Pembroke during the remainder of his uneventful life. He took a deep interest in Norton Nicholls, then a student of Trinity Hall, later rector of Lound and Bradwell, who became a warm friend and

---

[1] See Gray's letter to Wharton, October 21, 1760, *Letters*, ii. 167; and cf. Miss Speed's letters to Gray, in Tovey's *Gray and His Friends*, pp. 197 ff.

[2] *Letters*, ed. Tovey, ii. 143.

ardent admirer. His *Reminiscences of Gray*, though written more than thirty years after the poet's death, are of great value. Gray's health grew steadily worse, until in 1764 he was obliged to undergo a severe operation,[1] which restored him to health. The next year we find him traveling in northern England and in Scotland, and delighted with the Gaelic songs and the sublimity of the Highlands. Other summer holiday tours were to Kent in 1766, to the Lakes in 1767 (a trip cut short by the illness of his companion, Wharton) and again in 1769, and to Worcester, Gloucester, and South Wales in 1770.

Of great significance were Gray's visits to the Lakes. His *Journal in the Lakes*, describing the journey of 1769, is one of the first narratives in which the magnificent landscape of the Cumberland lakes is described with modern feeling and appreciation. Equipped with a Claude Lorraine glass, Gray passed slowly through the region, delighting in the changing colors of sky and cloud and water and in the noble lines of mountain and vale; and then soberly and without hysteria recorded his impressions. Wordsworth, whom many credit with having "discovered" the scenery of the English Lakes, only followed, in this respect, in the wake of Gray.

In July, 1768, the chair of Modern History and Modern Languages at Cambridge, for which Gray had been an unsuccessful applicant in 1762, was offered to him by the Duke of Grafton and was accepted. Following the custom of his predecessors, he delivered no lec-

[1] Cf. *Works*, ed. Gosse, iii. 170; Myra Reynolds, *The Treatment of Nature in English Poetry*, 1909, pp. 225-233.

tures; he complied with the recommendation that the teaching of the languages be entrusted to a deputy, and employed Agostino Isola, later the editor of Tasso. In the following year, on the occasion of the installation of the Duke of Grafton as Chancellor of the University of Cambridge, Gray volunteered to write the Installation *Ode*. It was the last verse, apparently, that he wrote; echoing Milton and Dryden, as a Cambridge ode might properly do, and containing some noble lines.

The chief thing yet to be chronicled of Gray's last years is his friendship for Charles Victor de Bonstetten, a young Swiss, son of the Treasurer of Berne, who was sent to Gray by Nicholls from Bath in November, 1769. For nearly four months Bonstetten sat daily at the feet of Gray, reading the English classics and talking of his life and enthusiasms. When Bonstetten left England in March, 1770, he had secured Gray's promise to visit him in Switzerland the next summer. But Gray's health proved unequal to the effort. His strength and courage gradually declined until in May, 1771, he was attacked by gout of the stomach. He died on July 30, 1771, profoundly mourned by a small circle of friends who, in spite of his reserve and his isolation, had learned to love his noble and attractive nature.[1]

In *The London Magazine* for March, 1772 (xli. 140), appeared an estimate of Gray written by his friend William J. Temple, of Trinity Hall, Cambridge, in a letter to Boswell, and published by the latter without

---

[1] Cf., for example, Walpole, *Letters*, ed. Mrs. Toynbee, viii. 66 f., 72 f., 85 f. ; Norton Nicholls, quoted in Gosse's *Gray*, pp. 208 f.

authority. Temple's remarks, quoted by both **Mason** and **Johnson**, are as follows:

"Perhaps he was the most learned man in Europe. He was equally acquainted with the elegant and profound parts of science, and not superficially but thoroughly. He knew every branch of history, both natural and civil; had read all the original historians of England, France, and Italy; and was a great antiquarian. Criticism, metaphysicks, morals, politicks made a principal part of his plan of study; voyages and travels of all sorts were his favourite amusement; and he had a fine taste in painting, prints, architecture, and gardening. With such a fund of knowledge, his conversation must have been equally instructing and entertaining; but he was also a good man, a well-bred man, a man of virtue and humanity. There is no character without some speck, some imperfection; and I think the greatest defect in his was an affectation in delicacy, or rather effeminacy, and a visible fastidiousness, or contempt and disdain of his inferiors in science. He also had in some degree that weakness which disgusted Voltaire so much in Mr. Congreve: Though he seemed to value others, chiefly according to the progress they had made in knowledge; yet he could not bear to be considered himself merely as a man of letters, and though without birth or fortune, or station, his desire was to be looked upon as a private independent gentleman, who read for his amusement. Perhaps it may be said, what signifies so much knowledge, when it produced so little? Is it worth taking so much pains to leave no memorial but a few poems? But let it be considered that Mr. Gray was to others, at least innocently employed; to himself, certainly beneficially. His time passed agreeably; he was every day making some new acquisition in science; his mind was enlarged, his heart softened, his virtue strengthened; the world and mankind were shewn to him without a mask; and he was taught to consider every thing as trifling, and unworthy of the attention of a wise man, except the pursuit of knowledge, and the practice of virtue, in that state wherein God hath placed us."

II. GRAY'S PRODUCTIVITY

A good deal has been written on the subject of Gray's sterility. His poetry, interspersed with many notes, in Mr. Gosse's edition fills little more than two hundred small octavo pages; his letters, about eight hundred pages; and his other prose, a little over five hundred pages. For a life of fifty-five years almost exclusively devoted to scholarly and literary pursuits, this is certainly not a large product. Several explanations of its smallness have been offered. Matthew Arnold, writing especially of Gray's poetical output, and echoing the Rev. James Brown, Master of Pembroke, says, "he never spoke out"; he "fell upon an age of prose." "As regards literary production, the task of the eighteenth century in England was not the poetic interpretation of the world, its task was to create a plain, clear, straightforward, efficient prose. Poetry obeyed the bent of mind requisite for the due fulfilment of this task of the century. It was intellectual, argumentative, ingenious; not seeing things in their truth and beauty, not interpretative. Gray, with the qualities of mind and soul of a genuine poet, was isolated in his century. Maintaining and fortifying them by lofty studies, he yet could not fully educe and enjoy them; the want of a genial atmosphere, the failure of sympathy in his contemporaries, were too great." It has been more than once pointed out [1] that Arnold here shows less critical acumen than usual, and has indeed quite missed the truth of the matter. Gray was quite as much in sympathy with the age and had quite as many friends as would have been the case in the seventeenth or the nineteenth century. Had he lived a century earlier or later he would doubtless have found more zeal for learning, and possibly, in the nineteenth century, more wide-spread intelligence, with which he would have been delighted; but he would have been perplexed by other things — the leaden weight of Puritanism, or the theological doubts of the troubled age of Arnold and Clough.[2] Friends he had always, and their approbation was not withheld or stinted.

Yet from one point of view there is doubtless truth in Arnold's highly elaborated dogma. Gray's companions and friends were not of the kind adapted to stimulate his activity in either verse or prose. West, the one stimulating comrade of his youth, died in 1742, when Gray was twenty-six. Walpole, always a dilettante, was scarcely an inspired writer, except of letters, and besides, he and Gray gradually drifted apart. Of the 186 letters (1759–1771) printed by Mr. Gosse in his third

[1] See, for example, Phelps, *Selections*, p. xviii; Parrott, *Studies of a Booklover*, p. 176; Saintsbury, *A History of Criticism*, iii. 55; *Letters*, ed. Tovey, i. xxvii f.; Lounsbury, *The Nation*, xl. 205 f.

[2] On this point see also Tovey, *Gray and His Friends*, pp. 27–30.

volume, only six are to Walpole; while of Walpole's 1360 letters written before Gray's death, only seven are addressed to Gray. Of his other friends, Wharton was a busy physician; Conyers Middleton's theology repelled him; Stonehewer, Chute, and James Brown were not productive. Mason, it is true, was exceptionally productive, but his work reacted on Gray's critical rather than his creative faculty. Gray's aversion to Cambridge society is well known. "I converse with none but the dead here," he writes to Chute in 1742. Even had he been less averse to the society of the Cambridge dons, however, there were few (except Middleton, who died in 1750) whose conversation would have been especially suggestive or stimulating.

Professor Phelps has sought for other causes of Gray's meagreness of output: his scholarly and critical temperament, his lack of health, his abhorrence of publicity and popularity. Phelps's argument is answered by Professor Parrott, who, reasoning from analogy, doubts the adequacy of even this explanation, and who believes rather that Gray lacked the born poet's creative impulse as well as the capacity for profound reflection, for strong, lively, and passionate feeling, and for broad and deep sympathy. Professor Parrott argues forcibly and plausibly, and has well stated some points of the case. I am inclined to think, however, that he has not given us a wholly adequate explanation of the matter.

Professor Phelps would seem to be warranted in saying that Gray's scholarly temperament had much to do with his writing so little. The scholar's instinct in him was strong. He chose to continue living at Cambridge after taking his degree in law, partly, it is true, because living there was cheap, but mainly because there he had access to books and manuscripts. He took keen delight in reading. He planned editions of Greek classics. It is true that he did not complete them; and the reason will be considered presently. That he undertook these studies merely to allay regret at not being able to write, or to drive away ennui, there is very little evidence. Nor can we think of Gray as selfish in devoting himself to the acquisition of knowledge which would benefit himself alone. His plans for publishing books make against this view. An ardent apostle of Greek culture, he hoped, through better editions of his favorite authors, to spread the study of Greek literature. The effect of his steady and prolonged devotion to scholarship — and in this he may be likened to Darwin — was to dry up the poetic vein; and in prose, moreover, aside from his letters, and his *Journal in the Lakes*, virtually a letter-diary, he seems to have produced little in his later years, certainly after 1764.

Another reason for his producing so little was his fastidious taste. He polished and repolished his verses. He rigorously excised lines that many another poet would have been proud to retain. "He has left nothing finished," wrote Walpole[1] to Sir Horace Mann after Gray's death; "in truth, he finished everything so highly, and laboured all his works so long, that I am the less surprised." There are indications, too, that he did not compose readily or fluently — probably for the

[1] *Letters*, ed. Mrs. Toynbee, viii. 92.

same reason. He thus presents a striking contrast to his friend Mason, who was prolific but uncritical.

Doubtless his reticence and shyness had something to do with his writing so little, though it is easy to make too much of this circumstance.[1] A lyric poet — and Gray's genius was essentially lyric — must express himself, his own nature; must have felt what he utters. That Gray was capable of deep feeling — and here I must differ with Professor Parrott — is evident from several passages in his letters;[2] yet he was chary about expressing it, and indeed was singularly reticent in talking to others about himself. Bonstetten's failure to get the old poet to talk about his past life is well known.

That Gray's health was for long periods (except in his later years) so bad as to prevent or discourage authorship, we find in his letters very little evidence. He speaks frequently of low spirits, or melancholy; but there are also occasional remarks [3] about his improvement in health. In the greater number of the letters written in middle life, even in those written to intimate friends, there is no reference to his health.

A stronger reason than ill health has not been too often dwelt on: namely, his inertia, or indolence. Not being obliged to write, he could not bring himself to do what required an effort. The consciousness of this defect

---

[1] Cf., for example, Mason's anecdote about unwittingly retarding *The Progress of Poesy*, *Works*, ed. Gosse, ii. 110, n. 1.

[2] Cf. *Letters*, ed. Tovey, i. 44, 111, 203 f., 239, ii. 29, 143; *Works*, ed. Gosse, iii. 265, 369.

[3] E. g., *Letters*, ed. Tovey, i. 33, 351, ii. 81, 187, 205, 209, 269; *Works*, ed. Gosse, iii. 170, 179, 258.

was probably a chief cause of that despondency, or depression of spirits, of which he speaks many times, and which cannot have been entirely due to physical ill health.

Finally, a lack of ambition doubtless combined with other circumstances to render Gray indifferent to fame. After all, Phoebus' reply to the shepherd friend of Lycidas was not exactly convincing. As he mused in the quiet churchyard, Gray thought how

> Some village-Hampden, that with dauntless breast
> The little tyrant of his fields withstood,
> Some mute inglorious Milton here may rest,
> Some Cromwell guiltless of his country's blood;

and then, as in the Mason MS., thus advised himself:

> No more, with Reason and thyself at strife,
> Give anxious cares and endless wishes room;
> But thro' the cool sequester'd vale of life
> Pursue the silent tenour of thy doom.

Gray's sense of humor prevented him from attaching too much importance to personal memorials. He was a spectator of life; he did not care to be a too active participant. He was content that the victors should have the spoils.

III. HIS POSITION IN THE DEVELOPMENT OF CRITICISM

The early years of the eighteenth century contributed little that was new or important to the science of literary criticism. In this field, at least, the first half of the century was in general an era of orthodoxy. In his interesting thesis [1] on eighteenth century criticism, Paul

---

[1] *Die Kritik in der englischen Literatur des 17. und 18. Jahrhunderts*, Liége thèse, Leipzig, 1897, pp. 69 f.

Hamelius has shown that in the seventeenth century there rose in England four schools of critics, — the Romantic, the Christian, the Neo-Classic, and the Rationalistic, — which by the end of the century had combined to form two schools. The first, the Romantic, with which the Christian combined, "auf den ästhetischen Grundlagen der Romantik eine christliche Literatur zu einrichten versuchte"; it was represented by Steele and to some extent by Addison and Dennis. The second, the Neo-Classic, with which the Rationalists arrayed themselves, agreed with the first school in regarding morality as the source and aim of all literary activity; but it "fasste die Moral nicht als ein Erzeugnis historischer Bedingungen oder innerer Seelenvorgänge, sondern als eine Schöpfung der Vernunft auf, welche nicht schöne Empfindungen, sondern eine nützliche Einrichtung des praktischen Lebens zum Zweck hat." Of this school, which held the supremacy for many years after the death of Dryden, the champions were Pope and Shaftesbury. It is not to be supposed, of course, that these schools were always sharply distinguished. All critics looked with reverence upon the critical work of Dryden, whom Johnson calls "the father of English criticism";[1] and he may be ranged now on the one side, now on the other, though the general temper of his criticism is Romantic.[2]

The Neo-Classic creed, which had been gradually evolved in the course of the previous century,[3] was

[1] *Lives of the Poets*, ed. Hill, i. 410.
[2] Hamelius, p. 185.
[3] Cf. F. E. Schelling, "Ben Jonson and the Classical School," *Pub. M. L. Ass'n*, xiii. 221–249.

based upon the ancient critics, especially Aristotle and Horace, though they were frequently misunderstood or credited with views they never upheld. The tragic drama, properly unified with reference to time, place, and action, and the heroic poem, duly accredited with fable, epic unity, and machines for the intervention of gods, angels, and the like, became the supreme types or kinds of literature.[1] Shakespeare and Milton, when they had the good fortune to please the critic, gave pleasure chiefly because they exemplified the precepts of the great Greek and Roman critics. But Shakespeare and Milton, it was thought, frequently violated the fundamental laws of art. According to Dennis, Shakespeare showed a want of art, and failed to mete out poetical justice.[2] For Addison, Shakespeare's style is often marred by "sounding phrases, hard metaphors, and forced expressions";[3] likewise Milton's language "is often too much labored, and sometimes obscured by old words, transpositions, and foreign idioms."[4] Swift was not alone in wanting to correct and fix the English tongue,[5] so that an unalterable standard of Ciceronian eloquence for English might be established and main-

[1] On tragedy, cf. *The Spectator*, Nos. 39, 40, 42, 44; on the epic, *id.* Nos. 267, 273, 291, 297, 315.

[2] See *On the Genius and Writings of Shakespear* (1711), reprinted by D. Nichol Smith in his *Eighteenth Century Essays on Shakespeare*, 1903, pp. 24 ff.

[3] *The Spectator*, No. 39, April 14, 1711, quoted also by Saintsbury, *A History of Criticism*, ii. 441 f.

[4] *The Spectator*, No. 297, Feb. 9, 1712.

[5] See *A Proposal for Correcting, Improving, and Ascertaining the English Tongue*, 1712.

tained. Pope's celebrated *Essay on Criticism* (1711), as Saintsbury has said,[1] is little more than an echo of Horace, Boileau, and Vida. Pope counseled the writer to follow "Nature," but it was a Nature perfectly correct and proper according to the standards of the London critics. Just as Pope is the last great poet of the Neo-Classic school, so his criticism dominated the first decades of the eighteenth century, and summed up the leading ideas of the Neo-Classic creed. The watchword of this creed was correctness; its text-book, one might say, was Edward Bysshe's *Art of English Poetry* (1702), with its rigorous and business-like rules, ignoring (for example) or condemning dactylic movements altogether, and providing collections of "beauties" for imitation. Originality, inspiration, genius counted for little.

But even before the eighteenth century began, the note of a revolt can be clearly heard. To this revolt Professor Saintsbury has given the suggestive name of "The Nemesis of Correctness." There is no apparent cessation of homage at the shrine of antiquity; but in the writings of Steele and Addison this worship of Aristotle and Quintilian is unconsciously tempered by good taste and a desire for freer and more general discussion of literary art. Non-classical works, such as the Bible and the early ballads, begin to be discussed and are discovered to have elements of beauty. Addison[2] justifies the introduction of fairies and demons into poetry, even

---

[1] Cf. his *History of Criticism*, ii. 455.
[2] "The Fairy Way of Writing," *The Spectator*, No. 419, July 1, 1712.

though it violate the canons of "Nature methodized"; and ventures to approve of blank verse for epic poetry. In landscape, too, Nature, it is found, does not have to be much "helped and regulated," to give pleasure. Addison admires Versailles, but prefers Fontainebleau, "situated among rocks and woods, that give you a fine variety of savage prospects."[1]

At the time when Thomas Gray began to read poetry and criticism, the points of dispute between the two schools had become clearly formulated.[2] The poet should follow Nature, indeed; but how should Nature be defined? Should imitation be confined to the ancients? What was the value of poetic justice? Was "the fairy way of writing" justifiable? Should tragedy and comedy be separated? Was the use of blank verse immoral? Could the lyric and epic styles be mixed? Such questions continued to be discussed throughout Gray's lifetime.

In estimating Gray as a critic it must be borne in mind that he made no pretense to critical acumen. "You know I do not love, much less pique myself, on criticism," he writes to Mason, in January, 1758, "and think even a bad verse as good a thing or better than the best observation that ever was made upon it." His own critical utterances were all published posthumously, and much of the text in the present volume was doubtless written without thought of publication. If

[1] *The Guardian*, No. 101, July 7, 1713. But these "savage prospects" differ widely from those Addison saw in the Alps and the Apennines.
[2] The situation is well described by Hamelius, p. 140.

his criticism is important, then, it is so in spite of any ambition cherished by its author, who would doubtless be greatly surprised if he could now return and learn of his reputation as a critic.

Professor Phelps, in his *Selections from Gray*, p. xxii, says of him: "Beginning as a classicist and disciple of Dryden, he ended in thorough-going Romanticism." Phelps is probably thinking of Gray's poetry; some of his earlier pieces are certainly conventional enough in both style and thought. But his critical utterances at any time show little inclination toward the classical school. From the first we are aware of an independence of thought and tone and a freedom from conventional cant, which point toward the coming and early disappearance of the old standards of taste. From the first, his criticism was of the independent, Romantic order. He was only twenty-three when he wrote to West the celebrated passage referring to the Alps, "Not a precipice, not a torrent, not a cliff, but is pregnant with religion and poetry." At twenty-six we find him saying that "the language of the age is never the language of poetry; except among the French, whose verse, where the thought or image does not support it, differs in nothing from prose." Further on in the same letter he pays a tribute to the creative genius of Shakespeare and Milton, manifested in enriching our language with borrowed or coined words, and complains of the degeneracy of English. This is only another way of saying that the vocabulary of the Neo-Classic poets was worn out and could no longer stimulate the imagination or give pleasure. Gray, then, can scarcely be said to have been, on principle, a classicist. Although some of his earlier verses conform to the conventional form,[1] his sympathies were with the independents, who knew that poetic diction must grow and that poetic structure can no more be held in by rules than can a spring freshet.

Gray is not one of those who have left a large body of criticism. He set down no elaborate theory of poetry or prose; he did not attempt to bring Aristotle or Horace "up to date." What he did was, in his letters, to express himself, often casually, and rarely at any length, about writers chiefly contemporary; and in his other pieces, to estimate men and movements — in literature, painting, architecture, theology, and so on — with the illuminating common sense of a trained and unbiased scholar. Probably his general cautiousness would have sufficed to prevent him from making many generalizations about our early literature; but it must also be remembered that much of this literature was not easily accessible, indeed, had not yet been printed, and that to obtain any wide acquaintance with it from manuscripts would at that time have been impossible. Now it happens that Gray was especially interested in this literature — in Lydgate, Gawin Douglas, Chaucer — and gave much time to these authors; with his own hand he copied *The Palice of Honour* entire.[2] Realiz-

---

[1] It may be noted that of his poems only the following employ the heroic couplet: *The Alliance of Education and Government*, 1748; *Epitaph on a Child*, 1758; *Comic Lines*, 1768; *Couplet about Birds*; *Tophet*; — all the above being posthumously published; and the six passages translated from Statius, Tasso, and Propertius.

[2] Gosse, *Gray*, p. 151.

ing to some extent the vastness of the field, and feeling himself but a beginner and a pioneer, Gray, in his utterances on these writers and on subjects connected with them, speaks always with the air of a learner rather than with that of an expert or authority; and assuming this attitude [1] and thus teaching others to assume it was not the least of his services to literary criticism.

We must not, then, look upon Gray as a protagonist in the conflicts of criticism. Yet his chance remarks have a permanent value as coming from an ardent scholar and a sympathetic reader. His whole attitude toward letters served to emphasize the importance to criticism of a sound basis in scholarship and of openness of mind and heart. In general, Arnold's definition of criticism would have suited him; would that he had had more of Arnold's militant ardor in making known what he considered the best that had been thought and written!

Gray holds a high place among the critics of his time partly because of his scholarship. Coming midway between Bentley and Porson (he was twenty-five when Bentley died and forty-three when Porson was born), he bridges the gap between these great lights of Trinity College; and what is more important, his deep interest in Greek studies may be said to herald the dawn of the modern study of Greek literature; with language studies for their own sake Gray was not especially concerned. The study of Greek was

---

[1] Cf. Saintsbury, *A History of Criticism*, iii. 63.

to do much to break down the narrow prejudices of the Neo-Classic creed; hence the importance of Gray's scholarly work and ambitions. His interest, too, in kindred studies — history and archeology, the Celtic and Scandinavian literatures — is significant of the growing desire to understand the past more fully, to sit at its feet and learn.

IV. HIS QUALIFICATIONS AS A CRITIC

Let us now see what were the qualities of Gray which fitted or unfitted him for the tasks of criticism. We have long heard that the fundamental quality of the true critic is that he is wholly disinterested, has no ax to grind. Surely this was true of Gray. We never find him wedded to a theory; he is never blinded by the brilliance of a particular meteor or comet; he scans the heavens steadily; and the differing magnitudes of the stars are evident to him. He knows all the stars of the first magnitude — Homer, Dante, Chaucer, Shakespeare, Milton — though Homer and Milton, he thinks, have some high-sounding words that mean little. Lydgate is ranked far below his master Chaucer, but is not denied some important merits. If Gray gave the reins to his admiration of any one, it was Dryden, whose sanity and clearness of judgment appealed to Gray's kindred temperament; yet he writes to Mason (December 19, 1757) that Dryden's character disgraced the laureateship. Gray's dislike of Johnson is well known;[1] we do not of course know when it began or whether he had

---

[1] Cf. Nicholls' *Reminiscences*, Gray's *Letters*, ed. Tovey, ii. 278.

seen Johnson when in 1748 he praised *London* as "one of those few imitations that have all the ease and all the spirit of an original." Yet Johnson was now well known in London; and it seems probable that Gray knew him by sight. Yet in spite of this dislike[1] of "Ursa Major," Gray respected Johnson's understanding, "and still more his goodness of heart."[2] These remarks do not imply that Gray was free from prejudices, or that he was more than human; what is meant is, that on important matters his prejudices did not bias him unduly. Aversion to Voltaire's moral character, Nicholls says, did not prevent Gray "from paying the full tribute of admiration due to his genius. He was delighted with his pleasantry; approved his historical compositions, particularly his *Essai sur l'histoire universelle*; and placed his tragedies next in rank to those of Shakespeare."[3]

Next in the category of Gray's critical virtues may be mentioned his broad and sound scholarship. If not the most learned man of his day, he was easily in the front rank of eighteenth century savants. His reading included virtually the whole range of Greek and Roman authors and all that was best in French, Italian, and English literature. Of German belles-lettres, like other Englishmen of his day, he knew little or nothing; but he knew something of Scaliger,[4] and being

[1] Cf. Horace Walpole's dislike of Johnson, frequently asserted, and with much greater violence.

[2] Nicholls, *Reminiscences*.

[3] *Letters*, ed. Tovey, ii. 278. See also 230 5 and the note. Cf. also his remark about Boswell, *id.* p. 287.

[4] Letter to West, May 8, 1742, ed. Tovey, i. 102.

familiar with the best German editions of the classics,[1] he was cognizant of German ideals of scholarship. Nor was his reading limited to literature alone. He read works on history, architecture, archeology, painting,[2] theology,[3] philology, botany,[4] medicine,[5] and travel.[6] His mind was thus not merely filled with that broad information necessary for criticism of any real worth, but was also trained in critical judgment. As his numerous annotations indicate, he was a careful and observant reader.

Moreover, it may be said that Gray possessed a well developed sense of humor. A person thus gifted is likely to see life in its true proportions. Gray's own humor is usually, though not always, of the genial, kindly sort which leaves no sting. Cambridge was for him at twenty, and we may suppose continued to be, the place, formerly known by the name of Babylon, of which "the prophet spoke when he said, 'The wild beasts of the desert shall dwell there and their houses shall be full of doleful creatures,'" etc.;[7] but he always took a good-natured interest in its petty squabbles — and especially

[1] Letter to Wharton, September 11, 1746, ed. of Tovey, i. 140 ff.

[2] *Letters*, ed. Tovey, ii. 286.

[3] *Id.*, i. 213, 330, ii. 282 ; and cf. the *Essay on the Philosophy of Bolingbroke*.

[4] *Works*, ed. Gosse, iii. 352 ; cf. also his annotation of Linnæus.

[5] "You do not mention Gray's study of physic, of which he had read much, and I doubt to his hurt." Walpole, letter to Mason, April 3, 1775, in his *Letters*, ed. Mrs. Toynbee, ix. 175.

[6] *Works*, ed. Gosse, iii. 311, 344 ; Gosse, *Gray*, pp. 204 f.

[7] Letter to West, December, 1736.

in the fortunes of "the high and mighty Prince Roger, surnamed the Long, Lord of the great Zodiac, the glass Uranium and the chariot that goes without horses," and a few similar "characters." Now and then he is more sarcastic, as when he translated *Non magna loquimur, sed vivimus*, the motto for Dr. Plumptre's picture, by the words, "we don't say much, but we hold good livings." [1] It shocks us when he speaks of his aged aunt as "an old Harridan, who is the Spawn of Cerberus and the Dragon of Wantley"; [2] but we do not know his provocation. For Mason, the voluminous writer of fourth-rate poems and dramas, he has the expressive nickname of "Scroddles." [3] Although he wrote to Mason long criticisms of *Elfrida* and *Caractacus*, he did not take Mason's effusions too seriously.

Finally, among the qualities that made Gray a critic was his sympathy. He saw another man's point of view and gave due weight to the inherited tendencies and prejudices which determined it. This is evident not so much from specific utterances as from the general tone of his writing and conversation. It was sympathy which led him to devote so much attention to the productions of Mason. It was this same quality which, in spite of his reserve of manner, brought him the devoted friendship of his little circle of intimates — Wharton, Chute, Stonehewer, Brown, and others.

---

[1] *Letters*, ed. Tovey, ii. 109.
[2] *Id.*, pp. 58 f.
[3] This seems to occur first in the letter of 1756, ed. Tovey, i. 298 ff.

V. HIS CRITICAL WORKS

Phædo

As we have seen, for several years after taking his degree in civil law, Gray read deeply and systematically in Greek literature. The notes which he made on Aristophanes and Plato were printed by Mathias in 1814 from manuscripts formerly in the possession of Richard Stonehewer, and by Gosse in 1884 (Gray's *Works*, iv. 1–338). Gosse says they had never been reprinted; he was unaware of the fact that a large selection of the notes on Plato was reprinted, with Mathias' introduction, in George Burges' translation of Plato, vi. 405–506, in 1854 (London, Bohn).

It is no disparagement of these notes to say that they contain little or no criticism of the two Greek authors. Criticism was not Gray's purpose. What he sought to do was to furnish such analyses of plots and stories, and such explanatory notes and comments, as would enable a student to read the original text with understanding. In the state of Greek scholarship in Gray's time, such work was vastly more useful than criticism would have been; for criticism read before the student has some independent knowledge of the original is, for the purpose of sound scholarship, of little worth.

As a specimen of Gray's remarks on Plato I have reprinted the section dealing with the *Phædo*, since this, perhaps more than any other section of Gray's notes, combines anaylsis of some important matters with a measure of criticism.

The edition of Plato used by Gray, according to Mathias, was that of Henry Stephens, 1578, three volumes, folio. It is interesting to note that the list of ancient authors sent by Gray to Wharton on September 11, 1746 [1] does not apparently include any edition of Plato. No doubt the omission was accidental.

In his letter to Wharton on the same date, Gray remarks: "The best Editions of ancient authors should be the first things, I reckon, in a library." With propriety, then, this short extract from Gray's commentaries on the ancients may head the list of selections in this volume.

Essay on the Philosophy of Lord Bolingbroke

The *Essay on the Philosophy of Lord Bolingbroke* is Gray's only published venture in theological controversy. It was probably written soon after the appearance of Lord Bolingbroke's works, edited by David Mallet,[2] and was published by Mason in 1775. The particular passages against which Gray directed his attack are to be found in the *Philosophical Works*, iv, sections 40, 41, 50.[3] Bolingbroke asserts that the chain of reasoning by which, from a knowledge of the phenomena, we arrive at a knowledge of God has never been broken. The ancients recognized a supreme God *a posteriori*; but there were some in ancient as in modern times who *a priori* made God after their own image.

---

[1] *Letters*, ed. Tovey, i. 140–143.
[2] Published March 6, 1754; cf. Boswell's *Johnson*, ed. Hill, i. 268 f.
[3] In the London edition of 1809, viii. 143–164, 226–239.

For such, God is only an infinite man. Among the most positive on this matter is Dr. Clarke. Bolingbroke then controverts Clarke's view that all the moral attributes are the same in God as in ourselves. Everything shows the wisdom and power of God conformably to our ideas; but everything does not, he holds, likewise show God's justice and goodness. These "artificial theology" has attempted to demonstrate. If God is good, the atheists have asked, how comes it that there is evil in the world? To answer this, the pagan theists absurdly supposed two co-existing principles; the modern theists fell back on the equally absurd story of the fall of man. . . . The defenders of this hypothesis, moreover, distort the moral attributes of God. Wollaston's exaggerations become burlesque. He unwarrantably exalts man above other animals. All animal and vegetable life is connected. The nature of every living creature is adapted to his condition and part in the action of the universe. Contrary to Wollaston's theory of universal misery, the general state of mankind is not only tolerable but happy. Whatever Wollaston's own circumstances may have been, any person offering to cut Wollaston's throat would have been ill received.

Such, in substance, is Bolingbroke's thought. Gray, in reply, frankly admits that only *a posteriori* reasoning is valid, then proceeds to demonstrate that we can comprehend God's goodness *a posteriori* much more easily than His wisdom and power; and if there is no analogy between God's attributes and our conceptions of them, then we can have no adequate conception of them at all. Gray's words are dignified, although he concludes with fine sarcasm.[1]

Essay on Norman Architecture

This piece was first published by Mathias in 1814, under the too general title of *Architectura Gothica*. Mr. Gosse (*Gray*, p. 115, *Works*, i. 294) has conjectured that it was written in 1754. There is nothing inconsistent with this date; and in its favor may be mentioned the fact, shown by his letters, that in this year Gray was especially interested in architectural matters.

In his biography (p. 116), Mr. Gosse has spoken of Gray as "the first modern student of the history of architecture." As such, we must not expect too much from him. Some of his views are no longer held. His theory that the intersection of semicircular arches led to the building of pointed arches was long accepted; but it is now known that the pointed arch was in use in the East in the early Christian centuries; it was used in Egypt as early as 861; it may have been borrowed then through Sicily (which the Normans occupied from 1060 to 1194), or possibly have been reinvented independently. It begins to appear in England as early as the time of Henry II.[2]

---

[1] Mr. Tovey prints this piece in the second volume of the *Letters*, pp. 43–46, with interesting notes. Bolingbroke's "philosophy" is well summed up by Sir Leslie Stephen in his *English Thought in the Eighteenth Century*, i. 177–184. For a summary of Wollaston, see the same, pp. 130–134; for Clarke, pp. 119–130.

[2] Cf. Bond, *Gothic Architecture in England*, pp. 262–266;

Again, niches are scarcely among "the improvements of another age"; they occur as early as the eleventh century in the west front of Lincoln Cathedral; in the twelfth century at Barfreston; and in the thirteenth century at Wells, Salisbury, and Lichfield.[1] Gray, therefore, is in error in supposing them to be later than the Romanesque Period.

With Gray's list of characteristics of the Norman style the general reader may conveniently compare the lists given by T. Roger Smith in his *Architecture, Gothic and Renaissance*, New York and London, 1880, pp. 23 f. Points characteristic of Romanesque and not referred to by Gray are the narrow windows, generally splayed only internally; the deeply recessed doorways; the massive square towers; and the wagon-headed or barrel vaulting. In Sturgis' *Dictionary of Architecture and Building*, iii. 330 (New York, 1902), Mr. R. Clipston Sturgis sums up the characteristics of English Romanesque as the great length of the nave, often six or seven times its span; the central tower; and the lack of ambition in scientific construction, which resulted in leaving the nave to be spanned with timber instead of being vaulted like the aisles.[2]

R. P. Spiers in *Encyclopædia Britannica*, 10th ed., xxv. 608 f. (1902); Russell Sturgis, *European Architecture, an Historical Study*, pp. 181, 183, 192 ff. (1896); C. H. Moore, *Development and Character of Gothic Architecture*, 2d ed., p. 62; F. M. Simpson, *A History of Architectural Development*, 1909, ii. 10.

[1] Cf. Bond, *Gothic Architecture in England*, pp. 84–87.

[2] See also F. M. Simpson, *A History of Architectural Development*, 1909, ii. 243 ff.; C. H. Moore, *Development and Character of Gothic Architecture*, 2d ed., 1899, pp. 191–236.

In a short criticism quoted by Mr. Gosse (*Works*, i. 301 f.), Mr. Basil Champneys remarks that "Gray does not seem to have perceived that Romanesque, to be appreciated, must be looked at from the Gothic point of view. His criticisms are what we should expect to read from an exclusively Classical standpoint. He notices the clumsiness and want of studied proportion as a note of deterioration, and no doubt it was, but he appears also to take exception to the variety of detail, which gives the style its essentially Gothic character, and is to lovers of Gothic, its redeeming feature." This predilection for the classical styles was no doubt the result of Gray's general attachment to the classics, and should only remind us that fondness of genuine Gothic was not a characteristic of Gray's time. Altogether, in spite of the errors and shortcomings of Gray's paper, we can only marvel at its general breadth of view and exhibition of pure taste, and wish with Mr. Gosse that he had left more essays on architectural topics.

Metrum

The remarks on metre and rhyme, to which Gray gave this general title, as well as the remarks on the poetry of Lydgate which follow, were probably among the fruits of Gray's sojourn at the British Museum in 1759–1761. Mr. Gosse believes they were written in the winter of 1760 and the spring of 1761, but there is apparently no more warrant for this year than for the preceding year, 1759–60. They were first printed by Mathias in 1814; the originals are preserved among the manuscripts of Pembroke College, Cambridge.

Introduction

A reference to Gray's letter of April 15, 1770, to Thomas Warton will make it clear that these fragments were to have been parts of the *History of English Poetry* which, unhappily, Gray never brought to completion. In the Preface to his *History of English Poetry* (1774), i. p. iv., Warton says:

"A few years ago, Mr. Mason, with that liberality which ever accompanies true genius, gave me an authentic copy of Mr. Pope's scheme of a *History of English Poetry*, in which our poets were classed under their supposed respective schools. The late lamented Mr. Gray had also projected a work of this kind, and translated some Runic odes for its illustration, now published: but soon relinquishing the prosecution of a design, which would have detained him from his own noble inventions, he most obligingly condescended to favour me with the substance of his plan, which I found to be that of Mr. Pope, considerably enlarged, extended, and improved."

Warton goes on to say that he found he could not use their plan,[1] but adopted one which "exhibits without transposition the gradual improvements of our poetry, at the same time that it uniformly represents the progression of our language" (p. v).

In no other respect are Gray's views so much out of date as in respect to metre. He is totally wrong in his understanding of "riding rhyme," and Puttenham, whom he thinks mistaken, was probably right. Likewise, although his remark about "doggerel verse" is

[1] Gray's plan is preserved in his letter to Warton, *Works*, ed. Gosse, iii. 364 ff.

true, that "it was consistent with the greatest exactness in the cæsura and in the measure," still Puttenham is also right; for the writer of doggerel verse is tied only to the rules of rhyme, cæsura, and number of accents, and it may be said that these are only the restrictions that belong to verse anyway. It is no reproach to Gray to say that his lists of poems in *The Measures of Verse* are now wholly antiquated; for in his day the great bulk of English poetry prior to Shakespeare's time remained unprinted. The lists are indeed remarkable for containing as many titles as they do; and are significant as a landmark in the history of English scholarship. Gray knows little or nothing of the metre of Old English (a subject which still has its cruces), as it appears from his remarks on the metre of *Piers the Plowman*, a modified form of Old English metre.[1] As regards the origin of rhyme, it is now known, of course, to have come into the Romance languages from the Greek and Latin popular poetry of the classical and Middle Ages. Wilhelm Grimm, in his *Zur Geschichte des Reims*,[2] collected many examples of rhyme, more or less perfect, from Lucretius, Catullus, Virgil, Horace, Tibullus, and other Latin poets. The Arabs can have had little to do with its introduction into French and English, since Germanic and French rhyme appeared before the Arabs entered into European history.[3] Nor is it

[1] "It is a sort of Indian Summer for the old Germanic metre." F. B. Gummere, *Handbook of Poetics*, 1890, p. 177.

[2] *Abhandlungen der Königlichen Akademie der Wissenschaften zu Berlin*, 1851, pp. 521–713, especially pp. 627 ff.

[3] Cf. M. Kawczynski, *Essai comparatif sur l'origine et l'histoire des rythmes*, Paris, 1889, pp. 93 f.

now thought likely that the Celts had much to do with it, though rhyme was a regular feature of early Irish and Welsh poetry.

On the other hand, in some matters Gray showed remarkable insight. His view that the apparent inequalities of Chaucer's metre were due to the mistakes of scribes is borne out by our modern study of manuscripts. His remarks against Puttenham in regard to cæsural freedom are sensible and are based on the right sort of reasoning. Finally, his general theory of the origin of rhyme among the common people, as far as it goes, may still pass as a fair statement of present-day views on the subject.

On the Poems of John Lydgate

Two things at once strike the reader of Gray's remarks on Lydgate: first, that he ranks Lydgate rather high, placing him in the class just below Chaucer, and above Gower and Hoccleve; and second, that his opinions of Lydgate as here expressed are based wholly on *The Fall of Princes*. As this work contains some 40,000 lines, however, if Gray read it through, he had some grounds on which to judge of the poet, even though Lydgate[1] be the longest-winded of all medieval English poets. Gray's opinion of Lydgate is shared by many who have probably read more widely in Lydgate's works than had Gray.[2]

[1] See the note on p. 96 2.
[2] Thus Dr. Schick, in his introduction to *The Temple of Glas*, p. clvi., says: "It certainly does not occur to me to claim for Lydgate a place in the realms of higher poetry; but I think we

Gray's treatment of Lydgate's life is of course quite inadequate; doubtless he would have amplified it before he was satisfied with it. Yet it is to be noted that none of his dates needs to be changed to-day. At the time of writing, the facts of Lydgate's life did not interest

must allow that not infrequently do we meet in his better works, especially in those of his youth, with passages which breathe true poetry, or at all events, lie on the borderlands of true poetry. . . . Moreover, his love of Nature, his humour, his earnest piety, his admiration of his betters or of genius beyond his reach — always tendered ungrudgingly — the love of his country, his national pride, his high reverence for women, cannot fail to win our hearts."

In *English Writers*, vi. 104 f. (1890), Henry Morley has this to say: "John Lydgate was a bright, pleasant, and earnest monk, who wrote clear, fluent verse in any style then reputable; but who was most apt at the telling of such moral stories as his public liked. Sometimes he was as prolix, and he always was as musical, as the old romancers who had been satirized by Chaucer in 'Sir Thopas'; but he preferred to take his heroes and heroines out of the Martyrology; and he could write cleverly to order, for the library of any monastery, the legend of its patron saint . . . John Lydgate was not a poet of great genius; but he was a man with music in his life. He was full of a harmony of something more than words, not more diffuse than his age liked him to be, and therefore, with good reason, popular and honoured among English readers in the fifteenth century."

Finally, ten Brink (*Geschichte der englischen Litteratur*, Strassburg, 1893, ii. 231) thus expresses himself: "Lydgate hatte von Haus aus das Zeug zu einem tüchtigen Volksdichter: eine weltfreudige, epische Stimmung, eine männlich derbe Natur, welche zarteren Empfindungen keineswegs verschlossen war, einen klar und richtig beobachtenden Blick, einen entwickelten Sinn für Naturschönheit. Was ihm fehlte, war die bedeutende Originalität, der weite Gesichtskreis, die geistige Tiefe und Feinheit, die dem Kunstdichter unentbehrlich sind, soll er sich über das Mittelmass erheben."

him; he hastened on to more important matters — Lydgate's knowledge of Latin, his "long processes," his facile rhymes, his ability to portray emotion, his satire on women and on monks. Gray's remarks on these topics are temperate and illuminating. So far as they go, in the main they have never been superseded, and there is nowhere to-day any better general estimate of Lydgate than that here furnished by the first modern student of the fifteenth century poet.

Samuel Daniel

The brief character sketch of the poet Daniel, like the observations on metre and on Lydgate, was intended to form a part of the projected *History of English Poetry*. It was first printed in *The Athenæum* for July 29, 1854 (No. 1396, pp. 941 f.), a few days before the sale of the Penn collection of Gray MSS., of which it formed a part, and so far as I know has never been reprinted. While somewhat sketchy and fragmentary in character, it nevertheless deserves to be incorporated into a collection of Gray's prose writings.

The Letters

Gray was a fairly industrious though by no means a voluminous letter-writer. Of his letters some 375 have been published, which were written between 1736 and 1771. His chief correspondents were his mother (until her death in 1753), West (1736–42), Walpole (1736–68), Thomas Wharton (1740–71), John Chute (1741–62), Mason (1753–70), James Brown

Introduction

(1757–70), and Nicholls (1764–71).[1] Of these the only one now remembered except for this connection with Gray is Walpole.

This is not the place for a characterization of Gray's letters as a collection. All the qualities of the best letters are exhibited — ease, familiar playfulness, sympathy with the point of view of the correspondent, the charm of good breeding, perfect truthfulness, — and to do justice to them would require more space than can here be given. The reader may be referred to Mr. Tovey's excellent introductions.

In this volume I have included from the letters a number of extracts pertaining mainly to literary criticism. Many of them, perhaps, are not to be taken too seriously, being merely off-hand first impressions. One of the most important letters, as Professor Saintsbury has pointed out, is the one [2] written to West in April, probably of 1742, in which Gray defends a cardinal principle of Romantic style: the principle of democratic freedom for the poet. In another interesting letter to Walpole (1748), he reviews Dodsley's *Miscellany*, bestowing praise and blame with taste and judgment. Important, too, are the remarks on the Letters Prefixed to Mason's *Elfrida*, in which he shows some of the limitations imposed by the presence of the chorus. Many illuminating comments are scattered throughout the criticisms of Mason's works, as, for example,[3]

---

[1] For interesting remarks on some of these men, see the introduction to the *Letters*, ed. Tovey, ii. pp. ix.-xxxv.
[2] See the text, p. 134.
[3] See the text, p. 221 f.

where Gray speaks, referring to Mador's song in *Caractacus*, of the difference between the lyric style and others, and explains why it cannot be long sustained. A number of letters touch on the Ossianic controversy, on which we find Gray with the will to believe, yet not blind to the evidence against the fragments. Notable, too, is his letter to Bonstetten in which he comments wisely on Plato's portrait of a philosopher. In its essential elements this portrait may well be applied to, and fairly describes, Gray himself. He too was gentle, magnanimous, temperate, generous, accustomed to large views of things. Other qualities he lacked of those necessary for "one who would govern the rest of mankind." But the noblest qualities of true manhood were generously meted out to him, and shine throughout his letters.

VI. SUMMARY

We may, then, recapitulate thus the points emphasized in this introduction: Gray lived the life of a recluse and a scholar, caring little for society and less for domestic life; absorbed in his books; deeply interested in antiquity, yet not indifferent to the spectacle of contemporary activity; viewing this spectacle, however, without a desire to engage actively in its struggles; caring little for fame and much for virtue. The smallness of his literary product was due not to the frigid atmosphere of the time which some have thought prevented him from "speaking out," but to other causes, — lack of stimulus from his friends, the growing predominance of the scholarly temperament and inclination, his highly critical and fastidious taste, his natural reticence, his indolence or aversion to active creative effort, and his lack of ambition. In criticism Gray ranged himself at the start with the Romanticists, and was never bound by tradition or undue veneration for authority. His critical prose is small in bulk but important and significant because of his attitude, that of the learner rather than the judge or arbiter, and because he possessed the qualities necessary for a great critic — disinterestedness, a sense of humor, sound learning, and sympathy. His critical utterances, though fragmentary, are always suggestive, and are among our valuable inheritances from the eighteenth century.

VII. BIBLIOGRAPHICAL NOTE

All of Gray's prose, we have seen, was published posthumously. The letters first appeared in the "Memoirs of His Life and Writings" prefixed by Mason to his edition of Gray's *Poems*, York, 1775. The *Observations on English Metre*, the *Notes on Aristophanes and Plato*, and other prose fragments were first printed by Thomas J. Mathias in his edition of the *Works*, London, 1814. Gray's correspondence with Norton Nicholls was published by the Rev. John Mitford in 1843; his correspondence with Mason, by the same editor in 1853. The most recent edition of his complete works is that of Mr. Edmund Gosse (4 volumes, London, 1884, revised in 1902), which in matters of detail is somewhat inaccurate. A selection from Gray's poetry and prose, edited by Professor William L. Phelps and including valuable critical matter, was published in Ginn's *Athenæum Press Series* in 1894. Gray's *Letters*, admirably edited by Mr. Duncan C. Tovey, are now being published in three volumes in Bohn's Library (vol. i., 1900, vol. ii., 1904). Appended to volume ii. are Nicholls' *Reminiscences of Gray*, written in 1805. The fullest life of Gray, though very inaccurate, is that by Gosse (*English Men of Letters* Series, 1882, new edition, 1889). The most trustworthy account of his life is by the late Sir Leslie Stephen (*Dictionary of National Biography*, xxiii. 22–28, 1890). Valuable essays on Gray are by Matthew Arnold (in Ward's *English Poets*, London, 1880), Lowell (*The New Princeton Review*, i. 153–177, March, 1886, reprinted in his *Latest Literary Essays*, 1892), Tovey in *Gray and His Friends* (Cambridge, 1890), T. H. Warren, "Gray and Dante" (*The Monthly Review*, iii. 147–164, June, 1901, reprinted in his *Essays of Poets and Poetry*, 1909), and Thomas M. Parrott in his *Studies of a Book-Lover*, 1904. A full bibliography of Gray by the editor of this volume will appear in *The Journal of English and Germanic Philology*.

Essays
and
Criticisms

Essays and Criticisms

PHÆDO

Η, ΠΕΡΙ ΨΥΧΗΣ

(Plat. Op. Serrani. Vol. 1, p. 57.)

This famous dialogue was supposed by Panætius [1] the stoick, a great admirer of Plato, not to be genuine, or at least interpolated, rather, as it seems, from his own persuasion [2] of the soul's mortality, than from any thing in the piece itself unlike the manner or the tenets of the philosopher, to whom it has always been ascribed. The whole course of antiquity has regarded it as one of his principal works; and (what seems decisive) Aristotle [3] himself cites it, as a work of his master.

The historical part of it is admirable, and, though written and disposed with all the art and management of the best tragick writer, (for the slightest circumstance in it wants not its force and meaning) it exhibits nothing to the eye but

---

[1] Anthologia, l. 1, 44.   [2] Cicero, Tusc. Quæst. l. 1, 32.
[3] Meteorolog. l. 2, 2.

the noble simplicity of nature. Every intelligent reader will feel what those who were eye-witnesses are said to have felt, namely, ἀήθη τινὰ κρᾶσιν, ἀπό τε τῆς ἡδονῆς συγκεκραμένην ὁμοῦ καὶ τῆς λύπης. The innocence, the humanity, the cheerfulness, and the unaffected intrepidity of Socrates, will draw some tears from him (as it did many from them) as for the loss of a father; and will, at the same time, better than any arguments, shew him a soul, which, if it were not so, at least deserved to be immortal.

The reasoning part is far inferior, sometimes weak, sometimes false, too obscure, too abstracted, to convince us of any thing; yet with a mixture of good sense and with many fine observations. The fabulous account of a future state is too particular and too fantastick an invention for Socrates to dwell upon at such a time, and has less decorum and propriety in it than the other parts of the dialogue.

Socrates attempts in this dialogue to prove, that true philosophy is but a continual preparation for death; its daily study and practice being to wean and separate the body from the soul, whose pursuit of truth is perpetually stopped and impeded by the numerous avocations, the little pleasures, pains, and necessities of its companion. *That*, as death is but a transition from its opposite,[1] life (in the same manner as heat is from cold, weakness from strength, and all things, both in the natural and in the moral world, from their contraries) so life is only a transition from death; whence he would infer the probability of a metempsychosis. *That*, such propositions,[2] as every one assents to at first, being self-evident, and no one giving any account how such parts of knowledge, on which the rest are founded, were originally conveyed to our mind, there must have been a pre-existent state, in which the soul was acquainted with these truths, which she recollects and assents to on their recurring to her in this life. *That*, as truth is eternal and immutable, and not visible to our senses but to the soul alone; and as the empire, which she exercises over the body, bears a resemblance to the power of the Divinity, it is probable that she, like her object, is everlasting and unchangeable, and, like the office she bears, something divine. *That*, it cannot be, as some have thought, merely a harmony resulting from a disposition of parts in the body, since it directs, commands, and restrains the func-

[1] This was an idea of Pythagoras. Ἐν βίῳ ἀρχὴ τελευτῆς· ἐν ζωῇ δὲ γένεσις φθορᾶς. Diog. Laert. l. 8, s. 22.
[2] Socrates has explained the same doctrine in the Meno, p. 81, &c. but rather as conjectural than demonstrable, for he adds, in the conclusion, p. 86. Τὰ μέν γε ἄλλα οὐκ ἂν πάνυ ὑπὲρ τοῦ λόγου διϊσχυρισαίμην, &c.

tions of that very body. *That*, the soul, being the cause of life to the body, can never itself be susceptible of death; and *that*, there will be a state of rewards and punishments, the scene of which he takes pains in describing, though he concludes, that no man can tell exactly where or what it shall be.

Dacier's superstition and folly are so great in his notes on the Phædo, that they are not worth dwelling upon.

ESSAY ON THE PHILOSOPHY OF LORD BOLINGBROKE

I WILL allow Lord Bolingbroke, that the moral, as well as physical, attributes of God must be known to us only à posteriori, and that this is the only real knowledge we can have either of the one or the other; I will allow too that perhaps it may be an idle distinction which we make between them: His moral attributes being as much in his nature and essence as those we call his physical; but the occasion of our making some distinction is plainly this: His eternity, infinity, omniscience, and almighty power, are not what connect him, if I may so speak, with us his creatures. We adore him, not because he always did in every place, and always will, exist; but because he gave, and still preserves to us our own existence by an exertion of his goodness. We adore him, not because he knows and can do all things, but because he made us capable of knowing and of doing what may conduct us to happiness. It is therefore his benevolence which we adore, not his greatness or power; and if we are made only to bear our part in a system, without any regard to our own particular happiness, we can no longer worship him as our all-bounteous parent. There is no meaning in the term. The idea of his malevolence (an impiety I tremble to write) must succeed. We have nothing left but our fears, and those too vain; for whither can they lead but to despair and the sad desire of annihilation? "If then, justice and goodness be not the same in God as in our ideas, we mean nothing when we say that God is necessarily just and good; and for the same reason it may as well be said that we know not what we mean when, according to Dr. Clarke, (Evid. 26th) we affirm that he is necessarily a wise and intelligent Being." What then can Lord Bolingbroke mean, when he says every thing shews the wisdom of God; and yet adds, every thing does not shew in like manner the goodness of God, conformably to our ideas of this attribute in either! By wisdom he must only mean, that God knows and employs the fittest means to a certain end, no matter what that end may be. This indeed is a proof of knowledge and intelligence; but these alone do not constitute wisdom; the word implies the application of these fittest means to the best and kindest end: or, who will call it true wisdom? Even amongst ourselves, it is not held as such. All the attributes then that he seems to think apparent in the constitution of things, are his unity, infinity, eternity, and intelligence; from no one of which, I boldly affirm, can result any duty of gratitude or adoration incumbent on mankind, more than if He and all things round him were produced, as some have dared to think, by the necessary working of eternal matter in an infinite vacuum: for what does it avail to add intelligence to those other physical attributes, unless that intelligence be directed, not only to the good of the whole, but also to the good of every individual of which that whole is composed?

It is therefore no impiety, but the direct contrary, to say that human justice and the other virtues, which are indeed only various applications of human benevolence, bear some resemblance to the moral attributes of the supreme Being. It is only by means of that resemblance, we conceive them in him, or their effects in his works. It is by the same means only, that we comprehend those physical attributes which his Lordship allows to be demonstrable. How can we form any notion of his unity, but from that unity of which we ourselves are conscious? How of his existence, but from our own consciousness of existing? How of his power, but of that power which we experience in ourselves?

Yet neither Lord Bolingbroke nor any other man, that thought on these subjects, ever believed that these our ideas were real and full representations of these attributes in the Divinity. They say he knows; they do not mean that he compares ideas which he acquired from sensation, and draws conclusions from them. They say he acts; they do not mean by impulse, nor as the soul acts on an organized body. They say he is omnipotent and eternal; yet on what are their ideas founded, but on our own narrow conceptions of space and duration, prolonged beyond the bounds of place and time? Either, therefore, there is a resemblance and analogy (however imperfect and distant) between the attributes of the Divinity and our conceptions of them, or we cannot have any conceptions of them at all. He allows we ought to reason from earth, that we do know, to heaven which we do not know; how can we do so but by that affinity which appears between one and the other?

In vain, then, does my Lord attempt to ridicule the warm but melancholy imagination of Mr. Wollaston in that fine soliloquy: "Must I then bid my last farewell to these walks when I close these lids, and yonder blue regions and all this scene darken upon me and go out? Must I then only serve to furnish dust to be mingled with the ashes of these herds and plants, or with this dirt under my feet? Have I been set so far above them in life, only to be levelled with them in death?"[1] No thinking head, no heart, that has the least sensibility, but must have made the same reflection; or at least must feel, not the beauty alone, but the truth of it when he hears it from the mouth of another. Now what reply will Lord Bolingbroke make to these questions which are put to him, not only by Wollaston, but by all mankind? He will tell you, that we, that is, the animals, vegetables, stones, and *other clods of earth*, are all connected in one immense design, that we are all Dramatis Personæ, in different characters, and that we were not made for ourselves, but for the action: that it is foolish, presumptuous, impious, and profane to murmur against the Almighty Author of this drama, when we feel ourselves unavoidably unhappy. On the contrary, we ought to rest our head on the soft pillow of resignation, on the immovable rock of tranquillity; secure, that, if our pains and afflictions grow violent indeed, an immediate end will be put to our miserable being, and we shall be mingled with the dirt under our feet, a thing common to all the animal kind; and of which he who complains

[1] Religion of Nature Delineated, sect. 9, p. 209, quarto.

does not seem to have been set by his reason so far above them in life, as to deserve not to be mingled with them in death. Such is the consolation his philosophy gives us, and such the hope on which his tranquillity was founded.

ESSAY ON NORMAN ARCHITECTURE

The characteristics of the old Norman or (as Sir Christopher Wren calls it) the Saxon Architecture, are great solidity, heaviness, and rude simplicity, better adapted to castles, walls of cities, and other places of defence, than to the purposes of habitation, magnificence, or religious worship. It seems indeed to be copied from the Roman style in that degenerate state to which it was reduced under the later emperors; for it seems but natural that the Franks [1] in Gaul, the Saxons in England, and other barbarous nations in the several countries which had made a part of the Roman empire (when they were once settled there, and found leisure to apply themselves to the arts of peace) should imitate those many monuments which were every where before their eyes, and especially (as they themselves were now become Christians) such as had been long consecrated to the uses of religion, and were filled with the miraculous relics and representations of those saints who were the

[1] Including the Normans, who soon learned the language and customs of the Franks.

principal objects of their worship. It may be asked, why then did they not rather imitate the beautiful remains of a better age, of which many were then in being, as some of them exist to this day? I answer, because taste had nothing to do in their choice; because the fabrics erected in the time and for the purposes of Christianity had a nearer connection with their own faith; and lastly, because the artizans employed in them were probably their subjects and natives of the country, who received these arts by tradition from their fathers, and were unaccustomed to any other style of building.

The particulars which distinguish this kind of architecture, which seems to have lasted in England from the time of the Conquest (if not earlier) to the beginning of Henry the Third's reign, that is, from A. D. 1066 to about 1216, are chiefly these.

First distinction. The *semi-circular, or round-headed,* [1] *arch*, generally, if not always, used in the

---

[1] I cannot absolutely affirm, that they never made use of the *pointed arch*, because the great western tower at Ely now rises upon four *such* arches; some of the ranges, too, which adorn the outside of this and of the Galilee adjoining, are of like form, and the grand arches in front under the middle tower of Peterborough are *pointed:* but yet I do suspect that all these were alterations and additions made in succeeding ages, which, I am persuaded, was a common practice with regard to windows, in order to let in more light, and

three orders which commonly compose the nave, namely, the lower great one that opens to the side aisles; the second, which runs in front of the two corridores over those aisles; and the uppermost, which forms a sort of arcade before the higher range of windows. The doors, the vault of the aisles, and even the windows, are in this form too, and the arch is usually wide beyond the just proportion of its height.

The same arching is frequently used to cover the long vacancy of a dead wall, and forms an arcade adhering to it with tall clumsy [1] pillars and extraordinary narrow intercolumns; and for a like purpose they frequently employed a wider archwork rising on short columns and interlaced, so that the curve of one arch intersecting that of its neighbour, their pillars or legs stand at only half the distance from each other that they otherwise would do. This, though only an ornament, might perhaps suggest the idea of building on *pointed arches*, afterwards in use, as the intersection of two circular ones produces the same effect to the eye.

Second distinction. The massy *piers*, or pillars, also to take off from the plain and heavy appearance of those thick walls.

[1] They have no swell, nor gradual diminution, which seems to be the cause of this clumsy appearance; besides this, they stand too close together.

either of an octagonal, round, or elliptical form, on which the arches rise. They are sometimes decagons, or duodecagons, or even a mixture of all these, without any correspondence or regularity at all, as in the choir at Peterborough: their height is generally far too short for their diameter, which gives them the appearance of great strength joined with heaviness. This latter fault seems to have struck even the eyes of that age itself, and, to conceal it, they added a flat pilaster on four sides of the pier, with a slender half-column projecting from it, or (to lighten it still more) covered the pier almost entirely with clustered pillars of small diameter, adhering to its surface, which in reality bear little or nothing of the weight, and serve merely for ornament. This latter had so good an effect, that it was adopted by all architects of succeeding times, and continued till the revival of the Greek and Roman style. There are very ancient examples of these cluster-piers to be seen, sometimes intermixed alternately with the plainer kind, as at Durham; sometimes interspersed among them, as it were by chance, as at Peterborough; and sometimes alone and unmixed, as in the views of old St. Paul's, and at Ely. From the capital of the piers usually rises a half-column of but small diameter, which, passing between the arches of the two upper orders in the nave or choir &c., reaches quite up to the roof, and is a principal grace of these buildings.

On the outside, as they have no buttresses, which were the invention of later ages, the walls are commonly adorned either with half-columns or with flat stripes of stone-work, resembling a plain pilaster, at regular distances.

Third distinction. The *capitals* of the piers and smaller columns have great variety in their forms; the square, the octagon, the cushioned, or swelling beneath, with four flat faces cut in a semicircle, the convex part downward, and sometimes adorned [1] with a mantling, or piece of drapery trussed like a festoon. Some of the large ones there are which, swelling like the last underneath, break above [2] into eight or sixteen angular projections, something like the rostra of an antique ship. Others are round, and decked with an awkward imitation [3] of acanthus leaves, curling at the point into a sort of volutes. These, and many other uncouth forms and inventions, may be seen in the arcade of the side aisles at Peterborough, where they have studied to vary all the capitals, as far as their art reached, and seem to have thought there was a beauty in this confusion:

---

[1] As at Durham.   [2] In the choir at Peterborough.
[3] In the Prebend's narrow way, and the south transept at Ely.

they are all in general too squat and too gross for the pillars which they are meant to adorn, not to mention the rudeness they have in common with every other member of these buildings, that required any sculpture or delicacy of workmanship.

Fourth distinction. The *ceilings*, at least in the wider and loftier parts, as of the nave, choir, and transepts, &c. were usually, I imagine, only of timber, perhaps because they wanted the skill to vault with stone in these great intervals, though they practised it in the smaller. They are either entirely flat, as at Peterborough, or gabel-fashioned with rafters, as in the transepts at Ely, or coved with frame-work made of small scantlings of wood, and lying open to the leads, as in the nave of the same church.

Fifth distinction. The *ornaments*, which are chiefly mouldings in front of the arches, and fasciæ or broad lists of carving, which run along the walls over them or beneath the windows, are without any neatness, and full as clumsy as the capitals above mentioned; the most frequent of them is the *zig-zag*, or chevron-work. There are also *billeted*-moulding, the *nail-head*, as in the great tower at Hereford and in the pendents of arches in the nave of old St. Paul's, resembling the heads of large nails drove in at regular distances; the *nebule*,[1] which I call by that name from its likeness to a coat nebulé in heraldry; and the *lozenge* and *triangle* lattice-work. These, with the ranges of arch-work rising one over another, with which they decorated the fronts of buildings and the sides of their towers on the outside, are the principal inventions which they employed for ornament. As to statues,[2] niches,[3] canopies, finialls, and tracery, they were the improvements of another age.

Such are the most obvious distinctions of this early style of building. An accurate inspection of those remains, which have their dates well ascertained, might possibly discover many other particulars, and also shew us the gradual advances of the art within the period which I have assigned; for it is not to be imagined that all the forms which I have described made their appearance at one and the same time, or that the build-

---

[1] Under the highest range of windows on the outside of Peterborough Cathedral, and elsewhere.

[2] There may be some figures extant in England, in stone or wood, older than the period which I have here assigned, but they made no part of the architect's design, and even on sepulchral monuments are very rare; besides that their originality may well be disputed; for example, that of King Ethelbald on Crowland Bridge, of King Osric at Worcester, of Robert Courthose at Gloucester, &c.

[3] These *niches*, when they had the figure of any saint in them, were called *perks*, whence comes our old phrase of being *perked* up, or exposed to public view.

ings, for example, in the first years of Henry the Second were exactly like those erected in the end of his reign. Any eye may perceive the difference between the body and aisles of the choir at Peterborough, with the east side of the transept, and the semicircular tribune which finishes the same choir, the two ends and west side of the transept, and the whole nave of the church: yet all these were built within the compass of five and thirty years by two successive abbots.

Upon the whole, these huge structures claim not only the veneration due to their great antiquity, but (though far surpassed in beauty by the buildings of the three succeeding centuries) have really a rude kind of majesty, resulting from the loftiness of their naves, the gloom of their aisles, and the hugeness of their massive members, which seem calculated for a long duration.

OBSERVATIONS ON ENGLISH METRE

Though I would not with Mr. Urry,[1] the Editor of Chaucer, insert words and syllables, unauthorized by the oldest manuscripts, to help out what seems lame and defective in the measure of our ancient writers, yet as I see those manuscripts, and the first [2] printed editions, so extremely inconstant in their manner of spelling one and the same word as to vary continually, and often in the compass of two lines, and seem to have no fixed orthography, I cannot help thinking it probable, that many great inequalities in the metre are owing to the neglect of transcribers, or that the manner of reading made up for the defects which appear in the writing. Thus the *y* which we often see prefixed to participles passive, *y*cleped, *y*hewe, &c. is not a mere arbi-

---

[1] See the Preface to Urry's Chaucer. Fol.

[2] This inconstancy of the manner of spelling one and the same word is not confined to the first printed copies, but is found equally in the MSS. themselves. This is no wonder, for the Italians themselves, contemporary with Chaucer, writing in an age when literature began to flourish, and in a language more regular and grammatical than that of any neighbouring country, had yet no fixed orthography, as appears from the original manuscripts of Francesco Barberino, Boccaccio, and Petrarch, which are still preserved. (See Crescimbeni, Comentarj, l. 6.)

trary insertion to fill up the verse, but is the old Anglo-Saxon augment, always prefixed formerly to such participles, as g*e*lufod (loved) from lufian (to love), g*e*ræd, from rædan (to read), &c. which augment, as early as Edward the Confessor's time, began to be written with a *y*, or an *i*, as *y*lufod, *i*seld, for g*e*lufod, g*e*seld, (loved, sold,) as Dr. Hickes[1] informs us in his Anglo-Saxon Grammar, C. 22, p. 136. This syllable, though (I suppose) then out of use in common speech, our poets inserted, where it suited them, in verse. The same did they by the final syllable of verbs, as bren*nin*, correc*tin*, dron*kin*, &c. (to burn, correct, drink,) which was also Saxon, all the infinitives in that tongue ending with an *an*, or *eon*, as

---

[1] And see Somner's Saxon Dictionary in Ge. Chaucer seems to have been well aware of the injustice that his copyists might chance to do to him: he says, towards the end of his Troilus,

"And for there is so great diversitie,
In English, and in writing of our tong;
So pray I to God, that none miswrite thee,
Ne thee mis-metre for defaut of tong
And redde where so thou be, or else song,
That thou be understond', God I beseech —"

Yet in another place he says,

"But for the rime is light and lewde,
Yet make it somewhat agreeable
Though some verse fayle in a syllable."

(3d b. of Fame.)

And so says Lydgate of himself:

"Because I know the verse therein is wrong,
As being some too short, and some too long."

(Chronicle of Troye, p. 316.)

*bebyrige*an, to bury, *magan*, to be able, *gefeon*, to rejoice, and most of the participles passive, and the plural persons terminating with the same letter, as, *gefund*en, found, *beswung*en, beaten, &c.; and *we, ge, hi, miht*on, (we, he, they, might), we *wold*on, we would; we *sceold*on, we should; we *a*ron, we are, &c. This termination began to be omitted after the Danes were settled among us; for in the Cimbrick tongue the verbs usually finished in *a*, as *greip*a, to gripe, *hab*a, to have, which in the Saxon were *greip*an, *hab*an; the transition is very apparent thence to the English which we now speak. As then our writers [1] inserted

---

[1] The same thing is observable in the MSS. and first editions of the Italian Poets. Even in Dante's and in Petrarch's time, as,
"Nello stato primaio non si rinselva."
Purgatorio, c. 14, v. 66.
And,
"Ecco Cin da Pistoia, Guitton d' Arezzo."
Trionfo dell' Amore, capit. 4, v. 32.
In both which verses there is a syllable too much, on which Crescimbeni observes, "Costumavano gli antichi rimatori, ogni volta che in fin d' una voce s' incontrava la vocale *i* tra due altri vocali, troncar la voce, e pronunziarla fino alla sillaba accentuata acutamente, benchè la voce ad arbitrio la scrivessero or tronca con l'apostrofe, ed ora intera." (Istor: della Volg: Poesia, l. 1, p. 9.) And one would think that they occasionally practised the same thing in syllables not consisting of a vowel only, by that verse of an ancient poet, which he cites,
"Tu sei quel arma*tura*, per cui vencimmo,"
where in reading they probably sunk the last syllable of *armatura*, because the accent did not fall upon it. This might less offend them, because their ears were so used to the Provençal dialect, in which abundance of words are the same with the Italian, were not the last

these initial and final letters, or omitted them; and, where we see them written, we do not doubt that they were meant to fill up the measure; it follows, that these Poets had an ear not insensible to defects in metre; and where the verse seems to halt, it is very probably occasioned by the transcriber's neglect, who, seeing a word spelt differently from the manner then customary, changed or omitted a few letters without reflecting on the injury done to the measure. The case is the same with the genitive case singular and the nominative plural of many nouns, which by the Saxon inflection had an additional syllable, as *word*, a word, *wordis*, of a word: *smith*, a smith, *smithis*, of a smith, *smithas*, smiths, which, as Hickes observes, is the origin of the formation of those cases in our present tongue; but we now have reduced them, by our pronunciation, to an equal number of syllables with their nominatives singular. This was commonly done too, I imagine, in Chaucer's and Lydgate's time; but, in verse, they took the liberty either to follow the old language in pronouncing the final syllable, or to sink the vowel and abridge it, as was usual, according to the necessity of their versification.

syllable cut off, as pie*tat* for pie*tate*, sequ*ent* for seguente, poder*uz* for poder*oso*, *fach* for fatto, &c. and doubtless from that language the Italians borrowed their custom of sinking the vowel in the end of many words at pleasure, when the next begins with a consonant, which they now do in prose, as well as in verse.

For example, they would read either vĭŏlēttĕs with four syllables, or violets with three; ban*kis*, or banks; triŭmphys, or triŭmphs, indifferently. I have mentioned (in some remarks on the verses of Lydgate) the *e* mute, and their use of it in words derived from the French, and I imagine that they did the same in many words of true English origin, which the Danes had before robbed of their final consonant, writing *bute* for the Saxon *butan* (without), *bifora* for *biforan* (before), *ondrede* for *ondreadan* (to dread), *gebringe* for *gebringan* (to bring), *doeme* for *deman* (to deem), and abundance of other words. Here we may easily conceive, that though the *n* was taken away, yet the *e* continued to be pronounced faintly, and though in time it was quite dropped in conversation, yet when the poet thought fit to make a syllable of it, it no more offended their ears than it now offends those of a Frenchman to hear it so pronounced, in verse.

Puttenham, in his Art of Poetry, addressed to Queen Elizabeth in 1587, tells us, l. 2, c. 4, that " Chaucer, Lydgate, and others used *Cesures* either very seldom, or not at all, or else very licentiously; and many times made their meetres (they called them *riding Rhyme*) of such unshapely words as would allow no convenient cesure; and therefore did let their rymes run out at length, and never staid till they came to the end; which manner, though it were not to be misliked in some sort of meetre, yet in every long verse the cesure ought to be kept precisely, if it were but to serve as a law to correct the licentiousness of Rymers. Besides that it pleaseth the eare better, and sheweth more cunning in the maker by following the rule of his restraint, for a Rymer that will be tied by no rules at all, but range as he list, may utter what he will; but such manner of Poesy is called in our Vulgar, [1] '*Ryme Dogrell*,'

---

[1] It appears from Alderman Fabian's Prologue to the second volume of his Chronicle, written in Henry the Seventh's reign, that the free verse, where no exact number of syllables was observed, was then called *doggrell*. Thus,

"Now would I fayne
In wordes plaine
Some honour sayne,
  And bring to mynde
Of that auncient citye,
That so goodly is to se,
And full trewe ever hath be,
  And also full kynde, &c.

For though I shuld all day tell,
Or that with my *ryme dogerell*
Myght I not yet halfe do spell
  This townes great honour, &c.

To the Reader.
Whoso hym liketh these versys to rede,
Wyth favour I pray he wyll theym spell,
Let not the rudeness of them hym lede
For to desprave this *ryme dogerell*," &c.

with which rebuke we will that in no case our Maker shall be touched."

Then Puttenham gives rules for the Cesura, which he tells us, "In a verse of twelve syllables should always divide it exactly in the middle; in one of ten, it should fall on the fourth, in one of eight on the same, in one of seven on the same, or on none at all," &c. I mention no[1] more than these, as they are now the only measures admitted into our serious poetry, and I shall consider how his rules hold in modern practice.

Alexandrines,[2] or verses of twelve syllables, it is true, though Spenser sometimes does otherwise, must, if they would strike the ear agreeably, have their pause in the middle, as,

And after toilsome days | a soft repose at night.

[1] Lines of six, five, or four syllables are intermixed in lyric compositions, but, as Puttenham says, "they need no cesure, because the breath asketh no relief."

[2] Puttenham says, "The Alexandrine is with our modern rhymers most usual, with the auncyent makers it was not so. For before Sir Thomas Wyatt's time they were not used in our vulgar: they be for grave and stately matters fitter, than for any other ditty of pleasure. — If the cesure be just in the middle, and that ye suffer the verse to run at full length, and do not (as common rimers do, or their printer, for sparing of paper) cut them off in the middest, wherein they make in two verses but halfe rime, they do very wel." Art of Poesie, l. ii. c. 3. — The poets of Henry the Eighth's time mixed it with the line of fourteen syllables alternately, which is so tiresome, that we have long since quite banished it. Thus many things of Wyatt's and Lord Surrey's are written, and those of Queen Elizabeth on the Queen of Scots.

Or,

> He both her warlike Lords | outshined in Helen's eyes.

And this uniformity in the cesura is just the reason why we no longer use them but just to finish a lyric stanza: they are also sometimes interspersed arbitrarily among verses of ten syllables. This is an odd custom, but it is confirmed by the sanction which Dryden and Pope have given to it, for they soon tire the ear with this sameness of sound; and the French seem to have judged ill in making them their heroic [1] measure.

Verses of *eight* syllables are so far from being obliged to have their cesura on the fourth, that Milton, the best example of an exquisite ear that I can produce, varies it continually, as,

> To live with her, | and live with thee . . On the 4th.
> In unreproved | pleasures free . . ———— 5th.
> To hear the lark | begin his flight . . ———— 4th.
> And singing | startle the dull night . . ———— 3d.

---

[1] They were not so till towards the end of the sixteenth century. "Quant aux vers de *douze* syllabes, que nous appellons Alexandrins, combien qu'ils proviennent d'une longue ancienneté, toutefois nous en avions perdu l'usage. Car, lorsque Marot insère quelques uns dedans ses Epigrammes ou Tombeaux, c'est avec cette suscription, Vers Alexandrins; comme si c'étoit chose nouvelle et inaccoustumée d'en user.— Le premier des nôtres, qui les mit en credit, fut Baïf en ses Amours de Francine, suivy depuis par Du Bellay au livre de ses Regrets, et par Ronsard en ses Hymnes, et finalement par Du Bartas, qui semble vouloir renvier sur tous les autres en ses deux Semaines." (See Pasquier, l. vii. c. 8 and 11.) Yet Ronsard, in his Art of Poetry, continues to call the Decasyllabic measure only *Heroic Verse*, and uses it in his Franciade and other long compositions.

Whĕre thĕ grēat sūn | bĕgīns hĭs stāte . . ———— 4th.
The clouds | in thousand liveries dight . ———— 2d.
With masque | and antique pageantry . . ———— 2d.

The more we attend to the composition of Milton's harmony, the more we shall be sensible how he loved to vary[1] his pauses, his measures, and his feet, which gives that enchanting air of freedom and wildness to his versification, unconfined by any rules but those which his own feeling and the nature of his subject demanded. Thus he mixes the line of eight syllables with that of seven, the Trochee and the Spondee with the Iambic foot, and the single rhyme with the double. He changes the cesura as frequently in the heptasyllabic measure, as,

Oft ŏn ă plāt | of rising ground   (Octosyll.)
I hear | the far-off curfew sound,   (Oct:—)   On the 2d.
Ŏvĕr sōme | wide-water'd shore   . . ———— 3d.
Swinging slow | with sullen roar: . . . ———— 3d.
Or if the air | will not permit, &c. (Oct:—) ———— 4th.
Far from all resort | of mirth   . . . ———— 5th.
Save the cricket | on the hearth . . ———— 4th.
Or the bellman's | drowsy charm . . . ———— 4th.

---

[1] Lord Surrey (who was Puttenham's example for sweetness and proportion of metre) generally, though not always, makes his Cæsura on the fourth; as,
"True wisdom join'd | with simpleness,
The night | discharged of all care, . . On the 2nd.
Where wine the wit | may not oppresse
The faithful wife | without debate,
Such slepes | as may beguile the night,
Content thyself | with thine estate,
Ne wish for death, | ne feare his might."

But the greatest confinement which Puttenham would lay on our verse is that of making the Cæsura constantly fall on the fourth syllable of our decasyllabic measure, which is now become our only heroic [1] metre for all poems of any length. This restraint Wyatt and Lord Surrey submitted to, though here and there you find an instance of their breaking through it, though rarely. So,

> From these hye hilles | as when a spring doth falle,
> It trilleth down | with still and subtle course,
> Of this and that | it gathers aye, and shall
> Till it have just | downe flowed to stream and force:
> So fareth Love, | when he hath ta'en a course;
> Rage is his raine; | resistance 'vaileth none;
> The first eschue | is remedy alone.   *Wyatt.*

---

[1] We probably took it from the Italians. Their heroic measure has indeed eleven syllables, because of the rhyme, which is double; but as our language requires single rhyme, the verse was reduced to ten syllables; the run of it is the same to the ear. The Italians borrowed it from the Provençals, there being verses extant still of this kind by Arnauld Daniel, who died in 1189, and is celebrated by Petrarch, under the title of Gran Maestro d'amor, and of Arnauld de Merveille, who flourished about 1190, as,
> "Fazes auzir vostras castas preguieras
> Tant doussament, qu'a pietat sia moguda
> De s' inclinar a ma justa demanda," &c.

Crescimbeni, Istor. della Volg. Poesia, l. i, p. 6. Dante judges it the best adapted of any metre to noble subjects. "Quorum omnium Endecasyllabum videtur esse superbius, tam temporis occupatione quam capacitate sententiæ, constructionis, et vocabulorum, &c. — et omnes hoc Doctores perpendisse videntur, Cantiones illustres principiantes ab illo." (De Vulgari Eloquentiâ, l. ii, c. 5.)

And these verses of Surrey:

> In active games | of nimbleness and strength
> Where we did strain, | trained with swarms of youth,
> Our tender limbs, | which yet shot up in length:
> The secret groves, | which oft we made resound
> Of pleasant plaint, | and of our Lady's praise,
> Recording oft, | what grace each one had found,
> What hope of speed, | what dread of long delays;
> The wild forèst, | the clothed holts with green,
> With reines availed, | and swift-ybreathed horse,
> With cry of hound, | and merry blasts between,
> Where we did chase | the fearful hart of force, &c.

But our poets have long since got loose from these fetters. Spenser judiciously shook them off; Milton in his Paradise Lost, is ever changing and mingling his pauses, and the greatest writers after him have made it their study to avoid what Puttenham regarded as a rule of perfect versification.

These reflections may serve to shew us, that Puttenham, though he lived within about one hundred and fifty years of Chaucer's time, must have been mistaken with regard to what the old writers called their *Riding Rhyme;* for the Canterbury Tales, which he gives as an example of it, are as exact in their measure and in their pause as in the Troilus and Cresseide, where he says, "*the metre is very grave and stately*"; and this not only in the Knight's Tale, but in the comic Introduction and Characters; as,

> A monke ther was | fair for the maistery,
> An outrider | that loved venery,[1]
> A manly man, | to ben an abbot able,
> Many a dainty horse | had he in stable;   (On the 6th.)
> And when he rode, | men might his bridle heare,
> Gingiling in a whistling wind, | as cleare   (On the 8th.)
> And eke as loud, as doth the chapell-bell, &c.

I conclude, that he was misled by the change which words had undergone in their accents since the days of Chaucer, and by the seeming defects of measure which frequently occur in the printed copies. I cannot pretend to say what it was they called *Riding Rhyme*, but perhaps it might be such as we see in the Northern Tale of Sir Thopas in Chaucer.

> Sir Thopas was | a doughty swaine,
> White was his face, | as pain[2] de maine,[3]
> His lippis red as rose, |
> His rudd[4] is like | scarlet in graine,
> And I you tell | in gode certaine
> He had a seemly nose. | &c.

But nothing can be more regular than this sort of stanza, the pause always falling just in the middle of those verses which are of eight syllables, and at the end of those of six. I imagine

---

[1] Venerie, Fr. hunting.

[2] "When thou beholdest before thy Lord *peyne-mayne*:
   A baker chosen, and waged well forthe,
   That only he should that businesse applye," &c.
            Alexander Barclay's Eclogues,
       Written in the beginning of Henry ye 8th's reign.

[3] The whitest bread.   [4] *Rudu*, Sax. colour of the cheek.

that it was this very regularity which seemed so tedious to *mine host of the Tabbarde*, as to make him interrupt Chaucer in the middle of his story, with

> No more of this for Goddis dignitè—
> Mine earès akin of thy draftie [1] speeche,
> Now such a rime the Devil I beteeche,[2]
> This may well be clepe *Rime Dogrell*, quoth he, &c.

Hence too we see that Puttenham is mistaken in the sense of *Rhyme Dogrell*, for so far was it *from being tied to no rule at all*, that it was consistent with the greatest exactness in the Cæsura and in the Measure; but as he himself has said very well in another place, (b. ii. ch. 9,) "the over busie and too speedie returne of one manner of tune doth too much annoy and, as it were, glut the eare, unless it be in small and popular musickes, sung by these Cantabanqui [3]

---

[1] Tedious, from *drof*, Sax. dirty, filthy.

[2] *Betæcan*, Sax. to give, or commit to.

[3] Doubtless the degenerate successors of those ancient *Jongleurs* in Provence, Italy, and other countries described by Crescimbeni, where he is speaking of the old romances. "Or questi Romanzi non v' ha dubbio che si cantavano, e forse non s'ingannò colui, che fu di parere, che i Romanzatori in panca vendessero l'opere loro cantando, imperocchè fioriva anticamente in Francia un' arte detta de' Giuglari, i quali erano faceti e spiritosi uomini, che solevano andar cantando i loro versi per le corte alle mense de' grandi, colla viuola, o' coll' arpa, o' con altro stromento.— Molti de' poeti Provenzali de' primi tempi questa stessa esercitarono ed anco de' nostri Italiani, che in quella lingua poetarono."

upon benches and barrels-heads, where they have none other audience than boys and country fellows, that pass by them in the street; or else by blind harpers or such like tavern-minstrels, that give a fit of mirth for a groat; and their matters being for the most part stories of old time, as the Tale of Sir Thopas, the reportes of Bevis [1] of Southampton, Adam Bell, and Clymme

(Comentarj del Crescimbeni, l. v. c. 5, p. 333.) And he cites on this occasion these verses in a Romance composed about the year 1230:
"Quand les tables ostées furent
Cil Jugleur en pies esturent,
S'ont Vielles et Harpes prises;
Chansons, sons, vers, et reprises,
Et de Gestes chanté nos ont," &c.

These verses are in the Tournoyement d'Antichrist, by Huon de Mari, a monk of St. Germain. (Fauchet, l. i. ch. 8.)

And Huon de Villeneuve, a writer of the same age, addresses himself to the company whom he is going to entertain in these words:

"Gardez, qu'il n'i ait noise, ne tabor, ne criée,
Il est ensinc coustume en la vostre contrée.
Quant uns Chanterres vient entre gent honorée
Et il a en droit soi la Vielle attrempée;
Je tant n'aura mantel, ne cotte desramée,
Que sa premiere * laisse ne soit bien escoutée:
Puis font chanter avant, se de riens lor agrée,
Ou tost sans vilenie puet recoillir s'estrée," &c.

* *Couple, ou* Entrée.

[1] The English Romance, so called, is in rude verse, seemingly of great antiquity. The Italians have one which is named *Buovo d' Antona*, probably on the same story, mentioned by Gio. Villani, who died in 1348. (See Crescimbeni, Comentarj, l. v. c. 6.)

This English Romance is in free octosyllabic rhyme, written, of the Clough, and such other old romances and historical rhymes, made on purpose for the recreation of the common people at Christmas dinners and bride-ales in taverns and ale-houses, and such other places of base resort," &c. This was therefore *Dogrell*, whose frequent return of rhyme and similarity of sound easily imprinted it in the memory of the vulgar; and, by being applied of old to the meanest uses of poetry, it was grown distasteful to the ears of the better sort.

But the *Riding Rhyme* I rather take to be that which is confined to one measure, whatever that measure be, but not to one rhythm; having sometimes more, sometimes fewer syllables, and the pause hardly distinguishable, such as the Prologue and History of Beryn, found in some MSS. of Chaucer, and the Cook's Tale of Gamelyn, where the verses have twelve, thirteen, or fourteen syllables, and the Cæsura on the sixth, seventh, or eighth, as it happens. This having

as Mr. Thomas Warton observes (in his Observations on the Fairy Queen, Lond. 1754, 8vo) in that short measure which was frequently sung to the harp in Queen Elizabeth's days, a custom which descended from the ancient bards (p. 36). Bevis is supposed to have been Earl of Southampton about the time of the Norman Invasion; his residence was at Duncton in Wiltshire; his sword, called *Morglay*, is kept as a relic in Arundel Castle, not equalling in length that of Edward the Third at Westminster. (See Selden's notes on Drayton's Polyolbion, canto iii.)

an air of rusticity, Spenser has very well adapted it to pastoral poetry, and in his hands it has an admirable effect, as in the Eclogue called March, which is in the same metre as Chaucer's Tale of Sir Thopas; and in February and May, where the two fables of the Oak and Bryer, and the Fox and Kid, for humour and expression are equal to any thing in our language. The measure, like our usual verse of eight syllables, is Dimeter-Iambic, but admits of a Trochee, Spondee, Amphybrachys, Anapæst, &c. in almost every place. Thus,

Sēĕst hŏw brāg yŏn bullock bears . . .	Trochee in the 1st.
So smirk, so smooth, his pricked ears? .	Pure Iambic.
His horns bĕen ăs brāde, as rainbow bent,	Anapæst in the 2d.
Hĭs dēwlăp ăs līthe, as Lass of Kent! . .	The same.
Seē hŏw hĕ vēntĕth intŏ thĕ wind . . .	Anapæst in the last.
Wēenĕst, ŏf lŏve is not his mind? &c. .	Trochee in the 1st.

And,

Though marked him, with melting eyes,	Pure Iambic.
A thrilling throb frŏm hĕr heārt did rise,	Anapæst in the 4th [3d].
And intĕrrūptĕd āll hĕr ŏthĕr spēech .	Amphibrachys the 2d. Tribrachys in the 3d.
With sŏme ōld sŏrrŏw, thăt māde ă nĕw brēach,	
Sēemĕd shĕ sāw ĭn hĕr yōunglĭng's fāce,	Trochee in the 1st. Anapæst in the 3d.
The' ōld lĭnĕāmēnts ŏf hĭs Fāther's grāce.	Anapæst in 2d and 3d.

In these last six lines, the first has eight syllables, and the second nine, the third and fourth ten, the fifth nine, and the last ten: and this is the only English measure which has such a liberty of choice allowed in its feet, of which Milton has taken some little advantage, in using here and there a Trochee in his octosyllabics, and in the first foot only of his heroic verses. There are a very few instances of his going farther for the sake of some particular expression, as in that line,

> Būrnt āftĕr thĕm tŏ thĕ bŏttŏmlĕss pīt,

where there is a Spondee in the first place, a Pyrrhic in the third, and a Trochee in the fourth, and that line,

> Wĭth ĭmpĕtŭoŭs recoil and jarring sound,

with an Anapæst in the first place, &c.

Spenser has also given an instance [1] of the decasyllabic measure with an unusual liberty in its feet, in the beginning of his Pastoral called August, thus,

> Thĕn lŏ, Pĕrĭgōt, thĕ plĕdge whĭch I plīght,
> Ă māzĕr ȳwroūght ŏf thĕ māplĕ wāre,
> Whĕreĭn ĭs ĕnchāsĕd mānȳ ă faĭr sīght
> Ŏf beārs ănd tȳgĕrs, thăt mākĕn fiĕrce wār, &c.,

---

[1] And after him Dr. Donne (in his Satires) observes no regularity in the pause, or in the feet of his verse, only the number of syllables is equal throughout. I suppose he thought this rough uncouth measure suited the plain familiar style of satirical poetry.

where there are Trochees, &c. in every foot but the last. I do not doubt that he had some ancient examples of this rhythm in his memory, when he wrote it. Bishop Douglas, in his Prologue to the eighth Æneid, written about eighty years before Spenser's Calendar, has something of the same kind.

I make no mention of the Hexameter, Sapphic, and other measures which Sir Philip Sidney and his friends [1] attempted to introduce in Queen Elizabeth's reign, because they soon dropped into oblivion. The same thing had happened in France a little before, where, in 1553, Etienne Jodelle began to write in this way, and was followed by Baïf, Passerat, Nicholas Rapin, and others, but without success. (See Pasquier, Recherches, l. vii. c. 12.) And in Italy this was attempted by Claudio Tolomei,[2] and other men of learning, to as little purpose. (See Crescimbeni, Comment. vol. i. p. 21.)

[1] We see from Spenser's Letters, that he himself, his friend Mr. Harvey, and Mr. Dyer, one of his patrons, approved of this method and practised it. Mr. Drant (he says) had derived the rules and principles of the art, which were enlarged with Mr. Sydney's own judgment, and augmented with his (Spenser's) Observations. This was in 1580.

[2] Bishop of Corsola; he flourished in 1540. He was five years Ambassador from the Republic of Sienna in France, and died soon after his return in 1557.

THE MEASURES OF VERSE

THE Measures which I find principally in use among our writers are as follow, being in all *fifty-nine*.

VERSE.	ORDER OF THE RHYMES.
Decasyllabic. As in Chaucer's Prologue to the Canterbury Tales, and many of the principal tales themselves: his Legende of Good Women, &c. Lydgate's Story of Thebes. Gawen Douglas's Translation of the Æneid, &c. Spenser, Mother Hubberd's Tale, and almost all our modern heroic poetry.	Successive, in Couplets; called by the old French writers *Rime plate*. (See Pasquier, Recherches de la France, l. vii, ch. 8.
Decasyllabic. Blank; as, The Death of Zoroas, The Death of Cicero, } published with Lord Surrey's and Sir T. Wyatt's Poems in 1574, 8vo. Anonym. Milton's Paradise Lost and Regained, &c.	Without Rhyme. (Versi [1] Sciolti of the Italians.) The invention [2] is attributed to Trissino, about the year 1525.

[1] Thus Trissino's Italia Liberata, the Georgic poems of L. Alamanni and Rucellai, the Sette Giornate of Tasso, &c. and many of the Italian Tragedies are written. It was attempted too by the French in the sixteenth century, as Ronsard in some odes, Blaise Viginelle in his Seven Psalms, &c. but was soon dropped again.

[2] i. e. As far as relates to the verse of eleven syllables, or Italian

| VERSE. | ORDER OF THE RHYMES. |

Stanzas of Four Lines.

| Lord Surrey's Verses written in Windsor Castle, Epitaph on Sir Thomas Wyatt, &c.
Dryden's Annus Mirabilis.
Spenser. Colin Clout's come Home again, and April. Gascoyne's Councel on Traveling. His Woodmanship. | Alternate: called by the French, Rime croisée, or entrelassée. Whether there were two or more rhymes which answered one another, as in all which we call Stanzas, see Pasquier, as above. |

Stanzas of Seven, on Three [1] Rhymes.

| Chaucer's Man of Honour, Clerk of Oxenford, Second Nun and Prioress's Tales. Troilus and Cresseide. Assembly of Fowls. Annelida and Arcite. Flower and Leaf. Assembly of Ladies. Complaint of the Black Knight. Lamentation of Magdalen. | The 1st and 3d. — 2d 4th and 5th. — 6th and 7th. |

heroic measure. But in shorter verses it had been practised sometimes by the most ancient writers of that nation, particularly in the beginning of the thirteenth century St. Francis wrote an irregular ode, or canticle, without rhyme, for music, in no contemptible strain of poetry. It begins,

"Altissimo Signore
Vostre sono le lodi,
La gloria, e gli onori," &c.

(See Crescimbeni, Comentarj, l. i. c. 10.)

[1] There is also a rough stanza of seven, free in its feet, as Dingley's Battle of Brampton, in the Mirrour of Magistrates.

| VERSE. | ORDER OF THE RHYMES. |

Stanzas of Seven, on Three Rhymes (continued).

Remedy of Love. Several Ballads,[1] &c. John Hardynge's Chronicle.

Gower's Epistle to Henry the 4th.

Occleve, de Regimine Principis. Letter of Cupid. Ballade of our Lady. Of Pride, and wast[2] Clothing. (In Camden's Remains.) Lydgate's Fall of Princes. Churl and Bird. Tale of the Merchant's, Ballades, &c. Assemblé de Dyeus. Gawen Douglas. Prologue to the 2d and 4th Book of the Æneid. Sir David Lyndsay's Testament of the Papingo. His Dream. Complaint of Scotland. Prologue to Experience and the Courtier. Fabyan's Ballad Royal on Edward the First. W. Caxton's Work on Sapience. Angel's Song. Sir T. Wyatt's Complaint on Love. The Govern-

} The 1st and 3d. — 2d 4th and 5th. — 6th and 7th.

---

[1] "The Staff of seven verses hath seven proportions, whereof one only is the usual of our vulgar, and kept by our old Poets, Chaucer and others, in their historical Reports and other ditties." (Puttenham, l. ii. c. 10.)

[2] This is a part De Regimine Principis.

VERSE.	ORDER OF THE RHYMES.

Stanzas of Seven, on Three Rhymes (continued).

ment of Kings and Princes, Anonymous.
Spenser's Hymns of Love and Beauty. Ruins of Time. Milton's Hymn on the Nativity, &c.

The 1st and 3d.
— 2d 4th and 5th.
— 6th and 7th.

Another Stanza of Seven Lines.

Some Poems of Chaucer.
Spenser's Daphnaida.

The 1st and 3d.
— 2d 4th and 6th.
— 5th and 7th.

Stanzas of Six, on Three Rhymes.

Chaucer, in some Envoys. Dr. Lodge, some Sonnets. Spenser, Tears of the Muses, Astrophel, December, and part of August. Gascoyne's Passion.

Four alternate, and the Two last together.

Another Stanza of Six, on *Two* Rhymes.

Spenser's October.

The 1st 4th and 6th.

Stanza of Eight, on Three Rhymes.

Chaucer. Monk's Tale. Belle Dame sans mercy. Envoys. His A.B.C. or Prayer to the Virgin. Lydgate's Ballads, &c.
Scogan's Letter to the Lords of the King's House. Spenser's November. G. Douglas's Prologue to the Sixth Æneid.

The 1st and 3d.
— 2d 4th 5th and 7th.
— 6th and 8th.

VERSE.	ORDER OF THE RHYMES.

Another.

Some Poems of Chaucer and Lydgate.

Gawen Douglas's Prologue to the Eleventh Æneid.

{ The 1st and 3d.
— 2d 4th 5th and 8th.
— 6th and 7th. }

Another.[1]

Spenser's Muiopotmos and Culex.

{ The 1st 3rd and 5th.
— 2d 4th and 6th.
— 7th and 8th. }

Another, on Two Rhymes.

Spenser's June.

{ The 1st 3d 6th and 8th.
— 2d 4th 5th and 7th. }

Stanza of Nine, on Three Rhymes.

G. Douglas's Prologue to the Fifth Æneid, and his Exclamation against Detractors. The Third Part of the Palice of Honour.

Sir D. Lindsay's Prologue to the Papingo's Testament.

{ The 1st 2d 4th and 5th.
— 3d 6th and 7th.
— 8th and 9th. }

---

[1] This is the *Ottava Rima* of the Italians, the Stanza of Ariosto and Tasso in their heroic poems, and that of an infinite number of authors. It was first introduced in Italy by Boccaccio, who wrote in this measure his Teseide, Filostrato, &c. in the fourteenth century; though he in reality appears to have borrowed it from Thibaut, King of Navarre and Count of Champagne, who had written in the same stanza in the year 1235. (See Crescembeni, Comentarj, vol. i. l. v. c. 7, p. 339.)

VERSE.   ORDER OF THE RHYMES.

Another, on Two Rhymes.

Chaucer's Complaint of Annelida. G. Douglas's Prologue to the Third Æneid, and the two first Parts of the Palice of Honour.	The 1, 2, 4, 5, and 8. — 3, 6, 7, and 9.

Stanza of Five, on Two Rhymes.

Chaucer's Cuckoo and Nightingale. Gawen Douglas's Prologue to the Tenth Æneid.	The 1st 2d and 5th. — 3d and 4th.

Another.

Some of Sir Thomas Wyatt's Verses.	The 1st and 3rd. — 2d 4th and 5th.

Terzetti,[1] or Terza Rima.

Lord Surrey's Restless State of a Lover. Sir T. Wyatt's [Epist.] to J. Poynes, and Sir Fr. Bryan. Milton. Second Psalm.	The 1st and 3d rhyme — 2d 4th and 6th, and so on by threes alternate, till the last and last but two, which answer like those at first.

---

[1] This is the measure of Dante in his Inferno, &c., of Petrarch's Trionfi, &c. The invention has usually been ascribed to the former, but there is a Poem (called Il Pataffio) extant, written in this very measure by Ser Brunetto Latini, who was Dante's master, and who died in 1294. It was probably the invention of the Provençals, who used it in ther Syrvientes (or Satires), whence the Italians have commonly called it *Serventese*. See Crescimbeni, Coment. vol. i. l. 2, c. 13)

VERSE.	ORDER OF THE RHYMES.

Sonnets of Fourteen,[1] on Five Rhymes.

Milton's 7th, 9th, 10th, and 13th Sonnets.
- The 1, 4, 5, and 8th.
- — 2, 3, 6, and 7th.
- — 9th and 12th.
- — 10th and 13th.
- — 11th and 14th.

Another.

Spenser's Amoretti.
- The 1st and 3rd.
- — 2, 4, 5, and 7th.
- — 6, 8, 9, and 11th.
- — 10th and 12th.
- — 13th and 14th.

Another.

Sir T. Wyatt's Sonnets of the Lover waxeth wiser, &c.
- 8 first lines, as of the first sort above.
- 4 next alternate.
- Couplet in the end.

Sonnets of Four Rhymes.

Milton's Sonnets, 8th, 11th, 12th, and 14th.
- Eight first lines as of the first sort, or else alternate: the six last alternate, or at pleasure.

Another, of Two Rhymes.

Lord Surrey on the Spring: Complaint by Night, &c.
- The 12 first alternate, and end with a couplet.

---

[1] This, and the fourth kind, are the true Sonnet of the Italians. Petrarch uses only these two measures. The invention of the regular Sonnet is ascribed to Fra Guittone d'Arezzo, who flourished about the year 1250; nor do we find any of this form among the Provençals till seventy years after. What they called *Sonet* was only a short Canzone, unconfined in the number of verses, the measure, and the order of the rhymes. (Crescimb. Coment. l. ii. c. 14, 15.)

VERSE.   ORDER OF THE RHYMES.

Another, of Seven Rhymes.

Lord Surrey's Vow to Love. On Sir T. Wyatt's Death, &c. Daniel's Delia. } The 12 first by 4 and 4 alternate.

Madrigals of Eight, on Three Rhymes.

Sir T. Wyatt. { Six first alternate; and end with a Couplet.

Madrigals on Two Rhymes.

Sir T. Wyatt. { The 1st 3d 6th and 8th.
— 2, 4, 5, and 7th.

Stanza of Fourteen, on Seven Rhymes.

Spenser's Visions of Petrarch, Bellay, &c. } Like the last kind of Sonnet.

Another, on Five Rhymes.

Spenser, Visions of the World's Vanity. { The 1st and 3d.
— 2, 4, 5, and 7th.
— 6, 8, 9, and 11th.
— 10th and 12th.
— 13th and 14th.

Sestine, of Six.[1]

Spenser, in his August. { No rhyme. The art consists in ringing changes on six words only, in the end of a line: the whole is finished in six stanzas only, and three verses over.

[1] The invention of the *Sestine* is ascribed to Arnauld Daniel

The Measures of Verse

VERSE.	ORDER OF THE RHYMES.
Decasyllabic, Mixed.	
Stanza of Nine, with an Alexandrine at the end, on Three Rhymes. Spenser's Fairy Queen.[1]	The 1st and 3d. — 2, 4, 5, and 7. — 6, 8, and 9th.
Stanza of Eighteen,[2] with 4 verses (the 5th, 10th, 15th, and 16th) of Six syllables, and the last an Alexandrine, on Seven Rhymes. Spenser's Prothalamion and Epithalamion.	The 1, 4, and 5th. — 2d and 3d. 4 next alternate (the 10th answers to the 9th.) — 11, 12, and 14th. — 13, 15, and 16th. — 17th and 18th.

in the middle of the twelfth century (see Crescimb. Coment. vol. i l. 2, c. 11), and from him the Italians borrowed it, though it must be always, both in sense and sound, a very mean composition.

[1] Spenser has also a stanza of eight, ending with an Alexandrine, where the 1st and 3d rhyme; the 2d, 4th, and 5th; the 6th, 7th, and 8th, as in Britain's Ida.

Sir Thomas Wyatt has a stanza of eight, where the 4th and 8th are of six syllables; it has three rhymes, the 1st, 2d, and 3d answering each other; the 4th and 8th; the 5th, 6th, and 7th.

[2] These resemble the Canzoni of the Italians, which are in stanzas of 9, 12, 13, or 14 verses, &c. in unequal measure. There is also a stanza (if it may be called so) not only of mixed measures but of an unequal number of verses, sometimes rhyming and sometimes not, as in Milton's Lycidas, and in the Choruses in his Samson Agonistes.

The Canzone is of very ancient date: the invention of it being ascribed to Girard de Borneil, of the School of Provence, who died in 1178. He was of Limoges, and was called *Il Maestro de' Trovatori*. The different kinds of Canzoni are infinite, many new ones being introduced by the Italians. The most ancient, which were extant in that tongue, were written by Folcacchio de' Folcacchieri, who lived before the year 1200. Nothing seems

VERSE.	ORDER OF THE RHYMES.
Stanza of Ten. The first an Alexandrine, the four next, and 9th, a decasyllabic, sixth and seventh octosyllabic, the eighth and tenth (being the Refrain or Burthen) tetrasyllabic. On four rhymes. Spenser's Lay, or Elegy of Dido, in the November.	The 1st and 3d. — 2, 4, 5, and 9th. — 6th and 7th. — 8th and 10th.
Stanza of Nine. The 1st, 3d, 5th, and 6th are decasyllabic, the 2d, 4th, 7th, and 8th are tetrasyllabic, the last octosyllabic. On four rhymes. Spenser's Lay to Eliza, in April.	The 1st and 3d. — 2d and 4th. — 5th 6th and 9th. — 7th and 8th.
Decasyllabic, free in their feet. Spenser, Proëme of his August. Baldwyn's Complaint of James the Fourth, King of Scotland. Donne's Satires.	In Couplets. With Trochees or Iambics in every foot indifferently.

essential to this species of poetry, but that the measures of every stanza should answer to the first, whether they be of equal or of unequal measures. It has generally been a rule that the stanzas should be not more than fifteen, and the verses in each stanza not fewer than nine, nor above twenty; but this rule is very often broken. Dante esteemed it the noblest species of poetry, and adds, "Quicquid de cacuminibus illustrium Capitum poëtantium profluxit ad labia, in *solis Cantionibus* invenitur." (De Vulg. Eloquent. l. ii. c. 3, b. 3.) He said they used all measures from eleven syllables to three, but particularly recommends the former, mixed with that of seven, which Petrarch has observed and approved.

The Measures of Verse

VERSE.	ORDER OF THE RHYMES.
The Same, Mixt, in Stanzas of thirteen, their four last verses are tetrasyllabic. On four rhymes. G. Douglas, Prologue to the Eighth Æneid.	The 1, 3, 5, and 7th. — 2, 4, 6, and 8th. — 9, and 13th. — 10, 11, and 12th. — I call them decasyllabic and tetrasyllabic, because they have that effect on the ear: but as they admit of Anapæsts, &c., they have sometimes eleven or five syllables.
Octosyllabic.[1] The Lord's Prayer, by Pope Adrian, in Henry the Second's time. Chaucer's Romaunt of the Rose. House of Fame. Book of the Dutchess. His Dream. Poem of the Owl and Nightingale (as old as the time of Henry the Third). Gower's Confessio Amantis. Lydgate's Story of Thebes. Sir David Lyndsay's Dialogue between Experience and a Courtier. Romaunce of Merlin.	Successive in Couplets.

[1] This measure is borrowed from the Welsh, or the Provençal and old French poets, with whom it was common. Robert Manning of Brunn, who towards the beginning of the fourteenth century translated Peter Langtoft's Chronicle out of the old French (or Roman tongue as it was then called) has prefixed a Prologue to it in Octosyllabic rhymes, wherein he mentions different kinds of

VERSE.	ORDER OF THE RHYMES.
Another kind.	
Lord Surrey's Restless State of a Lover. Means of a happy Life. Gascoyne's Good-Morrow. Wyatt's Prayer against Disdain; Lamentation, &c.	Alternate.
Another.	
Wyatt's Renunciation of Love.	Four successive rhymes.
Stanza of Eight, on Two Rhymes.	
Chaucer's Plowman's Tale and Prologue.	Alternate.
Stanza of Eight, on Three Rhymes.	
Chaucer's Ballade in praise of Women. Lydgate's Complaint of Tho. Chaucer.	The 1st and 3d. — 2, 4, 5, and 7th. — 6th and 8th.
Stanza of Seven, on Three Rhymes.	
Wyatt's Suit for Grace. Lover's Mistrust, &c.	The 1st and 3d. — 2d, 4th, and 5th. — 6th and 7th.

verse used in his days, as Entrelace, Baston, Couwe, Strangere, &c. The first of these is, as I suppose, the Rime croisée or enterlassée of the French; the second are unequal verse in *Staves* or Stanzas, answering one to the other. The French still say *Baston* de Balade for *Stance* de Balade. (See Menage Dictionnaire Etymol. v. Baston.) Couwe I take to be derived from the Welsh Cywydd (pronounced Couwyth) which is a peculiar stanza and composition of rhyme, described by Dr. David ap Rhys, p. 186; it may be perhaps the same with Chaucer's Tale of Sir Thopas.

VERSE.	ORDER OF THE RHYMES.

Stanza of Six, on Three Rhymes.

Lord Surrey's Lover's Comfort. Complaint of Absence, &c. Gascoyne's Arraignement. } 4 Alternate. 2 last together.

Stanza of Five, on Two Rhymes.

Wyatt, to his Lute. { The 1st 2d and 4th. — 3d and 5th.

Octosyllabic, Mixt.

Stanza of Six. The 3d and 6th are of six syllables; on Three Rhymes. (Doggerel.)

Chaucer's Sir Thopas. Frere and Boy; Sir Eglamore; Sir Triamore; The Green Knight; Sir Lybius Disconius. } The 1st and 2d. — 4th and 5th. — 3d and 6th.

Another. With Heptasyllabics mixed at pleasure. No Stanzas.

Milton's Allegro and Penseroso; Part of his Comus; Epitaph on the Marchioness of Winchester. } Successive.

Octosyllabics, with Verses of Six, alternate.

Spenser's July. Alternate.

Another, with Verses of Six or Five Syllables, alternate.

Spenser's Roundelay, in August. Alternate.

VERSE.	ORDER OF THE RHYMES.
Octosyllabic, Free.	
Spenser's February, May, and September. Bevis of Southampton. Sir Lambwell. Eger and Grime. Sir Degree. Earl of Carlisle.	Successive. The feet are Trochees, Spondees, Amphibrachys, and Anapæsts indifferently with the Iambic.
Octosyllabic, Free. Stanza of Six, Mixt and Free. On Three Rhymes.	
Spenser, Proëme of March.	The 1st and 2d. — 4th and 5th. — 3d and 6th.
Octosyllabic, Blank. Mixt with others of Six and Four Syllables.	
Spenser's Mourning Muse of Thestylis.	No Rhyme.
Verses of Six Syllables.	
Several Songs of Sir Tho. Wyatt and Lord Surrey.	
Others in Stanzas of Eight, on Two Rhymes.	Alternate. 1, 3, 6, and 8th. 2, 4, 5, and 7th.
The same. On Three Rhymes.	The 1, 3, 5, and 7th. — 2d and 4th. — 6th and 8th.
Pentasyllabic and Tetrasyllabic.	
These are rarely used alone.	

The Measures of Verse 53

VERSE.	ORDER OF THE RHYMES.
Alexandrines.[1] Lord Surrey's Ecclesiastes. Spenser's Envoy to the Shepherd's Kalendar. Drayton's Polyolbion.	Successive. There is also a Stanza of four Alexandrines with alternate rhyme, as Phœbe's Sonnet in Lodge's Euphues' Gold. Legacy.

[1] The Life of St. Margaret in very old Saxon (cited hereafter), and written above one hundred and seventy years before Chaucer was born, is in a sort of free Alexandrine measure: as is the Chronicle of Robert of Gloucester, and Peter Langtoft's Chronicle, translated by Robert Manning of Brunn, both of them older than Chaucer. The Alexandrine verse took its name from a poem written in this measure, called La Vie d'Alexandre by Jean li Nevelois and Pierre de St. Cloit, who lived in the thirteenth century (Pasquier, l. vii. c. 3). The *Roman d'Alexandre* was begun by Lambert li Cors and Alexandre de Paris; but some parts of it were executed by the two poets above mentioned. They all four (according to the President Fauchet) wrote between 1150 and 1193, in the reigns of Louis le Jeune and Philippe Auguste, and seem to have been of the Trouveures or Jongleurs, who then were in high esteem: their names appear in the work itself.

"La verté de l'histoir, si com li Roy la fit,
Un Clers de Chateaudun, Lambert li Cors, l'escrit,
Qui de Latin *la*[1] *trest*, et en Roman la mit."

See Fauchet, de la Langue et Poesie Françoise, l. ii. (A.D. 1581). The Latin, whence they translated, was (I imagine) the Alexandréis of Gualterus, (or Gautier de Châtillon, a native of Lisle in Flanders), a poet who lived about the same time, that is, in the middle of the twelfth century. It is observable, that none of these four Jongleurs was a Provençal, nor do they write in that dialect, yet they are contemporary with the most ancient Provençal poets, mentioned by Nôtredame.

[1] *tira.*

VERSE.	ORDER OF THE RHYMES.
Alexandrines, mixed with Verses of Fourteen Syllables,[1] alternately.	
Queen Elizabeth's Ditty on the Queen of Scots. Surrey's Description of Love. Complaint of a Lover. Dying Lover. The Warning. The careless Man, &c. Wyatt's Complaint of Absence. Song[2] of Iopas. Gascoyne's Gloze.	Successive.
Free Alexandrines, mixed in like manner.[3]	
Chaucer's Tale of Beryn and Prologue.	Successive: but with various feet.
Free Verse,[4] of Fourteen Syllables.	
Chaucer's Tale of Gamelin. Robin of Portingale; Ballade of Flodden Field; Adam Bell; Robin Hood; Nut-brown Maid; Childe Waters; Durham Field.	Successive. (Various.) There is also a verse of Sixteen, as Guy and Phillis, Thomas a Potts.

[1] "Some Makers (says Puttenham) write in verses of fourteen syllables, giving the cesure at the first eight, which proportion is tedious, for the length of the verse keepeth the ear too long from its delight, which is, to hear the cadence or tuneable accent in the end of the verse."

[2] There is also a mixed stanza of four (as in Baldwin's Complaint of Henry the Sixth, in the Mirrour of Magistrates), three verses of twelve and one of fourteen syllables. Rhymes in Couplets.

[3] And thus is written Robert of Gloucester's Chronicle, a work of Henry the Third's time, but without any regularity, the Alexandrine sometimes wanting a syllable or two, and the verse of fourteen coming in at random, as the writer thought fit.

[4] It is the very same measure with the Semi-Saxon moral poem

Of all these measures, which we may reduce to six, viz. the verse of fourteen, the Alexandrine, the decasyllabic, the octosyllabic,[1] the heptasyllabic, and verse of six; none are now used but the third and fourth; except it be interspersedly to vary our composition, and especially in lyric poetry. Our variety too in the rhyme is much circumscribed, never going further than the use of a triplet, and that rarely. As to any license[2] in the feet, it is only permitted in the beginning of a long verse, where we sometimes use a trochee, and the same foot more freely in shorter measures.

The Provençal poets either invented or made use of all these measures, from verses of three syllables to those of eleven and thirteen; but of these last we find no example till about the year 1321,

---

(cited hereafter) written almost two hundred years after Chaucer's time.

There was also the regular verse of fourteen used in Queen Elizabeth's time, and in this measure is written Dr. Phaer's Translation of the Æneid; (see Lambarde's Kent and Weever's Funeral Monuments) Arthur Goldynge's Ovid's Metamorphoses, Chevy Chase, Gill Morrice, Glasgerion, Launcelot du Lake, &c.

[1] We now use this as well on serious subjects as comic: the latter *we* call Doggerel, as Hudibras.

[2] We now and then in subjects of humour use a free verse of eleven or twelve syllables, which may consist of four Amphibrachees, or four Anapæsts, or the first may be an Iambic, &c.; so Prior:

"As Chlŏē cămē īntŏ thĕ rōom t'ŏthĕr dāy"—
"Tĭs enōugh thăt 'tĭs loādĕd wĭth bāublĕs ănd sēals," &c.

so that it is not certain that they were originally theirs, or borrowed from the French Alexandrine with the addition of a syllable, on account of the double rhyme. (See Crescimbeni, Comentarj, vol. i. l. 2, c. 14, and l. 1, c. 6.)

OBSERVATIONS ON THE PSEUDO-RHYTHMUS

THE most ancient instance of rhyming verse, as Sir W. Temple has observed, is that of the Emperor Adrian, about the 137th year of Christ.[1] It was undoubtedly borrowed from the barbarous nations, among whom, particularly in the east, it is said to have been in use from the remotest antiquity. The Welsh still preserve the works of the ancient British bards, Taliessin, Benbeirdh, and Lomarkk, who lived towards the end of the sixth century, and wrote in rhyme. It is possible that our ancesters, the Anglo-Saxons, might borrow it from the Britons, but it is much more probable that they brought it from Germany with them.

[1] There is a Hymn of St. Augustine, who lived about the year 420, in which are interspersed several verses which rhyme in the middle; as,

"Abest limus, | deest fimus, | lues nulla cernitur,
 Hymens horrens, | æstas torrens, | illic nunquam sæviunt.—
 Virent prata, | vernant sata, | rivi mellis influunt," &c.
                                    Augustin. Meditat. c. 26.

And in a treatise written by Theodulus (who lived in 480 under the Emperor Zeno), De Contemptu Mundi, are these lines:

"Pauper amabilis, | et venerabilis, | est benedictus,
 Dives inutilis, | insatiabilis, | est maledictus," &c.

It is true that we do not find any rhyming verses among them till towards the time of the Norman Conquest; all their poems now remaining being of a different contrivance, and their harmony consisting in alliteration,[1] or similar consonances in the beginning of three or more words in each distich; yet probably they might have had our *Pseudo-Rhythm*, (as Dr. Hickes and Wormius call it) beside this, though their performances in it are now lost; which is no great wonder, considering that we have not any specimen of their poetry in any kind [2] for three hun-

[1] This was the artifice of the Skalds, or old Danish poets in their *Drotquæt* (or vulgar song) described by Wormius, and observed sometimes strictly, sometimes with more liberty, by our old Saxons, both before and after the coming of the Danes. As to the measure, Hickes imagines that they had feet and quantity, but, as he owns, we have lost the pronunciation, and neither know the power of the diphthongs, nor of the vowel *e* in the end of words; we cannot tell of how many syllables their verse consisted; it appears to have from four to fourteen indifferently, but most usually from four to eight or nine.

[2] That is, from the first settlement of the Saxons in Britain to the coming of the Danes. (See Hickes's Gramm. Angl. Sax. c. xix.) This is his computation, I know not for what reason; for, from the arrival of Hengist, A.D. 449, to the settling of the Danes in Northumberland in 867, are 418 years. From that period to the Norman Conquest we have a good deal of their poetry preserved, but none of it in rhyme; the Ransom of Eigil (preserved by Olaus Wormius) written above one hundred and fifty years before the Conquest, is however in rhyme, as, "Vestur kom eg om ver | Enn eg vidris ber | Munstrindar mar | So er mitt offar | Dro eg eik a flot | Vid Isabrot |" &c. &c.

dred and thirty-seven years now preserved, except that fragment of Cædmon the Monk, extant in King Alfred's Saxon Translation of Bede's History, l. iv. c. 24, and the Harmony of the Evangelists paraphrased in verse, in the Cotton Library; nay, of these two it is doubtful if the latter be of that age or not.

What serves to confirm me in the opinion, that, beside their other species of verse, they might also use rhyme occasionally, is this: we have still extant in the language of the Franks a Paraphrase of the Gospels in rhyme, written by Otfrid, a monk of Weisenburgh, scholar to [1] Rhabanus Maurus, abbot of Fulde, before the year 876, and addressed [2] to Louis, the Germanic

---

[1] He was made Archbishop of Mentz in 847. His Latino-Theotische Glossary of the Bible is still preserved in the imperial library at Vienna. (See Lambecius, Comment. de Bibl. l. ii. p. 416 and 932.)

[2] A specimen of it, with notes and a Latin version, was published in 1701 by Schilterus of Strasburgh. There are also extant the Actions of Charlemagne by Stricher, and the Life of Anno, Archbishop of Cologne, both of them poems in rhyme, in the Franco-Theotische tongue, mentioned by Dr. Hickes in his grammar of that language, p. 109, and by Lambecius, l. ii. p. 422, who has published Otfrid's dedication of the work above-mentioned, in prose, which is very curious. In it he calls his own tongue "*barbara, inculta, et indisciplinabilis,*" he complains of its roughness and of the variety of its sounds, which the letters of the alphabet could not at all express, and adds, "Lingua enim hæc velut agrestis habetur, dum a propriis nec scripturâ, nec arte aliquâ, ullis est temporibus expolita, quippe qui nec historias antecessorum suorum, ut multæ gentes cæteræ, commendant memoriæ, nec

King of Austria (or East France) in stanzas, which begin thus:

"Lodovig their snéllo
Thes wisduames follo:
Er Ostarichi rihtit al
So Francono Kuning scal.
Ubar Francono lant gizalt
So gengit ellu sin giuualt.
Thas rihtit, so i thir zellu,
Thiu sin giuualt ellu," &c.

That is: Lewis the swift
Of wisdom full,
He Austrasia rules all
So as a Frankish king
becomes, &c.

And as the Saxons and Franks [1] were near neigh-

eorum gesta vel vitas exornant dignitatis amore. Quod si raro contigit, aliarum gentium linguâ, id est, Latinorum vel Græcorum, potius explanant." The President Fauchet had seen this poem and preface.

[1] The Franks under Clovis settled in Gaul about thirty-two years after the arrival of the Saxons in Kent. Hickes tells us that the Franco-Theotische and Anglo-Saxon (before the invasion of the Danes) were probably the same language. Gramm. Fr. Theot. p. 6, see also Carte, vol. i. p. 221.) It seems to appear from the words of Otfrid, in his preface, cited above, that the Franks of his time did still use some kind of metre distinct from rhyme, for he says: "Patitur quoque (Lingua Theotisca) nimiùm, non tamen assiduè, synalœphen, et hoc nisi legentes prævideant, rationis dicta deformius sonant, literas interdum scriptione servantes, interdum vero Ebraicæ linguæ more vitantes, quibus ipsas literas ratione synalœphæ in lineis, ut quidam dicunt, penitus amittere et transilire moris habetur. Non quo series scriptionis hujus metricâ sit subtilitate constricta, sed schema homoioteleuton assiduè quærit," &c. (Apud Lambecium, l. ii. c. 5, p. 425.)

There are no verses extant in the Romaun, or old French tongue, which are known to be more ancient than the middle of the twelfth century, and accordingly Fauchet begins his catalogue of poets with Maistre Wistace, or Eustace, who wrote the Romaunce of Brutt, the Trojan, in 1155: it is in octosyllabic rhymes.

The earliest of the Provençal writers (at least of those who

bours in Germany, and spoke a language only
have left any memorial behind them) lived about the middle of
the same century. The Sicilian poets, who first taught Italy to
write verse, lived very few years after; and in our own tongue,
we have, I believe, nothing extant in rhyme that can be with certainty judged to be more ancient than the reign of Stephen or Henry
the Second. The Germans have therefore preserved in their tongue
the most ancient monument of rhyming poesy, perhaps in Europe,
almost three hundred years older than any of those which I have
mentioned. The Welsh poetry only (if the remains of Taliessin
and Lowarkk be not fictitious) can pretend to a superior antiquity.

As to the Provençal writers, Crescimbeni observes, "Avvi cer-
tezza, che incominiciassero (i rimatori Provenzali) circa il 1100 sotto
il Guglielmo VIII. duca d'Aquitania, e l' istesso duca fosse il primo
verseggiatore, avendo composto in rima il viaggio di Gerusalemme,
e qualche cosa amorosa.— Non si truovano però rime più antiche
di quelle di Giusfredo Rudello, che molto scrisse in lode della Con-
tessa di Tripoli, che amò, e appresso cui morì l' anno 1162." (Crescimb. Istor. della Volg. Poesia, l. i. p. 6.) — Dante, who was born
in 1265, ascribes the origin of the old romances in prose to the
French nation, and that of the *volgare poesia* to the Provençale.
"Allegat ergo pro se lingua *Oil* (that is, the French) quod propter
sui faciliorem et delectabiliorem vulgaritatem, quicquid redactum
sive inventum est ad vulgare prosaicum, suum est, videlicet, biblia
cum Trojanorum Romanorumque gestibus compilata, et Arturi
Regis ambages pulcherrimæ, et quamplurimæ aliæ historiæ atque
doctrinæ. Pro se vero argumentatur alia, scilicet *Oc* (he means
the Provençale) quòd vulgares eloquentes in ea primitus poëtati
sunt, tanquam in perfectiori dulcioriqué loquelâ, ut puto, Petrus
de Alverniâ, et alii antiquiores doctores. Tertia, quæ Latinorum
est, (that is, the Italian) se duobus privilegiis attestatur præesse:
primo quidem, qui subtilius dulciusque poëtati sunt *vulgariter*,
hi familiares et domestici sui sunt, putà Cinus Pistoriensis et amicus
ejus (Dante himself): secundo, quia magis videntur inniti *gram-
maticæ*, quæ communis est." (He means the Latin or mother-
tongue.) Dante, De Vulgari Eloquentiâ, l. i. c. 10. — See also
Scaligerana 2da. vol. ii. p. 331.

differing in dialect, and alike derived from the old Gothic mother-tongue, it is likely that the same kinds of poetry were common to them both.

(N. B. It is remarkable that Walafrid Strabo, who died in 840, and other writers of that age, call themselves *Barbari,* and their own language *Barbarica Locutio.* See Goldastus's notes on Ekeckardus, Res Alamannicæ, tom. i. part 1, p. 113.)

However, we have not now among us any rhymes more ancient than that period, which extends from the Conquest in 1066 to the reign of Henry the Second, which begun in 1154; our tongue being then much mixed with the Norman-Gallic, and degenerating into what Hickes calls the Semi-Saxon, as in the Life of St. Margaret.[1]

> Olde ant yonge, I preit ou oure follies for to *lete,*[2]
> (*Old and young, I pray you your follies for to leave*)
> Thenchet on God, that yef ou wit oure sunnes to *bete.*[3]
> (*Think on God, that gave you wit your sins to correct.*)
> Here I mai tellen ou wid wordes faire ant swete
> (*Here I may tell you with words fair and sweet*)
> The vie of one meidan was hoten Maregrete.
> (*The life of a maiden was hight Margaret.*)
> Hire fader was a patriac, as ic ou tellen may,
> (*Her father was a patriarch, as I you tell may,*)
> In Auntioge wife *eches*[4] i the false lay,

[1] See other examples in Wanley's Catalogue, in John's or Henry the Third's reign, p. 79.

[2] *Lætan,* Saxon, to let, or permit, whence to let alone, to let go.

[3] *Betan,* Saxon, to amend, to make better.

[4] *Gecas,* Saxon, he chose.

> (*In Antioch a wife he chose in the false law*)
> Deve godes and doumbe he served nitt ant day,
> (*Deaf gods and dumb he served night and day,*)
> So deden mony othere, that singet *weilaway*.[1]
> (*So did many others, that sing wellaway.*) &c. &c.

And in those verses preserved in some MSS. in the Bodleian Library, and in Trinity College, Cambridge.

> Ic am elder than ic wes, a wintre ant ec a lore,
> (*I am elder than I was, in winters and eke in learning.*)
> Ic ealdi more than ic dede: mi wit oghte to bi more,
> (*I grow old more than I did: my wit ought to be more*)
> Wel longe ic habbe childe ibien on worde ant on dede,
> (*Very long I have a child been in word and in deed*)
> Thegh ic bi on winter eald, to giung ic am on *rede*,[2] &c. &c.
> (*Though I be in winters old, too young I am in counsel.*)

This is inscribed Parabolæ Regis Ælfredi. See J. Spelman's Life of Alfred, p. 98.

Other examples of ancient rhyme, within the period assigned, may be seen in Dr. Hickes, ch. xxiv. from whom I have transcribed the former. Yet though this kind of versification[3] prevailed

---

[1] *Wala-wa*, Saxon, Woe is me!

[2] *Rada*, Saxon, knowledge. *Ræd*, Counsel.

[3] It was towards the end of this period, about ninety years after the Conquest, that the Provençal poetry began to flourish, and continued in the highest esteem above two hundred years. They wrote in rhyme, and were the inventors of a variety of measures. Dante, Petrarca, &c. in Italy; Helinand, William de Lorry, Jean de Mehun, Thibaud, Count of Champagne, in France; and Chaucer, in our own tongue, first caught their fire from these writers, and imitated their manner, style, and versification. (See Jean de Nôtredame, Lives of the Provençal Poets, Lyons, 1575, 8vo.)

by degrees, and grew into general use, it is certain that we retained, even so late as Edward the

The Sicilians, about the end of the twelfth century, under the reign of Robert Guiscard the Norman, King of Naples, first began to imitate the Provençal writers in their own tongue, and as the most judicious Italians themselves inform us, such as Bembo, Varchi, Sansovini, Nicolo Villani, and Crescimbeni. The last of these has given us the names of these first Italian poets: "Le rime de' Siciliani a noi pervenute sono debolissime e scipite ed infelici, a segno che non possono leggersi senza estrema noia e rincrescimento, ancorche sieno de' più rinomati, cioè di Guido e d' Odo delle Colonne, di Jacopo da Lentino, dell' Imperador Federigo, e d' altri loro pari." (Istor. Volg. Poes. vol. i. l. 1, c. 2, p. 91.) He also mentions Ciullo dal Camo, and it appears that the art of versifying almost instantaneously diffused itself through Italy, from those verses inscribed in Gothic letters on a marble at Florence by Ubaldino Ubaldini, as early as the year 1184, which begin,

"De favore isto
Gratias refero Christo,
Factus in festo serenæ
Sanctæ Mariæ Magdalenæ;
Ipsa peculiariter adori
Ad Deum pro me peccatori.
Con lo mio cantare
Dallo vero vero narrare
Nulla ne diparto," &c.

It is not written in distinct verses, as here, upon the marble, but like prose, all confused together. (Crescimb. Coment. vol. i. l. 1, c. 4, p. 100.) — Dante observes, "Videtur *Sicilianum Vulgare* sibi famam præ aliis asciscere; eò quòd, quicquid poëtantur Itali, *Sicilianum* vocatur. — Quòd (i. e. tempore illustrium heroum Frederici Cæsaris et benegeniti ejus Manfredi,) quicquid excellentes Latinorum nitebantur, primitùs in tantorum coronatorum aulâ prodibat, et quia regale solium erat Sicilia, factum est, quicquid nostri predecessores *vulgariter* protulerunt, *Sicilianum* vocatur." (Dante de Vulg. Eloq. l. i. c. 12.)

The President Fauchet takes pains to prove that the people of

Third's reign, and above a hundred years after, our old Saxon or Danish verse without rhyme; for the Vision of Peirce Plowman, a severe satire

Normandy, of Provence, of Sicily, of Italy, of Spain, &c. all borrowed their rhyme from the Franks; and, I own, it wears a face of probability: but then it may be equally probable that the Franks borrowed it from the Latin church. He cites also the Life of Sancta Fides, in the Catalan dialect of the Spanish tongue (it is, he says, as old as the year 1100, and in rhyme), which calls the rhyming verses *a lei Francesca*, i. e. a la Françoise; (see Acad. des Inscript. vol. xxvi. p. 638) which is with allowance for some changes (which length of time will inevitably introduce in all languages) the true *Romaun*-tongue generally spoken throughout all the Roman Gaul, for many years before and after it fell into the hands of the Franks. This appears from the famous treaty in A.D. 843, between the sons of Lodovicus Pius, where the oaths in the original tongues (i. e. the Romaun, which was then the language of all who lay west of the Meuse, and the Theotische, or Frankish, spoken by all the people who lived east of that river,) are preserved to us by Nitard, the historian, grandson to Charlemagne: the first of these still nearly resembling the Provençal dialect, was then called *Rustica Romana*. The Council of Tours, assembled in the year 812, has this article: "Quilibet Episcopus habeat Omilias, &c. et easdem quisque apertè traducere studeat *in Rusticam Romanam linguam et Theotiscam;*" as being then the two languages most generally understood. The Provençal was only the Latin tongue corrupted and altered a little in its terminations by a mixture of the Celtic or Gaulish idiom, and afterwards of the Visigoth and Frankish. In the more northern provinces of Gaul it received a still stronger tincture of the latter, and of the Norman or Danish tongue, and formed the *Valonne*, or what is now called in France Vieille Gauloise, out of which time produced the modern French. But both this and the Provençale retained alike, till the fourteenth century, the name of *Langue Romande*. (See Fauchet, l. i. c. 3 and 4. Duclos, Mem. vol. xv. p. 565, et vol. xvii. p. 171. De l'Acad. des Inscript. et Huetiana, p. 41 and 189.

on the times, written by Robert Langland in
1350, is wholly in such measure, as, for instance:

> I *l*oked on my *l*eft halfe,
> As the *l*ady me taught,
> And *w*as *w*are of a *w*oman
> *W*orthylich clothed.
> *P*urfiled [1] with *p*elure,[2]
> The finest u*p*on erthe,
> *C*rowned with a *c*rowne
> The *k*ing hath no better;
> *F*etislich [3] her *f*ingers,
> Were *f*retted with gold wiers,
> And thereon *r*ed *r*ubies,
> As *r*ed as any glede,[4]
> And *d*iamonds of *d*earest price,
> And *d*ouble maner saphirs, &c.
> Passus 2^{dus} in princip.

and thus through the whole poem, which is a
long one, with very few exceptions, the triple
consonance is observed in every distich.

Robert Crowley, who printed the first edition
of Peirce Plowman's Vision in 1550 (dated by
mistake 1505) says, that Robert Langland, the
author of it, "wrote altogether in meter, but not
after the maner of our rimers that write now-
a-days, for his verses end not alike, for the nature of his meter is to have at least thre wordes

---

[1] *Pourfilé*, Fr. bordered.
[2] *Pelure*, furs, from pellis, Lat.
[3] *Fetislich*, handsomely.
[4] *Gled*, Sax. a burning coal.

in every verse, which begin with some one, and the same, letter. The author was a Shropshire man, born in Cleybirie, about eight miles from Malverne-Hills: his worke was written between 1350 and 1409."

In the same measure is the poem called "Death and Life in two fitts;" and another named *Scottish Field*, which describes the action at Flodden in Henry the Eighth's time, who was present in the action, and dwelt at Bagily. (I read them in a MS. Collection belonging to the Rev. Mr. Thomas Piercy in 1761.)

It cannot be supposed possible to fix exactly the time when rhyme was first introduced and practised in a country; but if we trace it back to the remotest monuments of the kind now extant, we shall find the æras nearly as follows:

	Anno Xti.
At Rome before the introduction of Christianity	137
In the Latin Church	420
In use among the Welsh	590
Among the Arabs earlier than	622
Among the Franks, in the old German tongue	873
In Provence, in the dialect of the country	1100
In Italy, in the Latin tongue, after the coming of the Normans	1032
In England, in our own tongue, before the year	1154
In France, in the French tongue	1155
In Sicily, and in the rest of Italy, in the Italian tongue, before	1187

Any one who considers these several dates, and sees that the fathers and priests of the Roman church wrote Latin rhyme early in the fifth century, and that the Franks did the same in their own tongue in the ninth, will scarcely give credit to P. Huet, who affirms, that the Provençals borrowed the art of rhyme from the Arabs. For though it is true that the Arabs had practised it before Mahomet's time, and perhaps from the remotest antiquity, and that they were in possession of part of Aquitaine from 732 to 738; which is the most probable of the two, that the Provençals should imitate the taste of a nation wholly different from themselves in language, religion, and manners, who were but for a small time conversant among them? or, that they should copy the Franks, who had reigned over them above two hundred years before the arrival of the Arabs, and still continue to do so to this day? Indeed, for my own part, I do believe, that neither the one nor the other of these nations was the immediate object of their imitation, but rather the hymns of the church, and the monkish Latin verses, which were even[1] then in vogue all over

[1] Crescimbeni observes that rhyming verses in Latin epitaphs, inscriptions, &c. first appeared in Italy, upon the arrival of the Normans, who served under Guimaro, Prince of Salerno, in 1032. In that city were composed, about the year 1100, the famous medical precepts of the Schola Salernitana, addressed to Robert, Duke of

France at the time, when the earliest Provençal writers attempted to rhyme in their own tongue.

This is the opinion of Crescimbeni (Istor. della Poesia, l. i. p. 13), and it will appear very natural, if we consider the near affinity of the Latin and Provençal tongues; and that they were accustomed to Latin rhymes in their books of religion, epitaphs, inscriptions, and other compositions of the learned in those days. Besides that in many old Provençal poems the rhyme not only appears at the end, but in the [1] middle of a verse, which

Normandy, son to William the Conqueror. They are in Latin rhyme, thus:

"Cœna brevis, | vel cœna levis | fit raro molesta,
 Magna nocet, | medicina docet, | res est manifesta," &c.

See also Fauchet (l. i. c. 7.) and Maffei (Journal Italien, t. i.) "On ne peut nier que la rime ne tire son origine des vers rimés et Leonins de la basse Latinité, connus uniquement dans des siècles barbares."

[1] Latin rhymes, as it may be well imagined, were nothing the less esteemed when people began to rhyme in their own tongue; indeed they flourished most when the Provençale poetry was in its dawn. In the year 1154 lived Leonius, a canon of St. Benedict at Paris, and afterwards a religious of St. Victor, who, for the age he lived in, wrote Latin verse in the regular way not contemptibly, as appears both in his elegies and in his heroics on sacred subjects; but he too gives in to the taste of those times, and writes epistles in rhyme to Pope Adrian the Fourth and Alexander the Third, which begin,

"Papa, meas, Adriane, preces, si postulo *digna*,
 Suscipe tam vultu placido, quam mente be*nignâ*," &c.

And,

"Summe Parens hominum, Christi devote Mi*nister*,
 Pastorum pastor, præceptorumque Ma*gister*," &c.

and upon such verses as these (it seems) he built his reputation;

manner was often imitated by the old Italians, Rinaldo d' Aquino, Dante da Majano, Guido Cavalcanti, and others, and is known by the name of "*Rima alla Provenzale*" (See Crescimbeni, Comentarj, vol. i. l. 2, c. 19, p. 178); and that this was the manner of the Latin rhymers is

so that they have ever since borne the name of Leonine verses; and the *rime riche* (or double rhyme) even in French verses was of old called *ryme Leonine*, or *Leonime*. The ancient Fabliau des trois Dames has these lines:

> "Ma peine mettray, et m'entente,
> A conter un fabliau par ryme
> Sans coulour, et sans *Leonime*," &c.

So that the rhyme-female was not looked upon as a rhyme of two syllables. An old book, printed in 1493, intitled, "L'Art et Science de Rhetorique pour faire Rhymes et Ballades," says, "Ryme Leonisme est, quand deux dictions sont semblables et de pareille consonance en syllabes, comme au chapitre de jalousie, de Jean de Meung:

> "Preude femmes, par St. Denis,
> Autant est, que de Fenis," &c.

But the word *Leonimetés* was more particularly applied (it seems) to such rhymes as run uninterrupted for many lines together; for the Life of St. Christina, written about the year 1300, after rhyming in couplets throughout, finishes with these lines:

> "Seigneurs, qui en vos livres par maistrie metez
> Equivocations et *leonismetéz*,
> Si je tel ne puis faire, ne deprisiez mon livre,
> Car qui a trouver n'a soubtil cuer et delivre,
> Et *leonismeté* veult par tout a consuivre
> Moult souvent entrelest, ce qu'il devoit en suivre."

(See Fauchet, l. i. c. 8, and Pasquier, l. vii. c. 2. Menage Dictionnaire Etymol. v. Leonins. Jul. Scaliger Poetice. Naude Mascurat, p. 332.)

plain from the Schola Salernitana, the Epitaph of
Roger, Duke of Sicily, in 1101;

> Linquens terrenas | migravit dux ad amœnas
> Rogerius sedes, | nam cæli detinet ædes:

and the poem De Contemptu Mundi, written by
Bernard, a monk of Cluny, about 1125, in this
measure:

> Hora novissima, tempora pessima sunt, vigi*l*emus:
> Ecce minaciter imminet arbiter ille Su*p*remus! &c.
>   Fauchet, l. i. c. 7.

Observe, that, if the date of this poem be true,
the general opinion, that the Leonine verse owes
its name to Leonius, seems to be false; for Bernard, in a preface prefixed to his own work, calls
his own measure " genus metricum, dactylum
continuum, exceptis finalibus, trochæo vel spondæo, tum etiam sonoritatem *Leoninicam* servans:"
and he mentions Hildebert de Laverdin, Bishop
of Mans and afterwards of Tours, and Wichard,
a canon of Lyons, as having written a few things
in this measure before him. It is not therefore
very likely, as Leonius flourished in 1154, that
he should give name to such Latin verses upwards
of thirty years before. Indeed some people have
thought that it was called after LEO, probably
the Second, who lived in 684, a pope who is said
to have reformed the hymns and the music of
the church. (See Fauchet, l. i. c. 16.)

What makes it still more probable that the ancient verses in Latin rhyme might give rise to the Provençal and Italian poetry is that mixture of different languages which appears in some old compositions, namely, the canzone of Rambald de Vacheres (before the year 1226) in five several tongues, the Provençal, Tuscan, French, Gascon, and Spanish; the strange rhymes of Ubaldino the Florentine; the canzone of Dante, which begins,

> Provenç. Ahi faulx ris, per qe trai haves
> Lat. Oculos meos? et quid tibi feci,
> Ital. Chè fatto m' hai così spietata fraude? &c. &c.

and the great work, or La Divina Comedia, of the same poet.

SOME OBSERVATIONS ON THE USE OF RHYME

THE oldest instance which we have of RHYME IN OUR TONGUE (if it be genuine) is that Tenure of the manor of Cholmer and Dancing, preserved in the Exchequer Rolls de anno 17 Edw. 2di, (at which time I suppose it was lodged there,) being the Grant of Edward the Confessor to Randolph Paperking. It begins:

> Iche, Edward Konyng,
> Have geven of my forest the keeping
> Of the hundred of Cholmer and Dancing
> To Randolph Paperking, and his kindling.
> With heort and hynd, doe and bocke,
> Hare and fox, cat and brocke,
> Wilde fowell, with his flocke,
> Partridge, Fesaunt-hen, and Fesaunt-cocke,
> With grene and wild stob and stocke,
> To kepen and to yemen by all her might, &c.

That King began his reign in 1043, and this grant must have been made before 1051, when Earl Godwyn rebelled; for Swein, the eldest son of Godwyn, and brother to Edward's wife, is named as a witness to it. From that time he was in arms against the king till he went to the Holy Land, whence he never returned. It is to be observed, that he is here called *Swein of Essex* (see

Camden); yet in reality not he, but his brother Harold, was earl of that county and East Anglia: which is a circumstance that may give cause to suspect the antiquity of this rhyming donation.

There is another of the same sort preserved by Stow in his Chronicle, and transcribed more perfectly by Blount (in his Ancient Tenures, p. 102) from a manuscript belonging to Robert Glover in Com. Salop:

> To the heyrs male of the Hopton lawfully begotten, &c.

There is also a poetical History of Great Britain extant, about the age of Henry the Third, written in Saxon verse without rhyme: it begins thus:

> A preost wes in leoden
> (*A priest was in the people*)
> Lazamon wes ihoten
> (*Lazamon was hight*)
> Lithe him beo drihten
> (*Gentle to him be the Lord!*) &c.

And another in like measure, as old as Henry the Second or Richard the First, on King Alfred, as follows:

> At Sifforde [1] seten
> (*At Sifford sate*)
> Theines manie
> (*Thanes many*)
> Fele [2] biscopes
> (*Many bishops*)

---

[1] Seaford, near Oxford. [2] *Fela*, Saxon, many.

Fele bok-lered
(*Many book-learned*)
Erles prude
(*Earls proud*)
Cnihtes egeleche [1]
(*Knights awful*)
Ther was Erl Alfric
(*There was Earl Alfric*)
Of the lage swuthe wis
(*Of the law very wise*)
Ec Alfrede Engle hirde
(*Eke Alfred England's shepherd*)
Engle dirling
(*England's darling*)
On Engelonde he was king
(*In England he was king*)
Hem he gan laren
(*Then he began to learn*)
Swo he heren mighten
(*So as they hear might*)
Hu hi here lif
(*How they their life*)
Leden scolden
(*Lead should*) &c.

There is a large fragment of this poem printed in J. Spelman's Life of Alfred, fol. Oxon., 1678, p. 96.

In the same manuscript volume, with the first of these specimens, are preserved "The Contention of the Owl and Nightingale," in rhyming verse of seven syllables, and "The Poem on Death," &c. in octosyllabic rhyme.

Ich was in one sumere dale
(*I was in a summer dale*)

[1] *Egeslice*, Saxon, *Egesa*, dread, fear.

In one snwe[1] digele[2] hale
(*In a hollow secret hole*)
I herde ich holde grete tale
(*Heard I hold great talk*)
An hule and one nightingale
(*An owl and a nightingale*)
That plait was stif and stare[3] and strong
(*The plea was stiff, and tight and strong*)
Sum wile soft and lud among
(*Some while soft and loud among*)
And other agen other sval[4]
(*And either against other raged*)
And let that whole mod[5] ut al
(*And let what would their anger out all*)
And either seide of otheres cust
(*And either said at the others cost*)
That alere worste that hi wuste[6]
(*All that ever worst they thought*)
And hure[7] and hure of othere song
(*And whore and whore each of the other sung*)
Hi holde plaidung suthe stronge
(*They hold pleading very strong*) &c.

ON DEATH, ETC.

Non mai longe lives wene,[8]
(*None may long lives ween*)
Ac ofte him lieth the wrench[9]
(*But oft for him lieth the snare*)

---

[1] Perhaps from *snidan*, to hew and hollow out.
[2] *Digel*, Saxon, secret.
[3] I imagine it should be *starc*: Saxon, stiff and hard; by a metaphor, inflexible and obstinate.
[4] *Swælan*, Saxon, to kindle, to burn.
[5] *Mod*, Saxon, mood, spirit.
[6] *Wis*, *Gewis*, Saxon, knowing, prudent.
[7] *Hure*, Saxon, a whore, from *hyran*, to hire.
[8] *Wenan*, Saxon, to suppose.
[9] *Wrence*, Saxon, a trap or wile.

Fair wether turneth oft into reine
(*Fair weather turneth oft into rain*)
An wunderliche hit maketh his blench

Tharfore, man, thu the biwench [1]
(*Therefore, Man, thou thee beware;*)
Al shal falewi [2] the gren
(*All shall fade away thy green*)
Weilawai nis kin ne quene
(*Wellaway there is nor king nor queen*)
That ne scal drinche of deathes drench
(*That shall not drink of Death's drench*)
Mon er thu falle of thi bench
(*Man ere thou fall off thy bench*)
Thine Sun thu aquench [3]
(*Thy Sun thou quench*) &c.

See also Pope Adrian the Fourth's Paraphrase of the Pater-noster, sent to Henry the Second, King of England (in Camden's Remains), and the Poetical Version of the Psalms (of Edward the Second's time) cited by Selden in his Titles of Honour, p. i. c. 3. The same may be seen in Weever's Funeral Monuments, p. 152; see also Scotch rhyme on Edward the First, and the answer (ibid. p. 458); Robert of Gloucester's Chronicle.

NOTE. — It appears from a story told by Ekkehardus junior, a monk of St. Gall, in his his-

---

[1] Perhaps from *Bewerigan*, Saxon, to beware.
[2] *Falewe*, Saxon, a yellow colour.
[3] *Acwencan*, Saxon, to quench.

tory of that monastery, that early in the *tenth* century the children who were educated there were taught to make Latin rhymes without regard to quantity and metre, and also verses strictly metrical in the same tongue. Ekkehardus says, that when Solomon, Bishop of Constance, a little before his death, came into their school, the boys addressed him in both these manners: " Parvuli Latinè *pro nosse* (perhaps, *prosaicè*), medii rhythmicè, cæteri vero metricè, quasi pro rostris rhetoricè etiam affantur; quorum duorum (quoniam a patribus verba recepimus) unus inquit,

> Quid tibi fecimus *tale*, | ut nobis facias *male?*
> Appellamus *regem*, | quia nostram fecimus *legem:*

at alter versificator inquit,

> Non nobis pia *spes* | fuerat, cum sis novus ho*spes*,
> Ut vetus in pe*jus* | transvertere tute velis *jus:*"

this prelate died in the year 919.

As to those rhyming epitaphs of Ethelbert, King of Kent, Laurentius the second Archbishop of Canterbury, &c. said by Weever (pp. 241 and 246) to be inscribed on their monuments, in the church of St. Austin's at Canterbury, they would carry back the date of Latin rhyme as far as the beginning of the seventh century, in England, but I suspect they are of a later date, written perhaps in the time of Abbot Scotland, soon after the Conquest; who, I find, rebuilt a great part of the church, and removed many of the ancient kings and abbots from the place in which they were first interred into the choir, where he erected princely monuments over them. (Weever, p. 253.)

ADDITIONAL OBSERVATIONS AND CONJECTURES ON RHYME

(*From an Essay entitled* "CAMBRI" *the following Remarks are selected as relating to the subject of* RHYME.)

IN the most ancient of the British poets and others, it appears that the *Cambri*, or Welsh, originally called themselves *Prydhain*, and their country Inis Prydhain, the Isle of Britain. The inhabitants of Wales removing their cattle and habitations from place to place, (which is still practised in some mountainous parts, and was so universally in former ages,) after the custom was disused in England, were called Wallenses, from *Walen*, a word synonymous to that of Nomades. (See Carte's Hist. vol. i. p. 5, and p. 108.)

The Druidical compositions, which served as a model to Taliessin, Llywark, and others of the most ancient and best of the British poets, whose works are preserved, and have since served for the foundation of that excellent prosodia which they have in the Welsh grammar, and which is perhaps the finest that any language affords, were admirably contrived for assisting the memory. They were all adapted to music, every word being harmonious, the strongest and most expressive repeated in a beautiful manner, and all of them ranged in an order established by rules well known and universally received in such compositions; each verse so connected with, and dependent on, those which either preceded or followed it, that, if any one line in a stanza be remembered, all the rest must of course be called to mind, and it is almost impracticable to forget or to mistake in any. "The British poetry, as well as the language, hath a peculiarity which no other language perhaps in the world hath; so that the British poets in all ages, and to this day, call their art *Cyfrinach y Beirdd*, or 'The Secret of the Poets.' Knowing this art of the poets, it is impossible that any one word of the language, which is to be found in poetry, should be pronounced in any other manner than is there used; so that without a transformation of the whole language, not one word could be altered."

These are the words of a very judicious antiquary, Mr. Lewis Morris, perfectly well versed in the ancient British poets. He adds, though at first sight it may be naturally thought that their poetry is clogged with so many rules, that it is impossible to write a poem of common sense in the language, yet the vast number of flexions of consonants in it, and the variations of declensions, &c. make it almost as copious as four or five languages added together; and consequently a poet in the Cambrian language, notwithstanding the strictness of his rules, hath as great a scope and use of words as in any other tongue whatsoever, as will appear from a perusal of the British poets. (Ibid. p. 33.)

This "*Secret of the Poets*" is explained to us at large by David ap Rhys (or Rhæsus) in his "Linguæ Cambro-Britannicæ Institutiones," p. 146, Lond. 1592, 4to. They had nine different measures from verses of three to those of eleven syllables, each distinguished by its proper appellation. Some of them have been from a very remote antiquity common among us in the English tongue, and not improbably might have been borrowed from the Britons, as I am apt to believe, that the use of rhyme itself was. I was once, I own, of Crescimbeni's opinion, that it was derived from the Roman Church in its hymns, and thence passed to the people of Provence. But if we consider that, some few slight traces of rhyme among the Romans excepted, there is nothing of their hymns, or sequentiæ, written in that manner earlier than the time of Pope Gregory the Great, in the end of the sixth century; and at the same time that it was regularly and very artificially practised among the Britons in a variety of measures, and these too of a peculiar contrivance, and (as men of letters acquainted with the language assure us) full of poetical spirit and enthusiasm: if we consider also how well adapted the division and rhyme of their poetry is to assist the memory, and that the British Druids (once the priesthood of the nation) delivered all the precepts of their doctrine in verse, which never was to be committed to writing, we may easily enough be induced to believe that these bards of the sixth century practised an art which they had received by tradition from the times of the Druids, and, though the precepts of their superstition had been laid aside and forgotten at the introduction of Christianity, yet the traces of their harmony did remain.

That the Saxons, who had no rhyme among them, might borrow both that and some of the measures still in use from their neighbours the Britons, seems probable to me, though at what time they did it is very uncertain. For above one hundred and fifty years after the Saxon invasion the two nations had no other commerce than in the rough intercourse of war, and seemed to breathe nothing but inextinguishable hatred and mutual defiance. But Christianity (it is likely) something softened their spirits, and brought the Britons to regard their bitter enemies, who were now no longer pagans, as their brethren and their fellow-creatures.

If any one ask, why (supposing us to have first borrowed our rhyme from the Britons) no memorial of it is left in England earlier than the Conquest, nay, perhaps than Henry the Second's reign, which is about four hundred and fifty years after our connection with the Welsh, I answer, the fact is not certainly true; for there are some few rhymes recorded as old as the beginning of the tenth century, witness Athelstan's donation to Beverley Minster; and, in the succeeding century, the freedom of Coventry granted to Earl Leofric, and the Tenure of Cholmer and Dancing in Essex, attributed to Edward the Confessor. But if these should be only the fictions of after-ages, can any one tell me why the Franks, who, as we know, wrote rhyme in their own [1] tongue

[1] As we have no reason to imagine that the Gothic nations of the north made any use of rhyme in their versification, and as the Franks appear to be the first who practised it (three hundred and fifty years after they conquered Gaul), it seems highly probable that they borrowed it from the natives of this country, to whom it must have been familiar at least three hundred years before. For, as we know that the Britons had it so early, who spoke the same tongue with the Gauls, and delivered to them the precepts of their religion and philosophy in verse, these latter could not possibly be ignorant of their poetry, which they imitated in their own country. Nor is it probable that the government of the Romans had obliterated all traces of their ancient arts and learning in the minds of the Gauls, since it had not made them forget their ancient language. It is plain, that in the fifth century the Arverni still spoke the Celtic tongue, from a letter of Sidonius Apollinaris (l. iii. ep. 3), and that it was still understood in the ninth century, appears from the Life

in the ninth century, should have nothing to produce of rhyme in the French or Provençal language till almost two hundred and fifty years afterwards? Why have they no monument at all, preserved in their ancient tongue, of the Gothic poetry, though for so many years they bordered on the Anglo-Saxons in Germany who practised it, a people of like origin and manners, and who probably spoke the same tongue? Why have these Saxons themselves, for above three hundred years after they landed in this island, no verses of this sort remaining, but a small fragment of Cædmon, preserved in a book of King Alfred's? Why have the Normans nothing at all of this kind extant among them after their arrival in France? Who can account for the caprice of time, and shew why one monument has, and another has not, escaped the wreck of ages? Perhaps rhyme might begin among the common people, and be applied only to the meaner species of poetry, adages, songs, and vulgar histories, passing by tradition from one to another; while the clergy and others, who possessed what literature there was in the nation, either wrote in the Latin tongue, or in the measures peculiar to their

of St. Germain, written in the reign of Charles the Bald, by Heric, a monk of Auxerre, wherein he interprets the names of several cities in Gaul. (See Mémoires de l'Académie des Inscriptions, vol. xx. pp. 43 and 44.)

country and language, which by a very natural prejudice they would prefer to those of a conquered people, especially as poesy had been cultivated among them, and in the highest esteem for ages past; and their *Scalds* were as necessary in their armies, and in the courts of their princes, as either Druid or bard among the Britons. After the Normans came over, and had introduced so much of the French (or Roman) tongue among us, rhyme must of course grow prevalent and familiar in England, especially when Henry the Second (himself an Angevin, and educated in France) had married the heiress of Aquitaine, where the Provençal school first began about fifty years before, and was at that time in the highest reputation.

SOME REMARKS ON THE POEMS OF JOHN LYDGATE

JOHN LYDGATE was born at a place of that name in Suffolk, about the year 1370.

> I followed after, fordulled for rudenèss,
> More than three scorè yerès set my date.
> Lustè of youth, passed his freshĕnesse,
> Colours of rhetorike, to help me translate,
> Were faded away; I was born in Lydgate
> Where Bacchus' licour doth ful scarsely flete,
> My dry soul for to dewè and to wete.
> Prologue to Book viii. by Bochas on the Fall of Princes.

This work, he tells us, was begun while Henry the Sixth was in France, where that King never was but when he went to be crowned at Paris in 1432, so that if Lydgate were then upwards of threescore, he must have been born at the time I have assigned; and Tanner says that he was ordained a deacon in 1393, which is usually done in the twenty-third year of a man's age. He was a monk of the Benedictine order at St. Edmund's Bury, and in 1423 was elected prior of Hatfield-Brodhook, but the following year had license to return to his convent again. His condition, one would imagine, should have supplied him with the necessaries of life, yet he more than once complains to his great patron the protector,

Humphry, Duke of Gloucester, of his wants, and he shews, particularly in the passage above, that he did not dislike a little more wine than the convent allowed him.

After enumerating the principal English poets who lived before him, whose merit he does not pretend to equal, he says,

> But I, who stand low downè in the vale,
> So grete a booke in Englyshe to translate,
> Did it by constrainte, and no presumption,
> Born in a village, which is called Lydgate
> By oldè time a famous castel towne,
> In Danès time it was beatè down,
> Time what St. Edmund's martir, maid and king,
> Was slaine at Oxford, récorde of writing, &c.   Epilogue.

There are a few other things in this work of Lydgate's which have no connection with his merit as a poet, but are curious as they relate to the history and manners of the times in which he lived. Thus in book viii. c. 24, we see that wine was still made in England in Henry the Sixth's reign, and that Hampshire was famous for it; so that the reason assigned for neglecting the culture of vines, I mean, that we could have so much better wines from our French dominions, is not true; and indeed a few years after this we lost all our conquests and territories in that country.

> London [1] hath shippis by the sea to saile,
> Bacchus at Winchester greatly doth availe,

[1] It may be worth while to compare this passage with a similar

> Worcester with fruits aboundeth at the full,
> Hertford with beastis, Cotiswold with wooll.
> Bath hath hot bathes holesome for medicine,
> Yorke mighty timber for great ávauntage,
> Cornĕwall miners in to mine,—
> And Salisbury has beastès full savàge,
> Wheate meale and hony plentie for every age:
> Kent and Canterbury hath great commoditie,
> Of sondrie fishes there taken in the sea.

We may remark too the notion then current in Britain, that King Arthur was not dead, but translated to Fairy-Land, and should come again to restore the Round Table:

> This errour [1] abideth yet among Britons,
> Which founded is upon the prophesie

one in Robert of Gloucester, who wrote (near two hundred years before) in the days of Henry the Third.

> In the country of Canterbury most plenty of fish is,
> And most chase of wild beasts about Salisbury, I wis,
> And London ships most, and wine at Winchester,
> At Hartford sheepe and oxe, and fruit at Worcester,
> Soape about Coventry, and iron at Glocester,
> Metall, lead, and tinne in the countie of Exeter,
> Everwicke* of fairest wood, Lincolne† of fairest men,
> Cambridge and Huntingdon most plentie of deep venne,
> Elie of fairest place, of fairest sight Rochester, &c.
>
> (In Camden's Remains, p. 8.)

* *Eboracum*, York.
† Testis Lincolnie, gens infinita decore,
   Testis Ely formosa situ, Roucestria visu.
(Liber Costumorum.)

[1] Peter of Blois, who lived in 1170, says ironically, in his Epistles, 57:

> "Quibus si credideris,
> Expectare poteris
> Arturum cum Britonibus."

> Of old Merlin, like their opinion;
> He as a king is crowned in faërie,
> With scepter and sworde, and with his regalie
> Shall resort as lord and soveraine
> Out of faerie, and reigne in Britaine, &c.
>
> B. viii. c. 24.

And we may remark also the opinion, then prevailing, that a decisive victory was a certain proof of the justice of the conqueror's cause, which was but natural among a people which for ages had been taught to refer even civil causes to a decision by combat.

It seems that Lydgate was little acquainted with the Latin tongue, whatever he might be with the Italian and French, in which Bishop Tanner says he was well skilled, having travelled in both those countries; for he says himself,

> I never was acquaintedde with Virgile,
> Nor with the sugared ditties of Homère,
> Nor Dares Phrygius withe his goldenne stile,
> Nor with Ovide in poetry most entère,
> Nor with the sovereign ballades of Chaucère,
> Which, amonge all that ever were redde or sunge,
> Excelled all other in our Englishe tungue.
>
> I cannot ben a judge in this mattère,
> As I conceive, following my fantaisie;
> In moral matter notable was Gowère,
> And so was Strode in his philosophie,
> In perfite living, which passith poesie,
> Richard Hermite, contemplatif of sentènce,
> Drough in Englishe, *the Pricke of Conscience.*
>
> As the gold-crested brightè summer-sunne
> Passith other sterres with his bemès cleare,
> And as Lucina chases setès downe

> The frostie nights when Hesperus doth appere,
> Righte soe my master haddè never peere,
> I mean Chaucère in stories, that he tolde,
> And he also wrote tragedïes olde.

But this perhaps [1] is only an affectation of great humility and modesty, which was common to all these ancient writers; for however little he might be *acquainted* with Homer and Virgil, it is certain that he was very much so with Chaucer's compositions, whom he calls his master, and who (as I imagine) was so in a literal sense. It is certain that Lydgate was full thirty years of age when Chaucer [2] died. But whatever his skill were in the learned languages, it is sure that he has not taken his "Fall of Princes" from the original Latin [3]

---

[1] So in Machabrées Daunce of Death, paraphrased from the French, he says:

> "Have me excused, my name is John Lydgate,
> Rude of languàge; I was not born in France,
> Her curious metres in Englishe to translate:
> Of other tongue I have noe suffisaunce."

[2] See Lydgate's Life of the Virgin Mary, cap. xxxiv. and in "The Pylgrimage of the Soul," printed by Caxton, 1483, c. xxxiv. which is the same, and seems to shew this latter translation to be Lydgate's also.

[3] Boccacius, de Casibus Illustrium Virorum is (like the rest of his Latin works and those of his master Petrarch) now little read or esteemed by any body; it is written in a kind of poetical prose; the parties concerned are introduced as passing in review before him, as in a vision, and recounting their own catastrophe, and it is interspersed with the author's moral reflections upon each of their histories.

prose of Boccaccio, but from a French translation of it by one Laurence, as he tells us himself in the beginning of his work. It was indeed rather a paraphrase than a translation, for he took the liberty of making several additions, and of reciting more at large many histories, which Boccaccio had slightly passed over:

> And he [1] sayeth eke, that his entencyon
> Is to amend, correcten, and declare,
> Not to condemne of no presumpcyon,
> But to supportè plainly and to spare
> Thing touched shortly of the storie bare,
> Under a stile briefe and compendious,
> Them to prolong when they be virtuous.
>   For a storye which is not plainly tolde,
> But constreyned under wordes few,
> For lacke of truth, wher they ben new or olde,
> Men by reporte cannot the matter shewe:
> These oakès greatè be not down yhewe
> First at a stroke, but by a *long processe*,
> Nor long stories a word may not expresse.

These "*long processes*" indeed suited wonderfully with the attention and simple curiosity of the age in which Lydgate lived. Many *a stroke* have he and the best of his contemporaries spent upon a *sturdy old story*, till they had blunted their own edge and that of their readers; at least a modern reader will find it so: but it is a folly to judge of the understanding and of the patience of

---

[1] i. e. Laurence.

those times by our own. They loved, I will not say tediousness, but length and a train of circumstances in a narration. The vulgar do so still: it gives an air of reality to facts, it fixes the attention, raises and keeps in suspense their expectation, and supplies the defects of their little and lifeless imagination; and it keeps pace with the slow motion of their own thoughts. Tell them a story as you would tell it to a man of wit, it will appear to them as an object seen in the night by a flash of lightning; but when you have placed it in various lights and in various positions, they will come at last to see and feel it as well as others. But we need not confine ourselves to the vulgar, and to understandings beneath our own. *Circumstance* ever was, and ever will be, the life and the essence both of oratory and of poetry. It has in some sort the same effect upon every mind that it has upon that of the populace; and I fear the quickness and delicate impatience of these polished times, in which we live, are but the forerunners of the decline of all those beautiful arts which depend upon the imagination.

Whether these apprehensions are well or ill grounded, it is sufficient for me that Homer, the father of *circumstance*, has occasion for the same apology which I am making for Lydgate and for his predecessors. Not that I pretend to make any more comparison between his beauties and theirs, than I do between the different languages in which they wrote. Ours was indeed barbarous enough at that time, the orthography unsettled, the syntax very deficient and confused, the metre [1] and

[1] I am inclined to think, (whatever Mr. Dryden says in the preface to his tales) that their metre, at least in serious measures and in heroic stanzas, was uniform; not indeed to the eye, but to the ear, *when rightly pronounced*. We undoubtedly destroy a great part of the music of their versification by laying the accent of words, where nobody *then* laid it; for example, in the lines cited above, if we pronounce enténcion, presúmpcion, compéndious, vértuous, prócesse, &c. in the manner in which we do in our own age, it is neither verse nor rhyme; but Lydgate and his contemporaries undoubtedly said, entenciōn, compendioūs, procēsse, &c. as the French (from whom those words were borrowed) do at this day, *intentiōn, compendieūx, procēs.*

We may every day see instances of this: the better sort of people affect to introduce many words from that language, some of which retain their original accent for many years, such as fracās, eclāt, ennūi, &c.: others, by coming more into vulgar use, lose it and assume the English accent, as rĭdicule, rāillery, éclāircissement, advĕrtisement, hāutgout, &c. Another peculiarity in the old pronunciation was that of liquefying two syllables into one, especially where there was a liquid consonant in either of them, as,

"Which among all that *ever* were redde or sunge"—

Or,

"Of right *consid'red* of truth and equitè."

Here undoubtedly "*ever*" in the first line was pronounced as one syllable, and "*consid'red*," in the second line, as two syllables. We cannot wonder at this, because we do it still; "*memo*ry, *heaven*ly, *eve*ry," &c. naturally of three syllables, are, when spoken, of two only; "*giv*en, *driv*en," &c. which should be of two, are reduced only to one syllable. It is true, that we are uniform in this, and pronounce such words always alike in prose and verse, and we have thrown out the vowel (to the great detriment of our language) in the

the number of syllables left to the ear alone; and yet, with all its rudeness, our tongue had then acquired an energy and a plenty by the adoption of a variety of words borrowed from the French, the Provençal, and the Italian, about the middle of the fourteenth century, which at this day our best writers seem to miss and to regret; for many of them have gradually dropped into disuse, and are only now to be found in the remotest counties of England.

end of all our participles-past, as "awaken'd, bless'd, damag'd, troubl'd," &c. by which they either lose a syllable quite, or (what is worse) that syllable is pronounced, and yet consists of nothing but consonants. The ancients, I imagine, did the same, but not uniformly, either opening or contracting such words to suit the necessities of *their* measure. They also at pleasure united two syllables, where one ended, and the other begun with a vowel; as,

"Ĭn pērfīt lĭvĭng, whĭch pāssĭth pŏĕsĭe"—

Or,

"Nor with Ŏvĭde ĭn *pŏ*etry mŏst ĕntēre—"

Poesie and *poetry* were dissyllables: and this they did even where the syllables were in two different words, as

"Shall follŏw *a* sprĭng-flŏŏde ŏf grăcĭoŭs plĕntĭe."—

The syllables I have marked were melted into one, as well in "follŏw *a*," as in "gracioŭs." They carried it still further, and cut off a syllable where the accent did not fall upon it, even before a consonant, as,

"Caŭse ŏf my̆ sŏrrŏwe, rōōte ŏf my̆ hēavĭnĕsse;"

here "sorrow" lost its last syllable entirely. These liberties may be justified by our use of the particle "*the*" in verse, which we sometimes sink, and sometimes pronounce distinctly before a vowel; and not many years ago it was frequently cut off even before a consonant.

Another thing, which perhaps contributed in a degree to the making our ancient poets so voluminous, was the great facility of rhyming, which is now grown so difficult; words of two or three syllables, being then newly taken from foreign languages, did still retain their original accent, and that accent (as they were mostly derived from the French) fell, according to the genius of that tongue, upon the last syllable;[1] which, if it had still continued among us, had been a great advantage to our poetry. Among the Scotch this still continues in many words; for they[2] say, envȳ, practīse, pensīve, positīve, &c.: but we, in process of time, have accustomed ourselves to throw back all our accents upon the antepenultima, in words of three or more syllables, and of our dissyllables comparatively but a few are left, as despāir, disdāin, repēnt, pretēnd, &c. where the stress is not laid on the penultima. By this mean we are almost reduced to find our rhymes among the monosyllables, in which our tongue

---

[1] Except in words which end with an *e* mute, which being always pronounced in verse by the French, and making a distinct syllable, the accent is laid upon the penultima: in such words our ancestors either pronounced the finishing *e*, or dropped it entirely, as the French themselves do in common conversation. This, I conceive, was one of our poetical licenses.

[2] In Waller's time only we said commērce, triūmph, &c. with the accent on the last syllable.

too much abounds, a defect which will for ever hinder it from adapting itself well to music, and must be consequently no small impediment to the sweetness and harmony of versification. I have now before me Pope's ethic epistles, the first folio edition, which I open at random, and find in two opposite pages (beginning with

> Who but must laugh, the master when he sees, &c.

in the Epistle on Taste to Lord Burlington) in the compass of forty lines only seven words at the end of a verse which are not monosyllables: there is indeed one which is properly a dissyllable, *hēavēn*, but cruel constraint has obliged our poets to make it but one syllable (as indeed it is in common pronunciation), otherwise it would not have been any single rhyme at all. Thus our too numerous monosyllables are increased, and consonants crowded together till they can hardly be pronounced at all; a misfortune which has already happened to the second person singular perfect in most of our verbs, such as, thou stood'st, gav'st, hurt'st, laugh'dst, uprear'dst, built'st, &c. which can scarcely be borne in prose. Now as to trissyllables, as their accent is very rarely on the last, they cannot properly be any rhymes at all: yet nevertheless I highly commend those who have judiciously and sparingly introduced them as such. DRYDEN, *in whose admirable ear the music of our old versification still sounded*, has frequently done it in his Tales, and elsewhere. Pope does it now and then, but seems to avoid it as licentious. If any future Englishman can attain that height of glory, to which *these two poets* have risen, let him be less scrupulous, upon reflecting, that to poetry languages owe their first formation, elegance, and purity; that our own, which was naturally rough and barren, borrowed from thence its copiousness and its ornaments; and that the authority of such a poet may perhaps redress many of the abuses which time and ill custom have introduced, the poverty of rhyme, the crowd of monosyllables, the collision of harsh consonants, and the want of picturesque expression, which, I will be bold to say, our language labours under *now* more than it did a hundred years ago.

To return to Lydgate. I do not pretend to set him on a level with his master, Chaucer, but he certainly comes the nearest to him of any contemporary writer, that I am acquainted with. His choice of expression, and the smoothness of his verse, far surpass both Gower and Occleve. He wanted not art in raising the more tender emotions of the mind, of which I might give several examples. The first is, of that sympathy which we feel for humble piety and contrition: Constantine is introduced making his confession and returning thanks to heaven in sight of the Roman people, after he had been cured of a grievous malady by the water of baptism;

> His crown he tooke, and kneeling thus he said,
> With wepinge eyen and voice lamentàble,
> And for sobbȳnge so as he might abbrayde;
> "O blessed Jesu, O Lord most merciàble,
> Lettè my teares to thee be acceptàble,
> Receive my prayer, my rèquest not refuse,
> As man most sinful, I may not me excuse.
>
> "I occupied the state of the emperoùr,
> Of thy martȳrs I shedde the holye blood,
> Sparèd no saintes in my cruel erròur,
> Them to pursue most furious and woode;
> Now blessed Jesu, gracious and most good,
> Peysed [1] and considred mine importàble [2] offènce,
> I am not worthy to come in thy presènce,
>
> "Nor for to enter into this holy place,
> Upon this ground unable for to dwell,
> To open my eyen, or lift up my face;
> Butte of thy mercy (so thou mee not repell)
> As man most sinfull I come unto the welle,
> Thy welle of grace and merciful pitȳe,
> For to be washed of mine iniquity."
>
> This example in open hath he shewed,
> His state imperial of mekeness laid aside,
> His purple garment with teares all bedewed,
> Sworde, nor sceptèrre, ne horse whereon to ride,
> There was none seen, nor banners splayed wide,
> Of martial triumphs was no token founde,
> But, crying mercy, the emperour lay plat on the ground.
>
> The people's gladness was meddled with wepìnge,
> And theire wepynge was meddled with gladnèss,

[1] *Pesè*, weighed.   [2] Insupportable.

> To see an emperour and so noble a king,
> Of his free choyce to shew soe great mekenèss;
> Thus intermeddled was joy and heavyness,
> Heavyness far passed oldè vengĕaŭnce,
> With newe rejoising of ghostly repentaunce.
>
> Book viii. fol. 184.

Of the same kind is the prayer of Theodosius before he engaged in battle with Arbogastes (in the same book, fol. 188). A second instance of the pathetic, but in a different way, I shall transcribe from the first book, fol. 39, to shew how far he could enter into the distresses of love and of maternal fondness. Canace, condemned to death by Æolus her father, sends to her guilty brother Macareus the last testimony of her unhappy passion:

> Out of her swoonè when she did abbraide,
> Knowing no mean but death in her distrèsse,
> To her brother full piteouslie she said,
> "Cause of my sorrowe, roote of my heavinesse,
> That whilom were the sourse of my gladnèsse
> When both our joyes by wille were so disposed,
> Under one key our hearts to be inclosed.
> . . . .
> This is mine end, I may it not astarte;
> O brother mine, there is no more to saye;
> Lowly beseeching with all mine whole hearte
> For to remember specially, I praye,
> If it befall my littel sonne to dye,
> That thou mayst after some mynd on us have,
> Suffer us both be buried in one grave.
>
> I hold him streitly twene my armès twein,
> Thou and natùre laidè on me this charge;

> He, guiltlesse, mustè with me suffer paine:
> And sith thou art at freedome and at large
> Let kindness oure love not so discharge,
> But have a minde, wherever that thou be,
> Once on a day upon my child and me.
>
> On thee and me dependeth the trespàce,
> Touching our guilt and our great offence,
> But, welaway! most àngelik of face
> Our childè, young in his pure innocence,
> Shall agayn right suffer death's violence,
> Tender of limbes, God wote, full guiltĕless,
> The goodly faire, that lieth here speechlèss.
>
> A mouth he has, but wordis hath he none;
> Cannot complaine, alas! for none outràge,
> Nor grutcheth not, but lies here all alone,
> Still as a lambe, most meke of his visàge.
> What heart of stele could do to him damàge,
> Or suffer him dye, beholding the manere
> And looke benigne of his tweine eyen clere?"
>
> B. i. fol. 39.

I stop here, not because there are not great beauties in the remainder of this epistle, but because Lydgate, in the three last stanzas of this extract, has touched the very heart-springs of compassion with so masterly a hand, as to merit a place among the greatest poets. The learned reader will see the resemblance they bear to one of the most admirable remnants of all antiquity, I mean the fragment of Simonides (unhappily it is but a fragment) preserved to us by Dionysius Halicarnassensis; and yet, I believe, that no one will imagine that Lydgate had ever seen, or heard of it. As to Ovid, from whom Boccaccio might borrow many of his ideas in this story, it will be easily seen, upon comparison, how far our poet has surpassed him. He finishes his narration in this manner:

> Writing her letter, awhapped all in drede,
> In her right hand her penne ygan to quake,
> And a sharp sword to make her heartè blede,
> In her left hand her father hath her take,
> And most her sorrowe was for her childes sake,
> Upon whose facè in her barme sleepy̆nge
> Full many a tere she wept in cõmplăyny̆ng.
>
> After all this, so as she stoode and quoke,
> Her child beholding mid of her peines smart,
> Without abode the sharpè sword she tooke,
> And rove herselfè even to the hearte;
> Her child fell down, which mightè not astert,
> Having no help to succour him, nor save,
> But in her blood the selfe began to bathe.
>
> B. i. fol. 39.

A third kind of pathos arises from magnanimity in distress, which, managed by a skilful hand, will touch us even where we detest the character which suffers. Of this too I shall produce an example in Olympias, the mother of Alexander, betrayed into the hands of the perfidious Cassander. It begins:

> His faith was laidè that time for hostàge—

And for five stanzas following.

And his reflections, after this, upon the fortitude of so cruel and imperious a woman shew something of penetration and insight into the human heart:

> But froward rancour and wode melancholie
> Gave her a sprite of feignèd patience,
> A false pretence of high magnificence;
> A scauncè she had been in virtue stronge,
> For truthe to have enduredde every wrong.
>   Contrarious force made her dispiteous
> Strong in her errour to endure her payne,
> Of obstinate heart she was, fell and yròus,
> In death's constreintè list not to complaine,
> Counterfeit suffrance made her for to feigne,
> Nothing of virtue plainly to termìne,
> Nor of no manners that be feminine.
>
> B. iv. fol. 114.

Of the same kind are his description of Mithridates surrounded by the troops of Pompey in Armenia, (B. vi. fol. 153) the Speech of Regulus to the Senate, (B. v.) and that of Lucrece to her husband and father determining on death, (B. ii. fol. 48) and the same story repeated, for he has told it twice in a different manner (B. iii. fol. 74).

It is observable that in images of horrour, and in a certain terrible greatness, our author comes far behind Chaucer. Whether they were not suited to the genius or to the temper of Lydgate, I do not determine; but it is certain that, though they naturally seemed to present themselves, he has almost generally chosen to avoid them: yet is there frequently a stiller kind of majesty both in his thought and expression, which makes one of his principal beauties. The following instance of it (I think) approaches even to sublimity:

> God hath a thousand handès to chastÿse,
> A thousand dartès of punicĩon,
> A thousand bowès made in uncouthe wyse,
> A thousand arblastes bent in his doungeon,[1]
> Ordeind each one for castigacĩon;
> But where he fyndes mekeness and repentaùnce,
> Mercy is mystresse of his ordinaunce.
>
> B. i. f. 6.

There is also a particular elegance in his grave and sententious reflections, which makes a distinguishing part of his character: of this I shall give some examples out of a multitude. B. i. f. 6, &c. on pride; on literature, in the prologue to the fourth book; and on contented poverty (B. i. f. 34); and on the vices of persons meanly born, when raised to power (B. iv. f. 118); but examples of this kind are too many and too prolix for me to transcribe. I shall refer, however, also to those verses which recommend gentleness and mercy to women (f. 115); on the mischiefs of flattery (f. 44); on ingratitude (f. 139); on patience (f. 211); on avarice (f. 93); on the duties of a king (f. 190); and the allegor-

---

[1] *Doungeon* is a castle or palace: so in B. viii. c. 24, he calls heaven "the riche sterry bright doungeon."

ical, combat between fortune and glad poverty (f. 69).

Lydgate seems to have been by nature of a more serious and melancholy turn of mind than Chaucer; yet one here and there meets with a stroke of satire and irony which does not want humour, and it usually falls (as was the custom of those times) either upon the women or on the clergy. As the religious were the principal scholars of these ages, they probably gave the tone in writing or in wit to the rest of the nation. The celibacy imposed on them by the church had soured their temper, and naturally disposed them (as is observed of old bachelors in our days) to make the weaknesses of the other sex their theme; and though every one had a profound respect for his own particular order, yet the feuds and bickerings between one order and another were perpetual and irreconcileable. These possibly were the causes which directed the satire of our old writers principally to those two objects. On the first may be produced the passage (B. i. f. 26),

But Bochas here, &c.

for three stanzas.

In the dispute between Brunichilde, Queen of France, and Boccaccio, he is more direct and explicit:

> Soothely, quoth he, this is the condicion,
> Of you women, almostè every where, &c.

(B. ix. f. 198), and so for three stanzas: and surely his reflections on Orpheus, when he had lost Euridice, are neither deficient in spirit nor in expression (B. i. f. 32):

> If some husbands had stonden in the case
> To have lost their wives for a looke sodeine, &c.

and for five stanzas.

This kind of satire will, I know, appear to modern men to taste a little stale and unfashionable; but our reflections should go deeper, and lead us to consider the fading and transitory nature of wit in general. I have above attempted to shew the source whence the two prevailing subjects of our ancestors' severity were derived: let us also observe their different success and duration from those times to our own.

The first, I mean the frailties of women, are now become the favourite theme of conversation among country-gentlemen, fellows of colleges, and the lower clergy. Upon these (if we attend to it) commonly turns the archness and pleasantry of farmers, peasants, and the meanest of the people; for to them it is that modes of wit, as well as of dress and manners, gradually descend: and there (as they came to them by a very slow and insensible progress) from a peculiar sullenness and aversion in their nature to every thing which seems new; so, when they are once established, do they continue and obstinately adhere for ages; for, as it has been said of justice, it is in the country that

> *Fashion* lingers, ere she leaves the land.

Go but into some county at a distance from the capital; observe their table, their furniture, their habits; and be sure that there was a time (which a person of curiosity in the original and antiquity of national customs may frequently discover) when those meats with which they serve you, and those moveables which they use, were delicacies and conveniences of life, only seen in the houses of people of high distinction; and when those forms of dress, at which you now laugh, were newly imported or invented by some " ruffling gallant," or by some lofty dame of honour in the court of Elizabeth, perhaps, or, at latest, of Charles the Second. In the same manner, in their expressions of civility and compliment, and in their turn of reflection, their stories and their jokes all savour of a former age, and once belonged to the most polished and gayest people of our nation. Sometimes they were originally ridiculous and absurd, sometimes far more proper and more sensible than what has been since introduced in their room; and here it is only the misapplication of them, and somewhat of awkwardness which they may have contracted in the country, that can with justice make them objects of ridicule.

That general satire upon the female sex, of which I am speaking, is now banished from good company; for which there may be several reasons given. Celibacy is no more enjoined to our clergy, and as knowledge and writing diffused themselves among the body of the people, the clergy grew no longer to be the leaders of their taste and humour; and lastly, we have (as in most things) adopted in some measure that extreme politeness and respect which the French *pretend* to shew to their women. The case is nearly the same in that nation as in this, in one point; the clergy have less influence there than in any other catholic country, and, as erudition has spread among the laity, they are no more the models of wit and good sense to their countrymen. Their old *Fabliaux* and *Romans* were just as severe upon the women, and in the same way, as ours; and just so that humour has imperceptibly worn out with them. Yet we need but look into the tales of Fontaine in that tongue, borrowed from those old stories which I have mentioned, and from Boccaccio, Machiavel, Ariosto, and others, where all the naïveté and sly simplicity of the ancient writers are preserved and heightened with the correctness, elegance, and graces of the moderns; and (though far the greater part of their humour runs upon this very subject) we shall soon be convinced that it is a topic not to be exhausted, and full as susceptible of wit and of true ridicule as it was four hundred years ago. Instances of this in our own language may be seen in most of Dryden's tales, in Pope's January and May, the Wife of Bath's Prologue, and in other compositions.

But raillery on the priesthood has continued through every age, and remains almost as fashionable as ever. It was in its full force about the time of the Reformation, and a little before, upon the revival of learning and the invention of printing: afterwards it turned upon our established church, and the variety of sects produced the same effect that the variety of the religious orders had done formerly; not to mention the struggles for power between the Church and the Commonwealth in Charles the First's and in Charles the Second's reign, and at the Revolution, and in the last years of Queen Anne, and in the beginning of George the First, which have produced a lasting bitterness and rancour, which keeps this kind of satire alive and in countenance even to this day. Addison, who formed and influenced the national taste in a thousand instances, could not with all his efforts do it in this case; yet perhaps we may, in no long time, see the end of this fashion, for, if I am not greatly mistaken, the spirit is already subsiding.

The examples of this second kind of wit are much more frequent in Chaucer than in Lydgate: there are however some, as in B. ix. fol. 202, of the Fall of Princes:

> The poorè staff, and potent of doctrìne,
> When it was chaunged, and listè not abide
> In wilful povertie; but gan anon decline
> On statelie palfreys and highe horse to ride;
> Sharpe hairès then were also laide asyde,
> Turned to copes of purple and sanguìne,
> Gownès of scarlet furrèd with ermìne.
>
> Slenderè fare ot wine and water clere,
> With abstinence of bread ymade of wheat,
> Chaunged the days to many fat dinère
> With confit drink and Ippocrasè swete;
> All sobernessè did his boundès lete:
> Scarsness of foode leftè his olde estate,
> With new excess gan wexè delicate.

And in B. ix. f. 217:

> Priestès, prelàtes, and well-fed fat parsòns
> Richly avaunced, and clerkès of degree
> Reken up religions with all their brode crowns,
> And patriarches, that have great sovereigntie,
> Bishops, abbòts, confirmed in their see,
> Secular canons, with many a great prebènd,
> Behold of fortune the mutability,
> How sodeinly she made them to descend.

And in the Daunce of Machabree,[1] where Death is introduced as leading a measure, and compelling all sorts and degrees of mankind to join the dance, men of the church are represented as more loth and unwilling to die, than any other profession whatever.

The Pope, indeed, out of respect to his dignity, and the Chartreux and the Hermit, (who were entirely abstracted from worldly affairs, and exposed therefore to no one's malignity,) shew less repugnance to death, and the latter even welcomes him with great cheerfulness.

Lydgate, however, makes his apology to the ladies very handsomely for the hard things he has said of them:

> The richè rubye, nor the sapphire Ynde,
> Be not appairèd of their freshe beautèe,
> Thoughe amonge stones men counterfeitès finde:
> And semblaby, though some women be
> Not well govèrned after their degre,
> It not defaceth, nor doth violence
> To them, that never did in their life offence.
>   The whitè lilie, nor the wholesom rose,
> Nor violettès spredde on bankis thick
> Their swetènesse, which outward they unclose,
> Is not appaired with no wedès wicke, &c.
>
> B. i. f. 37.

---

[1] It is a translation, or rather a paraphrase from the French of Doctor Machabrée, and the subject of it was expressed on the wall of St. Innocent's at Paris in painting, where Lydgate had seen it. It is printed by Tothill at the end of Boccace in 1554, fol.

He defends the honour of his country with a laudable spirit against Boccaccio, who, though speaking of the victory when John, King of France, was made prisoner, calls the English "inertissimos et nullius valoris homines":

> Though the said Boccace flowred in poetrie,
> His partialle writinge gave no mortal wounde,
> Caughtè a quarrel in his melancholie,
> Which to his shame did afterwardes redounde, &c.
>
> Held them but smale of reputation,
> In his report; men may his writings see:
> His fantasie, nor his opinion
> Stode in that case of no authoritie:
> Their kinge was took; their knightès all did flee:
> Where was Bochas to help them at such nede?
> Save with his pen, he made no man to blede.
>
> B. ix. f. 216.

The epilogue addressed to the Duke of Gloucester, and the three envoyes which follow it, have much poetical expression in them, which was Lydgate's[1] peculiar merit. However his name

[1] Lydgate composed a great number of ballads, one of which I shall here transcribe, as, I imagine, it never was printed.

[LIKE A MIDSOMER ROSE.]

[1.]

Let no man boaste of cunnyng, ne virtù,
Of tresour, richesse, nor of sapience,
Of worldly sùpport, alle cummith of Jesù,
Counsel, comfòrt, discretion, and prudènce,
Promotion, foresighte, and providence;
Like as the lord of grace lyst to dispose,
Som man hath wisdom, som hath eloquence.
All stand on chaunge, like a midsòmer rose.

be now almost lost in oblivion, yet did his reputation continue flourishing above a hundred years

[2.]

Holsome in smellyng be the sotè flowers,
Full delectàble outwarde to the syght;
The thorn is sharpe, endued with freshe colòurs;
All is not gold, that outwarde sheweth bryght.
A stockfysch bone in darkeness giveth light,
Twene faire and fowle, as God list to dispose,
A difference atwyx the day and nyght.
All stand on chaunge, like a midsòmer rose.

[3.]

Flowerrès open upon every greene
Whannè the larkè, mesangere of day,
Saleweth the' upryst of the sunnis shene
Most amorosely in April and in May;
And Aurora, agayne the morrow gray,
Causith the daysy his crowne to unclose.
Worldly gladnèsse is medlyd with affray:
All stand on chaunge, like a midsòmer rose.

[4.]

Atwene the cukkow and the nightyngale
There is amayde a straungè difference.
On freschè branchys singyth the wood-wayle;[1]
Jays in musicke have small experience,
Chattering pyes, whan they cum in presènce,
Most malapert theire verdyte to propose.
All thyng hath favour brevely in sentènce
Of soft or sharp, like a midsòmer rose.

[5.]

The royal lion let call a parlament,
All beastis soone aboute him èn viron;

[1] Wood-pigeon. Some say it is the witwall or golden thrush.

after his death, and particularly we may see the esteem in which this work of "The Fall of

> The wolf of malice being ther presènt
> Upon the lambe complayns again resòn
> Saidè, he made his water ùnholsumme,
> Hys tendyr stomak to' hinder and undispose;
> Ravenors ravyne, the' innocent is bore downe.
> All stand on chaunge, like a midsòmer rose.
>
> [6.]
>
> All worldly thyngè braidyth upon time;
> The sunnè chaungith, so does the pale moone;
> The aureat noumbre in kalenders for prime:
> Fortune is double, doth favour for no boone;
> And who that hath with that qwene [1] to done,
> Contrariosely she will his chaunge dispose;
> Who sitteth hyghest, most like to fall sone.
> All stands on chaunge, like a midsòmer rose.
>
> [7.]
>
> The golden carr of Phebus in the aire
> Causith mists blake that they dare not appere,
> At whose upryst mountains be made so faire
> As they were new gylt with his bemys clere,
> The nyght doth follow, appallith all his chere,
> When westerne waves his stremys over close;
> Recken all beawty, all fresheness, that is here:
> All stand on chaunge, like a midsòmer rose.
>
> [8.]
>
> Constreynt of cold makith the fowlis *dare* [2]
> With wynter frost, that they dare not appere;
> All cladde in russett soil of greene is bare,
> Tellus and Juno dullyd of their chere

[1] Harlot.
[2] *Lie hid.* From the A. Saxon *dearn dearnan*, to hide.

Remarks on Poems of John Lydgate 115

Princes" was in, for eight poets in Queen Elizabeth's reign, and at the head of them Thomas

By revolution turnyng of the yere;
As grayè March his stoundys [1] doth disclose,
Now rayne, now storme, now Phebus bright and clere.
All stand on chaunge, like a midsòmer rose.

[9.]

Where is now David, the most worthy king,
Of Juda and Israel famous and notàble?
And where is Solomon, soveraine of cunnìng,
Richest of buyldìng, of tresour incomparàble?
Face of Absalom most faire most amiable?
Recken up echone, of truth make no close;
Recken up Jonathas of friendship ìmmutable.
All stand on chaunge, like a midsòmer rose.

[10.]

Where Julius, proudest in his empìre,
With his triumphis most imperial?
And where is Porus, that was lord and sire
Of Indè in hys hygh estate ròyal?
And where is Alisaund, that conquer'd all?
Fayld laisour his testament to dispose,
Nabucodnosor, or Sardanapal?
All stand on chaunge like a midsòmer rose.

[11.]

And wherè is Tullius wyth hys sugyrd tungue,
Or Chrìsostomus with his golden mouthe?
The aureat ditties that were redde or sunge
Of Hòmerus in Grece both north and south?
The tragediès divers and unkouth
Of moral Seneck the misteries to unclose?
By many' examplys this *matt*[2] is full kowth:
All stand on chaunge as a midsòmer rose.

[1] Times, weathers. Saxon.
[2] i. e. This motto is well known.

Sackville, afterwards Lord Buckhurst, joined their forces to write a supplement to it, called

[12.]

Where ben of Frauncè all the dousĕperes [1]
Which over allè had the governance?
(Wowis of the pecok with her prowdè chères!)
The worthy [2] nine with allè their beaunce
The Trojan knightes, greatest of àllyaunce?
The flece of gold conquered in Colchòse?
Rome and Carthàge most soverein of puissaùnce?
All stand on chaunge, like a midsòmer rose.

[13.]

Putt in a summe all martial policye,
Compleat in Afrik, and bowndis of Cartàge,
The Theban legion, example' of chivalry,
At Jordain's river was expert their coràge,
There thousand knightis born of hygh paràge,
There martyrd, redde in metre and in prose;
The golden crownes made in the heavenly stage,
Fresher than lily', or the midsòmer rose.

[14.]

The rémembraunce of every famose knyght,
Grownd considerd, is buylt on ryghtwysnesse.
Rose out eche quarrell that' is not buylt on right.
Withouten trouthe what vaylith high noblèsse?
Lawrer of martyrs foundyd on holynesse,
White was made rede their triumphs to disclose;
The whitè lilie was theire chast cleannèsse,
Theire bloody sufferaunce no midsòmer rose:

[1] Douze Pairs; the twelve peers of Charlemagne.
[2] The nine Worthies: they are Joshua, David, Judas Machabeus, Hector, Alexander, Julius Cæsar, Arthur, Charlemagne, and Godfrey of Boulogne.

"The Mirror of Magistrates." (See W. Baldwyn's preface, fol. 109 of the edition in 1587, in 4to.)

[15.]

It was the rosè of the bloodye field,
The rose of Jericho, that grew in Bethlèmm,
The fine posìes, purtreyed on the sheelde
Splayd in the banner at Jerusalem.
The sunne was clypsd and darke in every reame,[1]
When Jesu Crist five wellis list unclose
Toward Paradyse, and callid the rede streme,
Of whose five woundes print in your heart a rose.

From a MS. in the Public Library in the University of Cambridge [Hh. iv. 12].

[1] Realm.

SAMUEL DANIEL

His genius and style rarely if ever rise to that elevation, that the stronger and more terrific emotions of mind require. His figures and allusions are neither many nor bold; he had little invention in the design, or art in the arrangement of his ideas. His ear was good, his versification like his style flowing and unaffected. As his youth was passed in an age of better taste, fertile in genius and in poetry, he caught from the works he then admired, and the friendships he then form'd, a warm zeal and respect for his own art, and improv'd those abilities nature had given him to a certain pitch beyond which he never went, for his riper days were passed in an insipid court, nay worse, a court of bad taste, that affected out of policy a contempt for the favourite studies of the preceding reign, and that with a pedantic admiration and reverence for the ancients preferred to the brightest productions of genius such works as servilely and inelegantly copied their thoughts, or imitated more happily their puerilities. This may be sufficient to show why his natural talents, and the expectations Spenser had raised of him were blasted after the death of Elizabeth; he himself was sensible of it, and feelingly regrets the happier days he had once seen. Musoph. p. 88. 'But whereas he came planted in the spring,' &c., and Epist. to the prince before his *Philotas*. 'Tho' I the remnant,' &c., and this was probably the reason why he employed his latter days in writing history, indeed, his wars of York and Lancaster, (tho' wrote before Elizabeth's death) of which he never finish'd more than eight books, mark very strongly his transition from verse to prose. The disposition of events is in the same dull order that he found in the Chronicle, no attempt at poetical contrivance or design, except the raising Henry the Fifth's ghost (l. 5), which is merely an imitation of Lydgate (or rather Boccace), Lyndesay's Tragedie of Card. Betone, Drayton's Legends of Robert D. of Norm., Piers Gaveston, &c., and the Mirror of Magistrates, already copied by him in the Complaint of Rosamond, and a long Fable ill introduced (l. 6, st. 27) to account for the invention of gunpowder, it can hardly be known for verse but by the measure and the rhyme, and is doubtless the meanest among his performances; indeed, in all he has left us there are two defects (perhaps of his nature) very conspicuous, the want of imagination and the weakness of expression (see Drayton's Elegy to Mr. Reynolds), (faults nearly allied to those beauties for which I have celebrated him;) yet had his application been directed by some friend (like Spenser) of superior talents to those subjects that best suit a gentle and sensible nature, that move and warm without inflaming or transporting the heart, he might have doubtless merited the character of an amiable and even affecting writer. He had the more need of such assistance, because besides his usual coldness and redundancy of expression, he shows a remarkable want of judgment, I might instance his giving in to the conceits of Marino and the bad Italian writers (though it is but seldom he does this and in a manner that shows it is not natural to him), his choice of Seneca for a model, and his introduction of rhyming stanzas in tragedy,— but the fashion of that age in which he lived may serve to excuse the former, and the examples of Lord Buckhurst, Lord Brooke, and others the latter. Such writers as Seneca and Marino not only dazzle men of little imagination, who admire them as women do heroes, because they possess what themselves principally want, but those too of brighter parts who find in them something congenial to their own fancy, and whose mind is not comprehensive or attention cool enough to judge of the whole or discern the superior beauties of propriety in place, of time, and of character. It is chiefly from the Musophilus that I judge of his talents for Elegy, which requires no other order or invention than those of pure, simple nature, what is (or what ought to appear) the result of a feeling mind strongly possess'd by its subject, and surely he that is so in poetry has done more than half his work, but it is not every imagination that can throw itself into all the situations of a fictitious subject.

SELECTIONS FROM THE LETTERS

SOME FRENCH PLAYS

[*To Richard West, from Paris, April 12, 1739*]

... At night we went to the Pandore; a spectácle literally, for it is nothing but a beautiful piece of machinery of three scenes. The first represents the chaos, and by degrees the separation of the elements. The second, the temple of Jupiter, the giving of the box to Pandora. The third, the opening of the box, and all the mischiefs that ensued. An absurd design, but executed in the highest perfection, and that in one of the finest theatres in the world; it is the grande sale des machines in the Palais des Tuileries. Next day dined at Lord Waldegrave's; then to the opera. Imagine to yourself for the drama four acts entirely unconnected with each other, each founded on some little history, skilfully taken out of an ancient author, e. g. Ovid's Metamorphoses, etc., and with great address converted into a French piece of gallantry. For instance, that which I saw, called the Ballet de la Paix, had its first act built upon the story of Nireus. Homer having said he was the handsomest man of his time, the poet, imagining such a one could not want a mistress, has given him one. These two come in and sing sentiment in lamentable strains, neither air nor recitative; only, to one's great joy, they are every now and then interrupted by a dance, or (to one's great sorrow) by a chorus that borders the stage from one end to the other, and screams, past all power of simile to represent. The second act was Baucis and Philemon. Baucis is a beautiful young shepherdess, and Philemon her swain. Jupiter falls in love with her, but nothing will prevail upon her; so it is all mighty well, and the chorus sing and dance the praises of Constancy. The two other acts were about Iphis and Ianthe, and the judgment of Paris. Imagine, I say, all this transacted by cracked voices, trilling divisions upon two notes and a half, accompanied by an orchestra of humstrums, and a whole house more attentive than if Farinelli sung, and you will almost have formed a just notion of the thing. Our astonishment at their absurdity you can never conceive; we had enough to do to express it by screaming an hour louder than the whole dramatis personæ. We have also seen twice the Comédie Françoise; first, the *Mahomet Second*, a tragedy that has had a great run of late; and the thing itself does not want its beauties, but the actors are beyond measure delightful. Mademoiselle Gaussin (M. Voltaire's Zara) has with a charming (though little) person the most pathetic tone of voice, the finest expression in her face, and most proper action imaginable. There is also a Dufrêne, who did the chief character, a handsome man and a prodigious fine actor. The second we saw was the *Philosophe marié*, and here they performed as well in comedy; there is a Mademoiselle Quinault, somewhat in Mrs. Clive's way, and a Monsieur Grandval, in the nature of Wilks, who is the genteelest thing in the world. There are several more would be much admired in England, and many (whom we have not seen) much celebrated here. . . .

THEATRICAL NOTES

[*To Thomas Ashton, from Paris, May, 1739*]

. . . We have seen here your "Gustavus Vasa" that had raised the general expectation so high, long ago. A worthy piece of prohibited Merchandise, in truth! The Town must have been extreme mercifully disposed; if for the sake of ten innocent lines that may peradventure be picked out, it had consented to spare the lives of the ten thousand wicked ones, that remain. I don't know what condition your Stage is in, but the French is in a very good one at present. Among the rest they have a Mademoiselle Dumenil whose every look and gesture is violent Nature, she is Passion itself, incarnate.

I saw her the other Night do the Phædra of Racine, in a manner which affected me so strongly, that as you see, I can't help prattling about her even to you, that do not care two Pence. . . .

VERSAILLES

[To Richard West]

PARIS, *May 22, 1739.*

AFTER the little particulars aforesaid I should have proceeded to a journal of our transactions for this week past, should have carried you post from hence to Versailles, hurried you through the gardens to Trianon, back again to Paris, so away to Chantilly. But the fatigue is perhaps more than you can bear, and moreover I think I have reason to stomach your last piece of gravity. Supposing you were in your soberest mood, I am sorry you should think me capable of ever being so dissipé, so evaporé, as not to be in a condition of relishing anything you could say to me. And now, if you have a mind to make your peace with me, arouse ye from your megrims and your melancholies, and (for exercise is good for you) throw away your night-cap, call for your jack-boots, and set out with me, last Saturday evening, for Versailles — and so at eight o'clock, passing through a road speckled with vines, and villas, and hares, and partridges, we arrive at the great avenue, flanked on either hand with a double row of trees about half a mile long, and with the palace itself to terminate the view; facing which, on each side of you is placed a semi-circle of very handsome buildings, which form the stables. These we will not enter into, because you know we are no jockeys. Well! and is this the great front of Versailles? What a huge heap of littleness! It is composed, as it were, of three courts, all open to the eye at once, and gradually diminishing till you come to the royal apartments, which on this side present but half a dozen windows and a balcony. This last is all that can be called a front, for the rest is only great wings. The hue of all this mass is black, dirty red, and yellow; the first proceeding from stone changed by age; the second, from a mixture of brick; and the last, from a profusion of tarnished gilding. You cannot see a more disagreeable tout-ensemble; and, to finish the matter, it is all stuck over in many places with small busts of a tawny hue between every two windows. We pass through this to go into the garden, and here the case is indeed altered; nothing can be vaster and more magnificent than the back front; before it a very spacious terrace spreads itself, adorned with two large basons; these are bordered and lined (as most of the others) with white marble, with handsome statues of bronze reclined on their edges. From hence you descend a huge flight of steps into a semicircle formed by woods, that are cut all around into niches, which are filled with beautiful copies of all the famous antique statues in white marble. Just in the midst is the bason of Latona; she and her children are standing on the top of a rock in the middle, on the sides of which are the peasants, some half, some totally changed into frogs, all which throw out water at her in great plenty. From this place runs on the great alley, which brings you into a complete round, where is the bason of Apollo, the biggest in the gardens. He is rising in his car out of the water, surrounded by nymphs and tritons, all in bronze, and finely executed, and these, as they play, raise a perfect storm about him; beyond this is the great canal, a prodigious long piece of water, that terminates the whole: all this you have at one coup d'œil in entering the garden, which is truly great. I cannot say as much of the general taste of the place: every thing you behold savours too much of art; all is forced, all is constrained about you; statues and vases sowed everywhere without distinction; sugar loaves and minced pies of yew; scrawl work of box, and little squirting jets-d'eau, besides a great sameness in the walks, cannot help striking one at first sight, not to mention the silliest of labyrinths, and all Æsop's fables in water; since these were designed in usum Delphini only. Here then we walk by moonlight, and hear the ladies and the nightingales sing. Next morning, being Whitsunday, make ready to go to the Installation of nine Knights du Saint Esprit, Cambis is one: high mass celebrated with music, great crowd, much incense, King, Queen, Dauphin, Mesdames, Cardinals, and Court: Knights arrayed by his Majesty; reverences before the altar, not bows but curtsies; stiff hams: much tittering among the ladies; trumpets, kettle-drums and fifes. My dear West, I am vastly delighted with Trianon, all of us with Chantilly; if you would know why, you must have patience, for I can hold my pen no longer, except to tell you that I saw Britannicus last night; all the characters, particularly Agrippina and Nero, done to perfection; to-morrow Phædra and Hippolitus. We are making you a little bundle of petites pieces; there is nothing in them, but they are acting at present; there are too Crebillon's Letters, and Amusemens sur le langage des Bêtes, said to be of one Bougeant, a Jesuit; they are both esteemed, and lately come out. This day se'nnight we go to Rheims.

THE ALPS

[*To Richard West, from Turin, November 16, N. S., 1739*]

. . . I own I have not, as yet, anywhere met with those grand and simple works of Art, that are to amaze one, and whose sight one is to be the better for: but those of Nature have astonished me beyond expression. In our little journey up to the Grande Chartreuse, I do not remember to have gone ten paces without an exclamation, that there was no restraining: not a precipice, not a torrent, not a cliff, but is pregnant with religion and poetry. There are certain scenes that would awe an atheist into belief, without the help of other argument. One need not have a very fantastic imagination to see spirits there at noonday; you have Death perpetually before your eyes, only so far removed, as to compose the mind without frighting it. I am well persuaded St. Bruno was a man of no common genius, to choose such a situation for his retirement; and perhaps should have been a disciple of his, had I been born in his time. You may believe Abelard and Heloïse were not forgot upon this occasion. If I do not mistake, I saw you too every now and then at a distance among the trees; il me semble, que j'ai vu ce chien de visage là quelque part. You seemed to call to me from the other side of the precipice, but the noise of the river below was so great, that I really could not distinguish what you said; it seemed to have a cadence like verse. In your next you will be so good to let me know what it was. The week we have since passed among the Alps, has not equalled the single day upon that mountain, because the winter was rather too far advanced, and the weather a little foggy. However, it did not want its beauties; the savage rudeness of the view is inconceivable without seeing it: I reckoned in one day, thirteen cascades, the least of which was, I dare say, one hundred feet in height. I had Livy in the chaise with me, and beheld his "Nives cœlo propè immistæ, tecta informia imposita rupibus, pecora jumentaque torrida frigore, homines intonsi & inculti, animalia inanimaque omnia rigentia gelu; omnia, confragosa, præruptaque." The creatures that inhabit them are, in all respects, below humanity; and most of them, especially women, have the tumidum guttur, which they call goscia. Mont Cenis, I confess, carries the permission mountains have of being frightful rather too far; and its horrors were accompanied with too much danger to give one time to reflect upon their beauties. . . .

TACITUS; THE DUNCIAD

[*To Richard West, after March 25, 1742*]

. . . Pray do not imagine that Tacitus, of all authors in the world, can be tedious. An annalist, you know, is by no means master of his subject; and I think one may venture to say, that if those Pannonian affairs are tedious in his hands, in another's they would have been insupportable. However, fear not, they will soon be over, and he will make ample amends. A man, who could join the *brilliant* of wit and concise sententiousness peculiar to that age, with the truth and gravity of better times, and the deep reflection and good sense of the best moderns, cannot choose but have something to strike you. Yet what I admire in him above all this, is his detestation of tyranny, and the high spirit of liberty that every now and then breaks out, as it were, whether he would or no. I remember a sentence in his Agricola that (concise as it is) I always admired for saying much in a little compass. He speaks of Domitian, who upon seeing the last will of that General, where he had made him Coheir with his Wife and Daughter, "Satis constabat lætatum eum, velut honore, judicioque: tam cæca & corrupta mens assiduis adulationibus erat, ut nesciret a bono patre non scribi hæredem, nisi malum principem."

As to the Dunciad, it is greatly admired; the Genii of Operas and Schools, with their attendants, the pleas of the Virtuosos and Florists, and the yawn of dulness in the end, are as fine as anything he has written. The Metaphysicians' part is to me the worst; and here and there a few ill-expressed lines, and some hardly intelligible. . . .

JOSEPH ANDREWS; THE LANGUAGE OF POETRY

[*To Richard West, from London, after April 4, 1742*]

. . . I talked of the Dunciad as concluding you had seen it; if you have not, do you choose I should get and send it you? I have myself, upon your recommendation, been reading Joseph Andrews. The incidents are ill laid and without invention; but the characters have a great deal of nature, which always pleases even in her lowest shapes. Parson Adams is perfectly well; so is Mrs. Slipslop, and the story of Wilson; and throughout he shews himself well read in Stage-Coaches, Country Squires, Inns, and Inns of Court. His reflections upon high people and low people, and misses and masters, are very good. However the exaltedness of some minds (or rather as I shrewdly suspect their insipidity and want of feeling or observation) may make them insensible to these light things (I mean such as characterize and paint nature), yet surely they are as weighty and much more useful than your grave discourses upon the mind, the passions, and what not. Now as the paradisiacal pleasures of the Mahometans consist in playing upon the flute and lying with Houris, be mine to read eternal new romances of Marivaux and Crébillon.

You are very good in giving yourself the trouble to read and find fault with my long harangues. Your freedom (as you call it) has so little need of apologies, that I should scarce excuse your treating me any otherwise; which, whatever compliment it might be to my vanity, would be making a very ill one to my understanding. As to matter of style, I have this to say: the language of the age is never the language of poetry; except among the French, whose verse, where the thought or image does not support it, differs in nothing from prose. Our poetry, on the contrary, has a language peculiar to itself; to which almost every one, that has written, has added something by enriching it with foreign idioms and derivatives: nay sometimes words of their own composition or invention. Shakespear and Milton have been great creators this way; and no one more licentious than Pope or Dryden, who perpetually borrow expressions from the former. Let me give you some instances from Dryden, whom everybody reckons a great master of our poetical tongue. — Full of *museful mopings* — unlike the *trim* of love — a pleasant *beverage* — a *roundelay* of love — stood silent in his *mood* — with knots and *knares* deformed — his *ireful mood* — in proud *array* — his *boon* was granted — and *disarray* and shameful rout — *wayward* but wise — *furbished* for the field — the *foiled dodderd* oaks — *disherited* — *smouldering* flames — *retchless* of laws — *crones* old and ugly — the *beldam* at his side — the *grandam-hag* — *villanize* his Father's fame. — But they are infinite; and our language not being a settled thing (like the French) has an undoubted right to words of an hundred years old, provided antiquity have not rendered them unintelligible. In truth, Shakespear's language is one of his principal beauties; and he has no less advantage over your Addisons and Rowes in this, than in those other great excellences you mention. Every word in him is a picture. Pray put me the following lines into the tongue of our modern Dramatics:

> But I, that am not shaped for sportive tricks,
> Nor made to court an amorous looking-glass:
> I, that am rudely stampt, and want love's majesty
> To strut before a wanton ambling nymph:
> I, that am curtail'd of this fair proportion,
> Cheated of feature by dissembling nature,
> Deform'd, unfinish'd, sent before my time
> Into this breathing world, scarce half made up—

And what follows. To me they appear untranslatable; and if this be the case, our language is greatly degenerated. However, the affectation of imitating Shakespear may doubtless be carried too far; and is no sort of excuse for sentiments ill-suited, or speeches ill-timed, which I believe is a little the case with me. I guess the most faulty expressions may be these—*silken* son of *dalliance*—*drowsier* pretensions—wrinkled *beldams*—*arched* the hearer's brow and *riveted* his eyes in *fearful extasie*. These are easily altered or omitted; and indeed if the thoughts be wrong or superfluous, there is nothing easier than to leave out the whole. The first ten or twelve lines are, I believe, the best; and as for the rest, I was betrayed into a good deal of it by *Tacitus*; only what he has said in five words, I imagine I have said in fifty lines. Such is the misfortune of imitating the inimitable . . .

TACITUS

[*To Richard West, from London, April, 1742*]

... I think you have translated Tacitus very justly, that is, freely; and accommodated his thoughts to the turn and genius of our language; which, though I commend your judgment, is no commendation of the English tongue, which is too diffuse, and daily grows more and more enervate. One shall never be more sensible of this, than in turning an Author like Tacitus. I have been trying it in some parts of Thucydides (who has a little resemblance of him in his conciseness) and endeavoured to do it closely, but found it produced mere nonsense. If you have any inclination to see what figure Tacitus makes in Italian, I have a Tuscan translation of Davanzati, much esteemed in Italy; and will send you the same speech you sent me; that is, if you care for it ...

WEST'S ODE ON MAY

[*To Richard West*]

LONDON, May 8, 1742.

I REJOICE to see you putting up your prayers to the May: she cannot choose but come at such a call. It is as light and genteel as herself. You bid me find fault; I am afraid I cannot; however I will try. The first stanza (if what you say to me in it did not make me think it the best) I should call the worst of the five (except the fourth line). The two next are very picturesque, Miltonic, and musical; her bed is so soft and so snug that I long to lie with her. But those two lines "Great nature" are my favourites. The exclamation of the flowers is a little step too far. The last stanza is full as good as the second and third; the last line bold, but I think not too bold. Now, as to myself and my translation, pray do not call names. I never saw Broukhusius in my life. It is Scaliger who attempted to range Propertius in order; who was, and still is, in sad condition. . . . You see, by what I sent you, that I converse as usual, with none but the dead: they are my old friends, and almost make me long to be with them. You will not wonder, therefore, that I, who live only in times past, am able to tell you no news of the present. I have finished the Peloponnesian war much to my honour, and a tight conflict it was, I promise you. I have drank and sung with Anacreon for the last fortnight, and am now feeding sheep with Theocritus. Besides, to quit my figure, (because it is foolish) I have run over Pliny's Epistles and Martial ἐκ παρέργου; not to mention Petrarch, who, by the way, is sometimes very tender and natural. I must needs tell you three lines in Anacreon, where the expression seems to me inimitable. He is describing hair as he would have it painted.

> Ἕλικας δ' ἐλευθέρους μοι
> Πλοκάμων ἄτακτα συνθεὶς
> Ἀφὲς ὡς θέλουσι κεῖσθαι.

Guess, too, where this is about a dimple.

> Sigilla in mento impressa Amoris digitulo
> Vestigio demonstrant mollitudinem.

GARRICK, THE DUCHESS OF QUEENSBURY, ETC.

[To John Chute, from London, May 24, N. S., 1742]

. . . 'Tis true indeed Mr. Mann is not everywhere; I am shock'd to think of his sufferings, but he of all men was born to suffer with a good grace. He is a Stoick without knowing it, and seems to think pain a pleasure. I am very sorry to compliment him upon such an occasion, and wished with all my heart, he were not so pleased. I much fear his books are gone already; but if not, to be sure he shall have *Middleton* and the *Sofa*; it seems most people here are not such admirers of it as I was: but I won't give up an inch of it, for all that. Did I tell you about Mr.

Garrick, that the town are horn-mad after: there are a dozen Dukes of a night at Goodmansfields sometimes, and yet I am stiff in the opposition. Our fifth Opera was the *Olympiade*, in which they retained most of Pergolesi's songs, and yet 'tis gone already, as if it had been a poor thing of Galuppi's. Two nights did I enjoy it all alone, snug in a nook of the gallery, but found no one in those regions had ever heard of Pergolesi, nay, I heard several affirm it was a composition of Pescetti's. Now there is a 6th sprung up, by the name of *Cephalo and Procri*. My Lady of Queensbury is come out against my Lady of Marlborough, and she has her spirit too, and her originality, but more of the woman, I think, than t'other. As to the facts, it don't signify two pence who's in the right; the manner of fighting, and character of the combatants is all: 'tis hoped old Sarah will at her again. A play of Mr. Glover's I am told, is preparing for the stage, call'd *Boadicea*; it is a fine subject, but I have not an extreme opinion of him. . . .

THE STORY OF MASSINISSA

[To West, from London, May 27, 1742]

I SEND you an inscription for a wood joining to a park of mine (it is on the confines of Mount

Cithæron, on the left hand as you go to Thebes); you know I am no friend to hunters, and hate to be disturbed by their noise.

> Ἀζόμενος πολύθηρον ἑκηβόλου ἄλσος ἀνάσσας,
> Τᾶς δεινᾶς τεμένη λεῖπε, κυναγὲ, θεᾶς·
> Μοῦνοι ἄρ' ἔνθα κυνῶν ζαθέων κλαγγεῦσιν ὑλαγμοὶ,
> Ἀνταχεῖς Νυηφᾶν ἀγροτέραν κελάδῳ.

Here follows also the beginning of an Heroic Epistle; but you must give me leave to tell my own story first, because Historians differ. Massinissa was the son of Gala, King of the Massyli; and, when very young at the head of his father's army, gave a most signal overthrow to Syphax, King of the Masæsylians, then an ally of the Romans. Soon after Asdrubal, son of Gisgo the Carthaginian General, gave the beautiful Sophonisba, his daughter, in marriage to the young prince. But this marriage was not consummated on account of Massinissa's being obliged to hasten into Spain, there to command his father's troops, who were auxiliaries of the Carthaginians. Their affairs at this time began to be in a bad condition; and they thought it might be greatly for their interest, if they could bring over Syphax to themselves. This in time they actually effected; and to strengthen their new alliance, commanded Asdrubal to give his daughter to Syphax. (It is probable their ingratitude to Massinissa arose from the great change of affairs, which had happened among the Massylians during his absence; for his father and uncle were dead, and a distant relation of the royal family had usurped the throne.) Sophonisba was accordingly married to Syphax: and Massinissa, enraged at the affront, became a friend to the Romans. They drove the Carthaginians before them out of Spain, and carried the war into Africa, defeated Syphax, and took him prisoner; upon which Cirtha (his capital) opened her gates to Lælius and Massinissa. The rest of the affair, the marriage, and the sending of poison, everybody knows. This is partly taken from Livy, and partly from Appian. . . .

AKENSIDE'S PLEASURES OF THE IMAGINATION, ETC.

[To Thomas Wharton, from Cambridge, April 26, 1744]

. . . You desire to know, it seems, what Character the Poem of your young Friend bears here. I wonder to hear you ask the Opinion of a Nation, where those who pretend to judge, don't judge at all; and the rest (the wiser Part) wait to catch the Judgment of the world immediately above them, that is, Dick's Coffee-House, and the Rainbow; so that the readier Way would be to ask Mrs. This and Mrs. T'other, that keeps the Bar there. However, to shew you I'm a Judge, as well as my Countrymen, tho' I have rather turn'd it over, than read it (but no matter: no more have they), it seems to me above the middling, and now and then (but for a little while) rises even to the best, particularly in Description. It is often obscure, and even unintelligible, and too much infected with the Hutchinson-Jargon; in short its great fault is that it was published at least nine Years too early; and so methinks in a few Words, à la Mode du Temple, I have very pertly dispatch'd what perhaps may for several years have employed a very ingenious Man worth fifty of myself. Here is a small poem, called the Enthusiast, which is all pure Description, and as they tell me by the same Hand. Is it so, or not? Item, a more bulky one upon Health, wrote by a physician: do you know him? . . .

You are much in the Right to have a taste for Socrates, he was a divine Man. I must tell you, by way of the News of the Place, that the other day, Mr. Fraigneau (entering upon his Professorship) made an Apology for him an Hour long in the Schools, and all the world, except Trinity-College, brought in Socrates Guilty. . . .

ARISTOTLE

[*To Thomas Wharton, September 11, 1746*]

I take it very ill you should have been in the twentieth Year of the War, and yet say nothing of the Retreat from before Syracuse: is it, or is it not the finest Thing you ever read in your Life? And how does Xenophon, or Plutarch agree with you? For my Part I read Aristotle; his Poetics, Politics, and Morals, though I don't well know which is which. In the first Place he is the hardest Author by far I ever meddled with. Then he has a dry Conciseness, that makes one imagine one is perusing a Table of Contents rather than a Book; it tastes for all the World like chop'd Hay, or rather like chop'd Logic; for he has a violent Affection to that Art, being in some Sort his own Invention; so that he often loses himself in little trifling Distinctions and verbal Niceties, and what is worse leaves you to extricate yourself as you can. Thirdly, he has suffered vastly by the Transcribblers, as all Authors of great Brevity necessarily must. Fourthly and lastly he has abundance of fine uncommon Things, which make him well worth the Pains he gives one. . . .

WARTON AND COLLINS

[To Thomas Wharton, probably from Cambridge, December 27, 1746]

... Have you seen the Works of two young Authors, a Mr. Warton and a Mr. Collins, both Writers of Odes? It is odd enough, but each is the half of a considerable Man, and one the counterpart of the other. The first has but little Invention, very poetical choice of Expression, and a good Ear. The second, a fine fancy, model'd upon the Antique, a bad Ear, great Variety of Words, and Images with no Choice at all. They both deserve to last some years, but will not ...

COLLEY CIBBER'S CICERO

[To Horace Walpole, from Cambridge, 1747]

I had been absent from this place a few days, and at my return found Cibber's book upon my table: I return you my thanks for it, and have already run over a considerable part; for who could resist Mrs. Letitia Pilkington's recommendation? (By the way is there any such gentlewoman? Or has somebody put on the style of a scribbling woman's panegyric to deceive and laugh at Colley?) He seems to me full as pert and as dull as usual. There are whole pages of common-place stuff, that for stupidity might have been wrote by Dr. Waterland, or any other grave divine, did not the flirting saucy phrase give them at a distance an air of youth and gaity. It is very true, he is often in the right with regard to Tully's weaknesses; but was there any one that did not see them? Those, I imagine, that would find a man after God's own heart, are no more likely to trust the Doctor's recommendation than the Player's; and as to Reason and Truth, would they know their own faces, do you think, if they looked in the glass, and saw themselves so bedizened in tattered fringe and tarnished lace, in French jewels, and dirty furbelows, the frippery of a stroller's wardrobe?

Literature, to take it in its most comprehensive sense, and include everything that requires invention or judgment, or barely application and industry, seems indeed drawing apace to its dissolution, and remarkably since the beginning of the war. I remember to have read Mr. Spence's pretty book; though (as he then had not been at Rome for the last time) it must have increased greatly since that in bulk. If you ask me what I read, I protest I do not recollect one syllable; but only in general, that they were the best bred sort of men in the world, just the kind of *frinds* one would wish to meet in a fine summer's evening, if one wished to meet any at all. The heads and tails of the dialogues, published separate in 16mo, would make the sweetest reading in *natiur* for young gentlemen of family and fortune, that are learning to dance. I rejoice to hear there is such a crowd of dramatical performances coming upon the stage. . . .

SPENCE'S POLYMETIS

[To Horace Walpole, from Cambridge, 1747]

I have abundance of thanks to return you for the entertainment Mr. Spence's book has given me, which I have almost run over already; and I much fear (see what it is to make a figure) the breadth of the margin, and the neatness of the prints, which are better done than one could expect, have prevailed upon me to like it far better than I did in manuscript; for I think it is not the very genteel deportment of Polymetis, nor the lively wit of Mysagetes, that have at all corrupted me.

There is one fundamental fault, from whence most of the little faults throughout the whole arise. He professes to neglect the Greek writers, who could have given him more instruction on the very heads he professes to treat, than all the others put together; who does not know, that upon the Latin, the Sabine and Hetruscan mythology (which probably might themselves, at a remoter period of time, owe their origin to Greece too) the Romans ingrafted almost the whole religion of Greece to make what is called their own? It would be hard to find any one circumstance that is properly of their invention. In the ruder days of the republic, the picturesque part of their religion (which is the province he has chose, and would be thought to confine himself to) was probably borrowed entirely from the Tuscans, who, as a wealthy and trading people, may be well supposed, and indeed are known, to have had the arts flourishing in a considerable degree among them. What could inform him here, but Dio. Halicarnassus (who expressly treats of those times with great curiosity and industry) and the remains of the first Roman writers? The former he has neglected as a Greek; and the latter, he says, were but little acquainted with the arts, and consequently are but of small authority. In the better ages, when every temple and public building in Rome was peopled with imported deities and heroes, and when all the artists of reputation they made use of were Greeks, what wonder, if their eyes grew familiarised to Grecian forms and habits (especially in a matter of this kind, where so much depends upon the imagination); and if those figures introduced with them a belief of such fables, as first gave them being, and dressed them out in their various attributes, it was natural then, and (I should think) necessary, to go to the source itself, the Greek accounts of their own religion; but to say the truth, I suspect he was a little conversant in those books and that language; for he rarely quotes any but Lucian, an author that falls in everybody's way, and who lived at the very extremity of that period he has set to his enquiries, later than any of the poets he has meddled with, and for that reason ought to have been regarded as but an indifferent authority; especially being a Syrian too. His book (as he says himself) is, I think, rather a beginning than a perfect work; but a beginning at the wrong end: for if anybody should finish it by enquiring into the Greek mythology, as he proposes, it will be necessary to read it backward.

There are several little neglects, that one might have told him of, which I noted in reading it hastily; as page 311, a discourse about orange-trees, occasioned by Virgil's "inter odoratum lauri nemus," where he fancies the Roman Laurus to be our Laurel; though undoubtedly the bay-tree, which is *odoratum*, and (I believe) still called Lauro, or Alloro, at Rome; and that the "Malum Medicum" in the Georgic is the orange; though Theophrastus, whence Virgil borrowed it, or even Pliny, whom he himself quotes, might convince him it is the cedrato which he has often tasted at Florence. Page 144 is an account of Domenichino's Cardinal Virtues, and a fling at the Jesuits, neither of which belong to them. The painting is in a church of the Barnabiti, dedicated to St. Carlo Borromeo, whose motto is HUMILITAS. Page 151, in a note, he says, the old Romans did not regard Fortune as a Deity; tho' Servius Tullius (whom she was said to be in love with; nay, there was actually an affair between them) founded her temple in Foro Boario. By the way, her worship was Greek, and this king was educated in the family of Tarquinius Priscus, whose father was a Corinthian; so it is easy to conceive how early the religion of Rome might be mixed with that of Greece, etc. etc. . . .

LYTTELTON'S ELEGY, ETC.

[To Horace Walpole, from Cambridge, November, 1747]

. . . I am not totally of your mind as to Mr. Lyttleton's elegy, though I love kids and fawns as little as you do. If it were all like the fourth stanza, I should be excessively pleased. Nature and sorrow, and tenderness, are the true genius of such things; and something of these I find in several parts of it (not in the orange-tree): poetical ornaments, are foreign to the purpose; for they only shew a man is not sorry; — and devotion worse; for it teaches him that he ought not to be sorry, which is all the pleasure of the thing. I beg leave to turn your weathercock the contrary way. Your epistle I have not seen a great while, and Dr. M— is not in the way to give me a sight of it: but I remember enough to be sure all the world will be pleased with it, even with all its *faults upon its head*, if you don't care to mend them. I would try to do it myself (however hazardous), rather than it should remain unpublished. . . .

[*To Thomas Wharton, from Cambridge, November 30, 1747*]

. . . Have you seen Lyttelton's Monody on his Wife's Death? There are Parts of it too stiff and poetical; but others truly tender and elegiac, as one would wish. Dodsley is publishing three Miscellaneous Volumes; some new, many that have been already printed. Lyttelton, Nugent, and G. West have given him several Things of theirs. Mr. W[alpole] has given him three Odes

of mine (which you have seen before) and one of
Mr. West's (my friend who is dead) which in
spite of the Subject is excellent: it is on the late
Queen's Death. There is a Mr. Archibald
Bower, a Scotchman bred in Italy, Professor in
three Universities there, and of the Inquisition.
He was employed by the Court of Rome to write
a History of the Popes. As he searched into the
Materials, his eyes were open'd: he came to England, has changed his religion, and continues his
Work in our language under the patronage of Mr.
Pitt, the Yorks, &c. The Preface is come out
with the Proposals, and promises exceeding well.
Doubtless there is no part of history more curious, if it be well perform'd. . . .

LE MÉCHANT, LE SIDNEY, ETC.

[*To Thomas Wharton, probably from Cambridge, June 5, 1748*]

. . . Your opinion of Diodorus is doubtless
right; but there are Things in him very curious,
got out of better Authors, now lost. Do you remember the Egyptian History, and particularly
the account of the Gold-Mines? My own Readings have been cruelly interrupted. What I have
been highly pleased with is the new Comedy from
Paris, by Gresset; Le Méchant, one of the very

best Dramas I ever met with. If you have it not, buy his Works altogether in two little Volumes. They are collected by the Dutch Booksellers, and consequently there is some Trash; but then there are the Ver-vert, the epistle to P. Bougeant, the Chartreuse, that to his sister, an ode on his Country, and another on Mediocrity; and the Sidnei, another comedy, which have great beauties. There is a poem by Thomson, the Castle of Indolence, with some good Stanzas. Mr. Mason is my acquaintance: I liked that Ode very much, but have found no one else, that did. He has much Fancy, little Judgement, and a good deal of Modesty. I take him for a good and well-meaning Creature; but then he is really *in Simplicity a Child*, and loves everybody he meets with: he reads little or nothing, writes abundance, and that with a design to make his fortune by it. . . .

DODSLEY'S MISCELLANY

[To Horace Walpole, 1748]

I am obliged to you for Mr. Dodsley's book, and having pretty well looked it over, will (as you desire) tell you my opinion of it. He might, methinks, have spared the graces in his frontispiece, if he chose to be economical, and dressed his

authors in a little more decent raiment — not in
whited-brown paper, and distorted characters, like
an old ballad. I am ashamed to see myself; but
the company keeps me in countenance: so to begin with Mr. Tickell. This is not only a state-
poem (my ancient aversion), but a state-poem on
the peace of Utrecht. If Mr. Pope had wrote a
panegyric on it, one could hardly have read him
with patience: but this is only a poor short-
winded imitator of Addison, who had himself not
above three or four notes in poetry, sweet enough
indeed, like those of a German flute, but such as
soon tire and satiate the ear with their frequent
return. Tickell has added to this a great poverty
of sense, and a string of transitions that hardly
become a school-boy. However, I forgive him
for the sake of his ballad, which I always thought
the prettiest in the world.

All there is of M. Green here, has been printed
before; there is a profusion of wit everywhere;
reading would have formed his judgment, and har-
monised his verse, for even his wood-notes often
break out into strains of real poetry and music.
The "School Mistress" is excellent in its kind
and masterly; and (I am sorry to differ from you,
but) "London" is to me one of those few imitations that have all the ease and all the spirit of an
original. The same man's verses on the opening

of Garrick's theatre are far from bad. Mr. Dyer (here you will despise me highly) has more of poetry in his imagination than almost any of our number; but rough and injudicious. I should range Mr. Bramston only a step or two above Dr. King, who is as low in my estimation as in yours. Dr. Evans is a furious madman; and pre-existence is nonsense in all her altitudes. Mr. Lyttleton is a gentle elegiac person. Mr. Nugent sure did not write his own Ode. I like Mr. Whitehead's little poems, I mean the Ode on a Tent, the Verses to Garrick, and particularly those to Charles Townsend, better than anything I had seen before of him. I gladly pass over H. Browne and the rest, to come at you. You know I was of the publishing side, and thought your reasons against it none; for though, as Mr. Chute said extremely well, the *still small voice* of Poetry was not made to be heard in a crowd; yet satire will be heard, for all the audience are by nature her friends; especially when she appears in the spirit of Dryden, with his strength, and often with his versification, such as you have caught in those lines on the Royal Unction, on the Papal Dominion, and Convents of both Sexes; on Henry VIII. and Charles II. for these are to me the shining parts of your Epistle. There are many lines I could wish corrected, and some blotted out, but beauties enough to atone for a thousand worse faults than these. The opinion of such as can at all judge, who saw it before in Dr. Middleton's hands, concurs nearly with mine. As to what any one says, since it came out; our people (you must know), are slow of judgment; they wait till some bold body saves them the trouble, and then follow his opinion; or stay till they hear what is said in town, that is at some Bishop's table, or some coffee-house about the Temple. When they are determined I will tell you faithfully their verdict. As for the beauties I am their most humble servant. What shall I say to Mr. Lowth, Mr. Ridley, Mr. Rolle, the Reverend Mr. Brown, Seward, etc.? If I say Messieurs! this is not the thing; write prose, write sermons, write nothing at all; they will disdain me and my advice. What then would the sickly Peer have done, that spends so much time in admiring everything that has four legs, and fretting at his own misfortune in having but two; and cursing his own politic head and feeble constitution, that won't let him be such a beast as he would wish? Mr. S. Jenyns now and then can write a good line or two — such as these —

"Snatch us from all our little sorrows here,
   Calm every grief, and dry each childish tear," etc.

I like Mr. Aston Hervey's Fable; and an Ode

(the last of all) by Mr. Mason, a new acquaintance of mine, whose Musæus too seems to carry with it a promise at least of something good to come. I was glad to see you distinguished who poor West was, before his charming Ode, and called it anything rather than a Pindaric. The town is an owl, if it don't like Lady Mary, and I am surprised at it: we here are owls enough to think her eclogues very bad; but that I did not wonder at. Our present taste is Sir T. Fitz-Osborne's Letters. . . .

GRESSET, ETC.

[*To Thomas Wharton, from Stoke, August 19, 1748*]

. . . I am glad you have had any Pleasure in Gresset: he seems to me a truly elegant and charming Writer. The Méchant is the best comedy I ever read. Edward I could scarce get through: it is puerile; tho' there are good lines; such as this for Example:

Le jour d'un nouveau règne est le jour des ingrats.

But good Lines will make anything rather than a good Play. However you are to consider, this is a Collection made by the Dutch Booksellers. Many Things unfinish'd or wrote in his Youth, or designed not for the World, but to make a few Friends laugh, as the Lutrin vivant, &c.: there are two noble Verses, which as they are in the middle of an *Ode to the King*, may perhaps have escaped you:

> Le Cri d'un peuple heureux, est la seule Éloquence,
> Qui sçait parler des Rois.

which is very true, and should have been a Hint to himself not to write Odes to the King at all. . . .

MONTESQUIEU'S L'ESPRIT DES LOIX

[*To Thomas Wharton, from Cambridge, March 9, 1749*]

You ask for some Account of Books. The principal I can tell you of is a work of the President Montesquieu's, the Labour of twenty Years. It is called, L'Esprit des Loix, 2 vols. 4to. printed at Geneva. He lays down the Principles on which are founded the three Sorts of Government, Despotism, the limited Monarchic, and the Republican, and shews how from thence are deducted the Laws and Customs, by which they are guided and maintained: the Education proper to each Form, the influences of Climate, Situation, religion, &c.: on the Minds of particular Nations, and on their Policy. The Subject (you see) is as extensive as Mankind; the Thoughts perfectly new, generally admirable, as they are just, sometimes a little too refined: in short there are Faults, but such as an ordinary Man could never have committed: the Style very lively and concise (consequently sometimes obscure); it is the Gravity of Tacitus (whom he admires) temper'd with the Gayety and fire of a Frenchman. . . .

CRÉBILLON'S CATILINA, ETC.

[To Thomas Wharton, from Cambridge, April 25, 1749]

. . . Rosse's "Epistles of Tully ad Familiares" will come out in about a Week. It is in two handsome 8vo Volumes, with an Introduction and Notes in English, but no Translation, dedicated to Lord Gower. Now I am come to Books, there is a new edition of Montesquieu's Work (which I mentioned to you before) publishing in 2 vols. 8vo. Have you seen old Crébillon's "Catilina, a Tragedy," which has had a prodigious Run at Paris? Historical Truth is too much perverted by it, which is ridiculous in a Story so generally known: but if you can get over this, the Sentiments and Versification are fine, and most of the Characters (particularly the principal one) painted with great Spirit. Observe, if you chuse to send for it, not to have Brindley's Edition, which is all false Prints, but Vaillant's. There is a Work publishing in Denmark by Subscription (4 guineas) "Travels in Egypt," by Captain Norden. He was once in England (as Tutor to a young Count Daniskiold, hereditary Admiral of Denmark) and known to many Persons for a Man of Sense, and that understood Drawing extremely well: accordingly it is the Plates, that raise it to such a Price, and are said to be excellent. The Author himself is dead, and his papers are publish'd by the Academy at Copenhagen. Mr. Birch, the indefatigable, has just put out a thick 8vo of original papers of Queen Elizabeth's Time. There are many curious Things in it, particularly Letters from Sir Robert Cecil (Salisbury) about his Negotiations with Henry the Fourth of France; the Earl of Monmouth's odd Account of Queen Elizabeth's Death, several Peculiarities of James First, and Prince Henry, &c.; and above all an excellent Account of the State of France with Characters of the King, his Court and Ministry, by Sir G. Carew, Ambassador there. This, I think, is all new worth mentioning, that I have seen or heard of, except a natural History of Peru in Spanish, printed at London by Don —— something, a Man of Learning, sent thither by that Court on Purpose. . . .

MASON

[To Thomas Wharton, from Cambridge, August 8, 1749]

... Mason's Ode was the only Entertainment, that had any tolerable Elegance; and for my own Part, I think it (with some little abatements) uncommonly well on such an Occasion. Pray let me know your Sentiments, for doubtless you have seen it. The Author of it grows apace into my good Graces, as I know him more: he is very ingenious with great Good-Nature and Simplicity. A little vain, but in so harmless and so comical a Way, that it does not offend one at all; a little ambitious, but withal so ignorant in the World and its Ways, that this does not hurt him in one's Opinion. So sincere and so undisguised, that no Mind with a Spark of Generosity would ever think of hurting him, he lies so open to Injury. But so indolent, that if he cannot overcome this Habit, all his good Qualities will signify nothing at all. After all I like him so well, I could wish you knew him. . . .

ASHTON'S DISSERTATION

[To Horace Walpole, from Stoke, June 12, 1750]

... Now I have talked of writings, I have seen a book which is by this time in the press, against Middleton (though without naming him), by Ashton. As far as I can judge from a very hasty reading, there are things in it new and ingenious, but rather too prolix, and the style here and there savouring too strongly of sermon. I imagine it will do him credit....

BUFFON AND D'AUBENTON'S HISTOIRE DU CABINET DU ROI

[*To Thomas Wharton*]

Stoke, August 9, 1750.

MY DEAR WHARTON — Aristotle says (one may write Greek to you without scandal) that Οἱ [γὰρ] τόποι οὐ διαλύουσι τὴν φιλίαν ἁπλῶς, ἀλλὰ τὴν ἐνεργείαν. Ἐὰν δὲ χρόνιος ἡ ἀπουσία γένηται, καὶ τῆς φιλίας δοκεῖ λήθην ποιεῖν· ὅθεν εἴρηται,

πολλὰς δὴ φιλίας ἀπροσηγορία διέλυσεν.

But Aristotle may say whatever he pleases. I do not find myself at all the worse for it. I could indeed wish to refresh my Ἐνέργεια a little at Durham by a Sight of you, but when is there a Probability of my being so happy? It concerned me greatly when I heard the other Day, that your Asthma continued at Times to afflict you, and that you were often obliged to go into the Country to breathe. You cannot oblige me more than by giving me an account of the State both of your Body and Mind; I hope the latter is able to keep you cheerful and easy in spite of the Frailties of its Companion. As to my own, it can do neither one, nor the other; and I have the Mortification to find my spiritual Part the most infirm Thing about me. You have doubtless heard of the loss I have had in Dr. Middleton, whose House was the only easy Place one could find to converse in at Cambridge. For my Part I find a Friend so uncommon a Thing, that I cannot help regretting even an old Acquaintance, which is an indifferent Likeness of it, and though I don't approve the Spirit of his Books, methinks 'tis pity the World should lose so rare a Thing as a good Writer. My studies cannot furnish a Recommendation of many new Books to you. There is a Defense de l'Esprit des Loix, by Montesquieu himself. It has some lively things in it, but is very short, and his Adversary appears to be so mean a Bigot, that he deserved no Answer. There are three vols. in 4to of Histoire de Cabinet du Roi, by Messrs. Buffon and D'Aubenton. The first is a Man of Character, but (I am told) has hurt it by this Work. It is all a sort of Introduction to Natural History. The weak Part of it is a Love of System, which runs through it, the most contrary Thing in the World to a Science, entirely grounded upon Experiments, and that has nothing to do with Vivacity of Imagination. There are some microscopical Observations, that seem'd curious to me, on those Animalcula to which we are supposed to owe our Origin; and which he has discover'd of like Figure in Females not pregnant, and in almost every Thing we use for Nourishment, even Vegetables, particularly in their Fruits and Seeds. Not that he allows them to be animated Bodies, but *Molecules organisées*. If you ask what that is, I cannot tell; no more than I can understand a new System of Generation which he builds upon it. But what I was going to commend is a general View he gives of the Face of the Earth, followed by a particular one of all known Nations, their peculiar Figure and Manners, which is the best Epitome of Geography I ever met with, and wrote with Sense, and Elegance: in short these Books are well worth turning over. The Mémoires of the Abbé de Mongon in five vols. are highly commended, but I have not seen them. He was engaged in several Embassies to Germany, England, &c., during the Course of the late War. The Presid. Henault's Abrégé Chronologique de l'Histoire de France I believe I have before mention'd to you, as a very good Book of its Kind.

MASON'S ELFRIDA

[To Horace Walpole, from Cambridge, Ash-Wednesday, 1751]

... You will take me for a mere poet, and a fetcher and carrier of sing-song, if I tell you that I intend to send you the beginning of a drama, not mine, thank God, as you will believe, when you hear it is finished, but wrote by a person whom I have a very good opinion of. It is (unfortunately) in the manner of the ancient drama, with choruses, which I am to my shame the occasion of; for, as great part of it was at first written in that form, I would not suffer him to change it to a play fit for the stage, and as he intended, because the lyric parts are the best of it, they must have been lost. The story is Saxon, and the language has a tang of Shakespeare, that suits an old-fashioned fable very well. In short I don't do it merely to amuse you, but for the sake of the author, who wants a judge, and so I would lend him *mine:* yet not without your leave, lest you should have us up to dirty our stockings at the bar of your house, for wasting the time and politics of the *nation*.

THE FINE LADY, ETC.

[*To Horace Walpole, from Cambridge, March 3, 1751*]

... *Gil Blas* is the *Lying Valet* in five acts. The *Fine Lady* has half a dozen good lines dispersed in it. *Pompey* is the hasty production of a Mr. Coventry (cousin to him you knew), a young clergyman; I found it out by three characters, which once made part of a comedy that he shewed me of his own writing. Has that miracle of *tenderness and sensibility* (as she calls it) Lady Vane given you any amusement? *Peregrine*, whom she uses as a vehicle, is very poor indeed, with a few exceptions. In the last volume is a character of Mr. Lyttleton, under the name of "Gosling Scrag," and a parody of part of his Monody, under the notion of a Pastoral on the death of his grandmother.

REMARKS ON THE LETTERS PREFIXED TO MASON'S ELFRIDA

[*To William Mason, from Cambridge, 1751*]

I

Dear Sir — very bad; I am yours — equally bad: it is impossible to conciliate these passages to nature and Aristotle.

"*Allowed to modern caprice.*" — It is not caprice but good sense that made these alterations in the modern drama. A greater liberty in the choice of the fable and the conduct of it was the necessary consequence of retrenching the Chorus. Love and tenderness delight in privacy. The soft effusions of the soul, Mr. Mason, will not bear the presence of a gaping, singing, dancing, moralising, uninteresting crowd: and not love alone, but every passion, is checked and cooled by this fiddling crew. How could Macbeth and his wife have laid the design for Duncan's murder? What could they have said to each other in the hall at midnight not only if a chorus but if a single mouse had been stirring there? Could Hamlet have met the Ghost or taken his mother to task in *their* Company? If Othello had said a harsh word to his wife before *them*, would they not have danced to the window and called the watch?

The ancients were perpetually crossed and harassed by the necessity of using the Chorus, and, if they have done wonders notwithstanding this clog, sure I am they would have performed still greater wonders without it. For the same reason we may be allowed to admit of more intrigue in our drama, to bring about a great action — it is often an essential requisite; and it is not fair to argue against this liberty for that misuse of it which is common to us, and was formerly so with the French, namely, the giving in to a silly intimacy of plot, in imitation of the Spanish dramas. We have also, since Charles the Second's time, imitated the French (though but awkwardly) in framing scenes of mere insipid gallantry; but these were the faults of the writers and not of the art, which enables us, with the help of a little contrivance, to have as much love as we please, without playing the petits maîtres or building labyrinths.

I forgot to mention that *Comedy* continued to be an odd sort of farce, very like those of the Italian theatre, till the Chorus was dismissed, when nature and Menander brought it into that beautiful form which we find in Terence. *Tragedy* was not so happy till modern times.

II

I do not admit that the excellences of the French writers are measured by the verisimilitude or the regularities of their dramas *only*. Nothing in them, or in our own, even Shakespere himself, ever touches us, unless rendered *verisimile*, which, by good management, may be accomplished even in such absurd stories as the Tempest, the witches in Macbeth, or the fairies in the Midsummer

Night's Dream; and I know not of any writer that has pleased chiefly in proportion to his *regularity*. Other beauties may, indeed, be heightened and set off by its means, but of itself it hardly pleases at all. Venice Preserved or Jane Shore are not so regular as the Orphan, or Tamerlane, or Lady Jane Grey.

III

Modern Melpomene. — Here are we got into our tantarems! It is certain that pure poetry may be introduced without any Chorus. I refer you to a thousand passages of *mere* description in the Iambic parts of Greek tragedies, and to ten thousand in Shakspere, who is moreover particularly admirable in his introduction of pure poetry, so as to join it with pure passion, and yet keep close to nature. This *he* could accomplish with passions the most violent and transporting, and this any good writer may do with passions less impetuous; for it is nonsense to imagine that tragedy must *throughout* be agitated with the furious passions, or attached by the tender ones: the greater part of it must often be spent in a preparation of these passions, in a gradual working them up to the light, and must thus pass through a great many cooler scenes and a variety of *nuances*, each of which will admit of a proper degree of poetry, and some the purest poetry. Nay, the boldest metaphors, and even description in its strongest colouring, are the natural expression of some passions, even in their greatest agitation. As to moral reflections, there is sufficient room for them in those cooler scenes that I have mentioned, and they make the greatest ornaments of those parts, that is to say, if they are well joined with the character. If not, they had better be left to the audience than put into the mouths of a set of professed moralists, who keep a shop of sentences and reflections (I mean the Chorus), whether they be sages, as you call them, or young girls that learnt them by heart out of their samples and primers.

There is nothing ungracious or improper in Jane Shore's reflections on the fate of women, but just the contrary, only that they are in rhyme; and, in like manner, it is far from a beautiful variety when the Chorus makes a transition in the — from plain iambics to high-flown lyric thoughts, expressions, and numbers, and, when their vagaries are over, relapse again into common sense and conversation. A confidante in skilful hands might be a character, and have both sense and dignity. That in Maffei's Merope has as much as any Chorus.

The Greeks might sing better than the French, but I'll be burnt if they *danced* with more grace, expression, or even pathos. Yet who ever thought of shedding tears at a French opera?

IV

If modern music cannot, as you say, express poetry, it is not a perfection, but a deterioration. You might as well say that the *perfectionnement* of poetry would be the rendering it incapable of expressing the passions.

MIDDLETON'S WORKS, ETC.

[To Horace Walpole]

Cambridge, October 8, 1751.

I send you this (as you desire) merely to make up half a dozen; though it will hardly answer your end in furnishing out either a head or a tail-piece. But your own fable may much better supply the place. You have altered it to its advantage; but there is still something a little embarrassed here and there in the expression. I rejoice to find you apply (pardon the use of so odious a word) to the history of your own times. Speak, and spare not. Be as impartial as you can; and after all, the world will not believe you are so, though you should make as many protestations as bishop Burnet. They will feel in their own breast, and find it very possible to hate fourscore persons, yea, ninety and nine: so you must rest satisfied with the testimony of your own conscience. Somebody has laughed at Mr. Dodsley, or at me, when they talked of the *bat:* I have nothing more either nocturnal or diurnal, to deck his miscellany with. We have a man here that writes a good hand; but he has little failings that hinder my recommending him to you. He is lousy, and he is mad: he sets out this week for Bedlam; but if you insist upon it, I don't doubt he will pay his respects to you. I have seen two of Dr. Middleton's unpublished works. One is about 44 pages in 4to. against Dr. Waterland, who wrote a very orthodox book on the *Importance of the Doctrine of the Trinity*, and insisted that Christians ought to have no communion with such as differ from them in fundamentals. Middleton enters no farther into the doctrine itself than to shew that a mere speculative point can never be called a fundamental: and that the earlier fathers, on whose concurrent tradition Waterland would build, are so far, when they speak of the three persons, from agreeing with the present notion of our church, that they declare for the inferiority of the Son, and seem to have no clear and distinct idea of the Holy Ghost at all. The rest is employed in exposing the folly and cruelty of stiffness and zealotism in religion, and in shewing that the primitive ages of the church, in which tradition had its rise, were (even by the confession of the best scholars and most orthodox writers) *the æra of nonsense and absurdity*. It is finished and very well wrote; but has been mostly incorporated into his other works, particularly the enquiry; and for this reason, I suppose, he has writ upon it, " *This wholly laid aside.*" The second is in Latin, on miracles; to shew, that of the two methods of defending Christianity, one from its intrinsic evidence, the holiness and purity of its doctrines, the other from its external, the miracles said to be wrought confirm it; the first has been little attended to by reason of its difficulty; the second much insisted upon, because it appeared an easier task; but that, in reality, it can prove nothing at all. " Nobilis illa quidem defensio (the first) quam si obtinere potuissent, rem simul omnem expediisse, causamque penitus vicisse viderentur. At causæ hujus defendendæ labor cum tantâ argumentandi cavillandique molestiâ conjunctus, ad alteram, quam dixi, defensionis viam, ut commodiorem longè et faciliorem, plerosque adegit —— ego verò istiusmodi defensione religionem nostram non modo non confirmari, sed dubiam potiùs suspectamque reddi existimo." He then proceeds to consider miracles in general, and afterwards those of the Pagans compared with those of Christ. I only tell you the plan, for I have not read it out (though it is short); but you will not doubt to what conclusion it tends. There is another thing, I know not what, I am to see. As to the *Treatise on Prayer*, they say it is burnt indeed.

MEMOIRS BY FREDERICK II., ETC.

[*To Thomas Wharton, from Cambridge, December 18, 1751*]

His Prussian Majesty has published the *Suite des Memoires*, pour servir à l'Histoire de la Maison de Brandebourg, which includes a very free account of his Grandfather's Life, who was the first King of that House, reflections on the gradual Advance in science, Commerce, &c., of his Subjects, and on their Changes in Religion. It is much in Voltaire's Manner. The book itself is at present hard to be got, but you may see a good Extract of it in the *Mercure historique*, a Work publish'd Monthly: whether it is in that for October or September I cannot justly say. There is also an account of the History of Crusades, which seems to be Voltaire's, and promises

well. I hear talk of a Pamphlet, called Voix du
Sage et du Peuple, ascribed to Montesquieu; and
a book, styled only *Lettres*, by the Procureur
General, Fleury, on the Power of the Clergy in
France, but have not seen either of them, being
very scarce as yet. Mr. de Buffon has discovered
the Speculum of Archimedes, which burns at 200
Foot distance; and a chymist in . . .

MADAME DE MAINTENON'S LETTERS, ETC.

[To Thomas Wharton, from Cambridge, probably in 1752]

. . . de Maintenon's Letters; they are undoubtedly genuine. They begin very early in her
Life, before she married Scarron; and continue
after the King's Death to within a little while
of her own. They bear all the marks of a noble
Spirit (in her adversity particularly), of Virtue,
and unaffected Devotion, insomuch that I am
almost persuaded she indulged Lewis the 14th
in no Liberties, till he actually married her, and
this not out of Policy and Ambition, but Conscience; for she was what we should call a Bigot,
yet with great good-sense. In short she was too
good for a Court; Misfortunes in the beginning
of her Life had formed her Mind (naturally lively

and impatient) to reflexion, and a habit of piety;
she was always miserable, while she had the care
of Mad. de Montespan's children; timid and very
cautious of making Use of that unlimited power
she rose to afterwards for fear of trespassing on
the King's Friendship for her; and after his death,
not at all afraid of meeting her own. I don't
know what to say to you with regard to Racine:
it sounds to me as if anybody should fall upon
Shakespear, who indeed lies infinitely more open
to Criticism of all kinds, but I should not care to
be the person that undertook it. If you don't like
Athaliah, or Britannicus, there is no more to be
said. I have done. . . . Have you seen Bishop
Hall's Satires, called Virgidemiæ, republished
lately, they are full of spirit and poetry; as much
of the first, as Dr. Donne, and far more of the
latter. They were wrote at this University, when
he was about 23 years old, in Queen Elizabeth's
time. . . .

GOTHIC ARCHITECTURE

[*To Thomas Wharton*]

Stoke, September 18, 1754.

DEAR SIR — I rejoice to find you at last settled
to your heart's content, and delight to hear you
talk of giving your house *some Gothic ornaments*

already. If you project anything, I hope it will be entirely within doors; and don't let me (when I come gaping into Coleman-street) be directed to the Gentleman's at the ten Pinnacles, or with the Church-Porch at his door. I am glad you enter into the Spirit of Strawberry-Castle. It has a purity and propriety of Gothicism in it (with very few exceptions) that I have not seen elsewhere. The eating-room and library were not completed, when I was there, and I want to know what effect they have. My Lord Radnor's Vagaries (I see) did not keep you from doing justice to his situation, which far surpasses everything near it, and I do not know a more *laughing* Scene, than that about Twickenham and Richmond. Dr. Akenside (I perceive) is no Conjurer in Architecture, especially when he talks of the Ruins of Persepolis, which are no more Gothic, than they are Chinese. The Egyptian Style (see Dr. Pococke, not his discourses, but his prints) was apparently the Mother of the Greek; and there is such a similitude between the Egyptian, and those Persian Ruins, as gave room to Diodorus to affirm, that the old buildings of Persia were certainly perform'd by Egyptian Artists. As to the other part of his opinion, that the Gothic manner is the Saracen or Moorish, he has a great Authority to support him, that of Sir Christopher

Wren, and yet (I cannot help thinking) is undoubtedly wrong. The Palaces in Spain, I never saw but in description, which gives us little or no idea of things; but the Doge's Palace at Venice I have seen (which is in the Arabesque manner) and the houses of Barbary you may see in Dr. Shaw's book, not to mention abundance of other eastern Buildings in Turkey, Persia, &c., that we have views of, and they seem plainly to be corruptions of the Greek Architecture, broke into little parts indeed, and cover'd with little ornaments, but in a taste very distinguishable from that we call Gothic. There is one thing that runs through the Moorish Buildings, that an Imitator would certainly have been first struck with, and would have tried to copy, and that is the Cupolas, which cover everything, Baths, Apartments, and even Kitchens — yet who ever saw a Gothic Cupola? It is a thing plainly of Greek original. I do not see anything but the slender Spires, that serve for steeples, which may perhaps be borrowed from the Saracen Minarets on their Mosques. . . .

STROPHE AND ANTISTROPHE

[*To Thomas Wharton, from Cambridge, March 9, 1755*]

. . . I am not quite of your opinion with regard to Strophe and Antistrophe. Setting aside the difficulties, methinks it has little or no effect upon the ear, which scarce perceives the regular return of Metres at so great a distance from one another. To make it succeed, I am persuaded the stanza's must not consist of above nine lines each at the most. Pindar has several such odes....

BAIARDI AND VOLTAIRE

[*To Richard Stonehewer, probably from Stoke*]

August 21, 1755.

I thank you for your intelligence about Herculaneum, which was the first news I received of it. I have since turned over Monsignor Baiardi's book, where I have learned how many grains of modern wheat the Roman Congius in the Capitol, holds, and how many thousandth parts of an inch the Greek foot consisted of more or less (for I forget which) than our own. He proves also by many affecting examples, that an Antiquary may be mistaken: that for anything anybody knows, this place under ground might be some other place, and not Herculaneum; but nevertheless, that he can shew for certain that it was this place and no other place; that it is hard to say which of the several Herculeses was the founder; therefore (in the third volume) he promises to give us the memoirs of them all; and after that, if we do not know what to think of the matter, he will tell us. There is a great deal of wit too, and satire, and verses, in the book, which is intended chiefly for the information of the French King, who will be greatly edified without doubt.

I am much obliged to you also for Voltaire's performance; it is very unequal, as he is apt to be in all but his dramas, and looks like the work of a man that will admire his retreat and his Lemon-Lake no longer than till he finds an opportunity to leave it. However, though there be many parts which I do not like, yet it is in several places excellent, and everywhere above mediocrity. . . .

CHANGES IN THE BARD

[*To Thomas Wharton, from Stoke, August 21, 1755*]

. . . Though I allow abundance for your kindness and partiality to me, I am yet much pleased with the good opinion you seem to have of the *Bard*. You may alter that, *Robed in* the sable, &c., almost in your own words, thus,

> With fury pale, and pale with woe,
> Secure of fate, the Poet stood, &c.

Though *haggard*, which conveys to you the idea

of a *Witch*, is indeed only a metaphor taken from an unreclaimed Hawk, which is called a *Haggard*, and looks wild and *farouche*, and jealous of its liberty. I have sent now to Stonehewer a bit more of the *prophecy*, and desire him to shew it you immediately: it is very rough and unpolish'd at present. Adieu, dear Sir, I am ever

Truly Yours
T. G.

. . . .

 She-Wolf of France with unrelenting fangs,
 That tear'st the bowels of thy mangled Mate;
 From thee be born, who o'er thy country hangs
 The Scourge of Heaven. What Terrors round him wait!
 Amazement in his Van with Flight combined,
 And Sorrow's faded form and Solitude behind.

ANT. 2.
   Victor
Mighty Conqu'ror, mighty Lord,
   his
Low on the funeral couch he lies;
No   no
What pitying heart, what eye afford
A tear to grace his obsequies?
Is the sable Warrior fled?
Thy son is gone. He rests among the dead.
     in thy noontide beam were born
The swarm that *hover'd in thy noontide ray?*
     morn
Gone to salute the rising *day*
Mirrors of Saxon truth and loyalty,
Your helpless old expiring master view,
They hear not. Scarce Religion dares supply

Changes in The Bard

Her mutter'd Requiems and her holy Dew.
Yet thou, proud Boy, from Pomfret's walls shalt send
A sigh, and envy oft thy happy Grandsire's end.

Epode 2.

Fill high the sparkling bowl,
The rich repast prepare,
Reft of a crown he yet may share the feast.
Close by the regal chair
Fell Thirst and Famine scowl
A smile of horror on their baffled guest.
Heard ye the din of battle bray,
Lance to lance and horse to horse!
Long years of havock urge their destined course,
And thro' the kindred squadrons mow their way.
Ye
Grim towers of Julius, London's lasting shame,
With many a foul and midnight murther fed,
Revere his consort's faith, his Father's fame,
And spare the meek Usurper's hallow'd head.
Above, below, the Rose of snow,
Twined with her blushing foe we spread:
The bristled boar in infant gore,
Wallows beneath the thorny shade.
Now, Brothers, bending o'er the accursed loom,
Stamp we our vengeance deep, and ratify his doom.

Strophe 3.

Edward, lo! to sudden fate,
   (Weave we the woof. The thread is spun),
Half of thy heart we consecrate
   (The web is wove. The work is done).
        thus
Stay, oh stay, nor here forlorn
     me unbless'd. Unpitied here
Leave your despairing Caradoc to mourn!
     track
In yon bright *clouds* that fires the western skies,

melt
They sink, they vanish from my eyes.
But ah! what solemn scenes *of Heaven* on Snowdon's height,
                              glitt'ring
Descending slow their golden skirts unroll!
Visions of glory, spare my aching sight,
Ye unborn ages, crowd not on my soul.
From Cambria's thousand hills a thousand strains
Triumphant tell aloud, another Arthur reigns.

ANTIST. 3

Girt with many a
Youthful Knights and Barons bold
Sublime their starry fronts they rear
With dazzling helm, and horrent spear
And gorgeous Dames, and Statesmen old,
In bearded majesty appear.
In the midst a Form divine,
Her eye proclaims her of the Briton-Line;
Her   her
A Lyon-port, *an* awe-commanding face,
Attemper'd sweet to virgin-grace.
What strings symphonious tremble in the air!
What strains of vocal transport round her play!
Hear from the grave, great Taliessin, hear,
They breath a soul to animate thy clay.
Bright Rapture calls, and soaring, as she sings,
Waves in the eye of Heaven her many-coloured wings.

EPODE 3.

The verse adorn again,
    Fierce War, and Faithful Love,
And Truth severe by fairy-Fiction drest.
    In buskin'd measures move
Pale Grief and pleasing Pain,
With Horrour, tyrant of the throbbing breast.

A voice as of the Cherub-Quire,
  Gales from blooming Eden bear;
  And distant Warblings lessen on my ear,
That lost in long futurity expire.
Fond impious man, think'st thou yon sanguine cloud
  Rais'd by thy breath has quench'd the Orb of day?
To-morrow he repairs the golden flood,
  And warms the Nations with redoubled ray.
    Enough for me. With joy I see
    The different doom our fates assign,
    Be thine Despair, and scepter'd Care.
    To triumph and to die are mine.
He spoke, and headlong from the mountain's height
Deep in the roaring tide he sunk to endless night.

HENRY IV. OF FRANCE AND SULLY

[*To Thomas Wharton, from Cambridge, March* 25, 1756]

. . . The similitude between the Italian republics and those of ancient Greece has often struck me, as it does you. I do not wonder, that Sully's Memoirs have highly entertain'd you, but cannot agree with you in thinking him or his master two of the *best Men* in the world. The king was indeed one of the best natur'd Men, that ever lived. But it is owing only to chance, that his intended Marriage with Mad. d'Estrées, or with the Marquise de Verneuil, did not involve him and the kingdom in the most inextricable confusion; and his design upon the Princess of Condé (in his old age) was worse still. As to the

Minister, his base application to Concini after the murther of Henry has quite ruin'd him in my esteem, and destroy'd all the merit of that honest surly Pride, for which I honour'd him before. Yet I own, that as Kings and Ministers go, they were both extraordinary Men. Pray look at the end of Birch's State Papers of Sir T. Edmonde's for the character of the French Court at that time, written by Sir George Carew. . . .

TWO VOLUMES OF MEMOIRS

[*To Thomas Wharton, from Stoke, October 15, 1756*]

. . . I recommend two little French books to you, one called Mémoires de Monsieur de la Porte. It has all the air of simplicity and truth, and contains some few very extraordinary facts relating to Anne of Austria and Cardinal Mazarin. The other is two small volumes, *Mémoires de Madame Staal*. The facts are no great matter, but the manner and vivacity of it make it interesting. She was a sort of Confidente to the late Duchess of Maine, and imprison'd a long time in the Bastille on her account during the Regency. The first you may buy, and the latter borrow. . . .

BROWN'S ESTIMATE, ETC.

[To William Mason, from Cambridge, April 23, 1757]

. . . Dr. Brown's book (I hear) is much admired in town, which I do not understand. I expected it would be admired here; but they affect not to like it, though I know they ought. What would you have me do? There is one thing in it I applaud, which is the dissertation against trade, for I have always said it was the ruin of the nation. I have read the little wicked book about Evil, that settled Mr. Dodsley's conscience in that point, and find nothing in it but absurdity: we call it Soame Jenyns's, but I have a notion you mentioned some other name to me, though I have forgotten it. . . .

CHILD MAURICE, ETC.

[To William Mason, from Cambridge, June, probably 1757]

DEAR MASON — I send you inclosed the breast and merry-thought and guts and garbage of the chicken, which I have been chewing so long that I would give the world for neck-beef or cow-heel. I thought, in spite of *ennui*, that the ten last lines would have escaped untouched; for all the rest

that I send you I know is weakly, and you think
so too. But you want them to be printed and done
with; not only Mr. Hurd, but Mr. Bonfoy too
and Neville have seen them. Both these like the
first Ode (that has no *tout-ensemble*), the best of
the two, and both somehow dislike the conclusion
of the "Bard," and mutter something about an-
tithesis and conceit in "to triumph, to die," which
I do not comprehend, and am sure it is altered
for the better. It was before —

"Lo! to be free to die, are mine."

If you like it better so, so let it be. It is more
abrupt, and perhaps may mark the action better;
or it may be —

"Lo! liberty and death are mine."

whichever you please. But as to breaking the
measure, it is not to be thought of; it is an inviol-
able law of the Medes and Persians. Pray think
a little about this conclusion, for all depends upon
it; the rest is of little consequence. "In bearded
majesty," was altered to "of" only because the
next line begins with "In the midst," &c. I understand what you mean about "The verse adorn
again." You may read —

"Fierce War and faithful Love
Resume their," &c.

But I do not think it signifies much, for there is

no mistaking the sense, when one attends to it. "That chills the throbbing," &c. I dislike as much as you can do. "Horror wild," I am forced to strike out, because of "wild dismay" in the first stanza. What if we read

"With Horror, tyrant of the throbbing breast."

Why you would alter "lost in long futurity" I do not see, unless because you think "lost" and "expire" are tautologies, or because it looks as if the end of the prophecy were disappointed by it, and that people may think that poetry in Britain was some time or other really to expire, whereas the meaning is only that it was lost to his ear from the immense distance. I cannot give up "lost," for it begins with an *l*.

I wish you were here, for I am tired of writing such stuff; and besides, I have got the old Scotch ballad on which Douglas was founded; it is divine, and as long as from hence to Aston. Have you never seen it? Aristotle's best rules are observed in it in a manner that shews the author never had heard of Aristotle. It begins in the fifth act of the play. You may read it two-thirds through without guessing what it is about; and yet, when you come to the end, it is impossible not to understand the whole story. I send you the two first verses —

"Gil Maurice was an Earle's son,
　His fame it wexed wide.
It was næ for his grete riches,
　Nae for his mickle pride;
But it was for a ladie gay
　That lived on Carron's side.
' Where shall I get a bonny boy
　That will win hose and shoon,
That will gae to Lord Barnard's ha',
　And bid his ladie come?
Ye maun rin this errand, Willie,
　And ye maun rin with pride;
When other boys gae on their feet,
　On horseback ye sal ride,'
' Ah na, ah na, my master dear,' " &c. &c.

You will observe in the beginning of this thing I send you some alterations of a few words, partly for improvement, and partly to avoid repetitions of like words and rhymes; I have not got rid of them all. The six last lines of the fifth stanza are new; tell me if they will do.

I have seen your friend the Dean of S[alisbur]y here to-day in the theatre, and thought I should have sp[e]w[e]d. I am very glad you are to be a court chaplain nevertheless; for I do not think you need be such a one, — I defy you ever to be.

I have now seen your first Chorus, new-modelled, and am charmed with it. Now I am coming with my hoe. Of all things I like your idea of "the sober sisters, as they meet and whisper with their ebon and golden rods on the top of Snowdon;" the more because it seems like a new mythology peculiar to the Druid superstition, and not borrowed of the Greeks, who have another quite different moon. But yet I cannot allow of the word "nod," though it pictures the action more lively than another word would do. Yet, at the first blush, "See the sober sisters nod," taken alone without regard to the sense, presents a ridiculous image, and you must leave no room for such ideas; besides, a word that is not quite familiar to us in the sense it is used should never form a rhyme; it may stand in any other part of a line. The rest is much to my palate, except a verse (I have it not now before me) towards the end. I think it is "Float your saffron vestments here," because one does not at once conceive that "float" is "let them float;" and besides, it is a repetition of the idea, as you speak of the "rustling of their silken draperies" before, and I would have every image varied as the rest are. I do not absolutely like "Hist ye all," only because it is the last line. These are all the faults I have to find; the rest is perfect. I have written a long letter of poetry, which is tiresome, but I could not help it. . . .

CARACTACUS

[To William Mason]

Stoke, September 28, 1757.

DEAR MASON — I have, as I desired Stonehewer to tell you, read over *Caractacus* twice, not with pleasure only, but with emotion. You may say what you will, but the contrivance, the manners, the interests, the passions, and the expression, go beyond the dramatic part of your *Elfrida* many, many leagues. I even say (though you will think me a bad judge of this) that the world will like it better. I am struck with the Chorus, who are not there merely to sing and dance, but bear throughout a principal part in the action, and have (beside the costume, which is excellent) as much a character of their own as any other person. I am charmed with their priestly pride and obstinacy, when, after all is lost, they resolve to confront the Roman General, and spit in his face. But now I am going to tell you what touches me most. From the beginning the first opening is greatly improved. The curiosity of Didius is now a very natural reason for dwelling on each particular of the scene before him, nor is the description at all too long. I am glad to find the two young men are Cartismandua's sons; they interest me far more. I love people of condition. They were men before that nobody knew; one could not make them a bow if one had met them at a public place.

I always admired that interruption of the Druids to Evelina, " Peace, Virgin, peace," &c.; and chiefly the abstract idea personified (to use the words of a critic), at the end of it. That of Caractacus — " Would save my Queen," &c., and still more, that, " I know it, reverend Fathers, 'tis heaven's high will," &c., to " I've done, begin the rites!" This latter is exemplary for the expression (always the great point with me); I do not mean by expression the mere choice of words, but the whole dress, fashion, and arrangement of a thought. Here, in particular, it is the brokenness, the ungrammatical position, the total subversion of the period, that charms me. All that ushers in the incantation, from " Try we yet what holiness can do," I am delighted with in quite another way, for this is pure poetry, as it ought to be, forming the proper transition, and leading on the mind to that still purer poetry that follows it. You have somehow mistaken my meaning about the sober Sisters: the verb " nod " before " only," seemed to be a verb neuter; now you have made it absolutely such, which was just my objection to it; but it is easily altered, for if the accusative case come first, there is no danger of ambiguity. I read

> See! their gold and ebon rod
> Where the sober Sisters nod,
> And greet in whispers sage and slow.
> Snowdon, mark! 'tis Magic's hour;
> Now the mutter'd spell hath power,
> Power to rift thy ribs of rock,
> To burst thy base with thunder's shock,
> But, &c., &c.
>
>   Than those that dwell
> In musick's, &c.

You will laugh at my "these's" and "those's," but they strike my ear better. What Mador sings must be the finest thing that ever was wrote; and the next chorus, where they all go to sleep, must be finer still.

In the beginning of the succeeding act I admire the chorus again, "Is it not now the hour, the holy hour," &c.: and their evasion of a lie, "Say'st thou, proud boy," &c.: and "Sleep with the unsunn'd silver," which is an example of a dramatic simile. The sudden appearance of Caractacus, the pretended respect and admiration of Vellinus, and the probability of his story, the distrust of the Druids, and their reasoning with Caractacus, and particularly that, "'Tis meet thou should'st; thou art a king," &c., &c.; "Mark me, Prince, the time will come when destiny," &c., are well and happily imagined.

Apropos of the last striking passage I have mentioned, I am going to make a digression.

When we treat a subject where the manners are almost lost in antiquity our stock of ideas must needs be small, and nothing betrays our poverty more than the returning to and harping frequently on one image; it was therefore I thought you should omit some lines before, though good in themselves, about the scythed car, that the passage now before us might appear with greater lustre when it came; and in this, I see, you have complied with me. But there are other ideas here and there still that occur too often, particularly about the oaks, some of which I would discard to make way for the rest.

But the subjects I speak of, to compensate (and more than compensate) that unavoidable poverty, have one great advantage when they fall into good hands: they leave an unbounded liberty to pure imagination and fiction (our favourite provinces), where no critic can molest or antiquary gainsay us. And yet (to please me) these fictions must have some affinity, some seeming connection with that little we really know of the character and customs of the people. For example, I never heard in my days that midnight and the moon were sisters, that they carried rods of ebony and gold, or met to whisper on the top of a mountain; but now, I could lay my life it is all true, and do not doubt it will be found so in some Pantheon of the Druids that is to be discovered in the library at Herculaneum. The Car of Destiny and Death is a very noble invention of the same class, and, as far as that goes, is so fine, that it makes me more delicate than, perhaps, I should be. About the close of it, Andraste, sailing on the wings of Fame, that snatches the wreaths from oblivion to hang them on her loftiest amaranth, though a clean and beautiful piece of unknown mythology, has too Greek an air to give me perfect satisfaction.

Now I proceed. The preparation to the Chorus, though so much akin to that in the former act, is excellent. The remarks of Evelina, and her suspicions of the brothers, mixed with a secret inclination to the younger of them (though, I think, her part throughout wants re-touching), yet please me much; and the contrivance of the following scene much more. " Masters of wisdom, no," &c., I always admired, as I do the rocking-stone and the distress of Elidurus. Evelina's examination of him is a well-invented scene, and will be, with a little pains, a very touching one; but the introduction of Arviragus is superlative. I am not sure whether those few lines of his short narrative, " My strength repaired, it boots not that I tell," &c., do not please me as much as anything in the whole drama. The sullen bravery of Elidurus; the menaces of the Chorus, that "Think not, Religion," &c.; the trumpet of the Druids; that "I'll follow him, though in my chains," &c.; "Hast thou a brother, no," &c.; the placability of the Chorus when they see the motives of Elidurus' obstinacy, give me great contentment. So do the reflections of the Druid on the necessity of lustration, and the reasons for Vellinus' easy escape; but I would not have him seize on a spear, nor issue hastily through the cavern's mouth. Why should he not steal away unmarked and unmissed till the hurry of passions in those that should have guarded him was a little abated? But I chiefly admire the two speeches of Elidurus: — "Ah! Vellinus, is this thee," &c., and "Ye do gaze on me, Fathers," &c. The manner in which the Chorus reply to him is very fine, but the image at the end wants a little mending. The next scene is highly moving; it is so very good that I must have it made yet better.

Now for the last Act. I do not know what you would have, but to me the design and contrivance of it is at least equal to any part of the whole. The short-lived triumph of the Britons — the address of Caractacus to the Roman victims

— Evelina's discovery of the ambush — the mistake of the Roman fires for the rising sun — the death of Arviragus — the interview between Didius and Caractacus — his mourning over his dead son — his parting speech (in which you have made all the use of Tacitus that your plan would admit) — everything, in short, but that little dispute between Didius and him, " 'Tis well, and therefore to increase that reverence," &c., down to " Give me a moment" (which must be omitted, or put in the mouth of the Druid), I approve in the highest degree. If I should find any fault with the last Act it could only be with trifles and little expressions. If you make any alterations I fear it will never improve it, I mean as to the plan. . . . I reserve my nibblings and minutiæ for another day. . . .

[*To Thomas Wharton, from Cambridge, October 7,* 1757]

. . . I am greatly pleased with M[aso]n's *Caractacus* in its present state. The contrivance and arrangement of events, the manners of the country, the characters and passions, strike me wonderfully. The difficult part is now got over, nothing remains but to polish, and retouch a little: yet only the beginning of the first Chorus is done of the lyric part. Have you seen it? . . .

AN ODE BY MASON

[*To William Mason, from Cambridge*]

January 13, 1758.

DEAR MASON — Why you make no more of writing an Ode, and throwing it into the fire, than of buckling and unbuckling your shoe. I have never read Keysler's book, nor you neither, I believe; if you had taken that pains, I am persuaded you would have seen that his Celtic and his septentrional antiquities are two things entirely distinct. There are, indeed, some learned persons who have taken pains to confound what Cæsar and Tacitus have taken pains to separate, the old Druidical or Celtic belief, and that of the old Germans, but nobody has been so learned as to mix the Celtic religion with that of the Goths. Why, Woden himself is supposed not to have been older than Julius Cæsar; but let him have lived when he pleases, it is certain that neither he nor his Valhalla were heard of till many ages after. This is the doctrine of the Scalds, not of the Bards; these are the songs of Hengist and Horsa, a modern new-fangled belief in comparison of that which you ought to possess. After all, I shall be sorry to have so many good verses and good chimæras thrown away. Might we not be permitted (in that scarcity of Celtic ideas we labour under) to adopt some of these foreign whimsies, dropping however all mention of Woden and his Valkhyrian virgins, &c.? To settle this scruple of conscience, I must refer you to Dr. Warburton: if this should be his opinion (which I doubt), then I go on to tell you (first premising that a dirge is always a funeral service sung over persons already dead), that I would have something striking and uncommon in the measures, the rhythm, and the expression of this Chorus; the two former are not remarkable here, and the third is so little antiquated, that "murky" and "dank" look like two old maids of honour got into a circle of fleering girls and boys. Now for particulars. I like the first stanza; the image of Death in arms is very fine and gallant, but I banish "free-born train," and "glory and luxury" here (not the ideas, but the words), and "liberty and freedom's cause," and several small epithets throughout. I do not see how one person can *lift* the voice of another person. The imagery of the second stanza too is excellent. A dragon *pecks!* Why a cock-sparrow might do as much: in short, I am pleased with the Gothic Elysium. Do not think I am ignorant about either that, or the *hell* before, or the *twilight*. I have been there, and have seen it all in Mallet's Introduction to the

History of Denmark (it is in French), and many other places. "Now they charge," &c. looks as if the coursers rode upon the men. A ghost does not fall. These are all my little objections, but I have a greater. Extreme conciseness of expression, yet pure, perspicuous, and musical, is one of the grand beauties of lyric poetry; this I have always aimed at, and never could attain; the necessity of rhyming is one great obstacle to it: another and perhaps a stronger is, that way you have chosen of casting down your first ideas carelessly and at large, and then clipping them here and there, and forming them at leisure; this method, after all possible pains, will leave behind it in some places a laxity, a diffuseness; the frame of a thought (otherwise well invented, well turned, and well placed) is often weakened by it. Do I talk nonsense, or do you understand me? I am persuaded what I say is true in my head, whatever it may be in prose, — for I do not pretend to write prose.

I am extremely pleased with your fashionable Ode, and have nothing to find fault there, only you must say " portray'st " in the first stanza; and " it looks at best but skin," in the fourth, is not right. I have observed your orders, but I want to shew it everybody. Pray tell me when I may have the credit of doing so. I have never seen a prettier modernism: let it be seen while it is warm. You are in the road to fame; but do not tell your name at first, whatever you may venture to do afterwards. . . .

ELEGIES BY MASON

[To William Mason, from Cambridge, January, 1758]

DEAR MASON — I am almost blind with a great cold, and should not have written to you to-day if you did not hurry me to send back this Elegy. My advices are always at your service to take or to refuse, therefore you should not call them severe. You know I do not love, much less pique myself, on criticism, and think even a bad verse as good a thing or better than the best observation that ever was made upon it. I like greatly what you have now sent me, particularly the spirit and sentiment of it; the disposition of the whole too is natural and elegiac. As to the expression, I would venture to say (did you not forbid me) that it is sometimes too easy. The last line I protest against. This, you will say, is worse than blotting out rhymes. The descriptive part is excellent, yet I am sorry for the name of Cutthorpe. I had rather Vertumnus and Flora did not appear in person. The word "lopt" sounds like a farmer, or a man of taste. "A mountain hoar, the savage," &c. is a very good line: yet I always doubt if this ungrammatical construction be allowable; in common speech it is usual, but not in writing even prose; and I think Milton (though hard pressed by his short metre in Penseroso) yet finds a way to bring in his *that's*, his *who's*, and his *which's*. "Fair unfold the wide-spread," &c.; "fair," is weakly, "wide-spread" is contained in "unfold." By "amber mead," I understand the yellow gleam of a meadow covered with marsh-marigolds and butterflowers,— is it not so? The two first lines (the second especially) I do not admire. I read, "Did Fancy wake not — refuse one votive strain"; you will ask me why? I do not know. As to *votive*, it is like *delegated*, one of the words you love. I also read, "How well does Memory," &c.— for the same no reason. "It all was his," &c. I like the sense, but it is not sufficiently clear. As to the versification, do not you perceive that you make the pause on the fourth syllable in almost every other line?

Now I desire you would neither think me severe, nor at all regard what I say any further than it coincides with your own judgment; for the child deserves your partiality; it is a healthy well-made boy, with an ingenuous countenance, and promises to live long. I would only wash its face, dress it a little, make it walk upright and strong, and keep it from learning paw words.

I never saw more than two volumes of Pelloutier, and repent that I ever read them. He is an idle man of some learning, who would make all the world Celts whether they will or no. *Locus est et pluribus umbris*, is a very good motto; you need look no further. I cannot find the other passage, nor look for it with these eyes. Adieu! dear Mason, I am most sincerely yours.

You won't find me a place like Mr. Wood's.

Elegy I.

"Favour'd steps," useless epithet! Write "choir." Read "rank'd and met." "Cull living garlands," &c. too verbose. You love "garlands which pride nor gains": odd construction. "Genuine wreath — Friendship twine"; a little forced. "Shrink" is usually a verb neuter; why not "blight" or "blast"? "Fervid"; read "fervent." "When sad reflection"; read "till sad," &c. "Blest bower," "call on"; read "call we." "In vain to thee"; read "in vain to him," and "his" for "thy." Oh, I did not see: what will become of "thine"? "Timid" read "fearful." "Discreter part"; "honest part" just before "explore." "Vivid," read "warmest."

There is too much of the Muse here. "The Muse's genuine wreath," "the Muse's laurel," "the Muse full oft," "the Muse shall come," "the Muse forbids," — five times.

Elegy II.

"Laurel-circled"; "laurel-woven" sounds better. "Neglect the strings" is somehow naked: perhaps

"That rules my lyre, neglect her wonted strings."

Read "re-echo to my strain." "His earliest blooms" should be "blossoms." "Then to thy sight," "to the sight." Read "he pierced." "Modestly retire," I do not like. "Tufts" sounds ill.

"To moral excellence": a remnant of bad books you read at St. John's; so is the "dignity of man."

"Of genuine man glowing,"

a bad line. "Dupe" I do not approve. "Taste" too often repeated.

"From that great Guide of Truth,"

hard and prosaic.

Elegy III.

"Attend the strain," "quick surprise," better than "sweet." "Luxuriant Fancy, pause," "exulting leap." — Read

"The wint'ry blast that sweeps ye to the tomb."

"Tho' soon," — query? "His patient stand," better before. Read "that mercy." "Trace then by Reason's," — blot it out. "Dear as the sons," perhaps, "yet neither sons," &c.

"They form the phalanx," &c.
"Is it for present fame?"

From hence to "peasant's life," the thought seems not just, because the questions are fully as applicable to a prince who does believe the immortality of the soul as to one who does not; and it looks as if an orthodox king had a right to sacrifice his myriads for his own ambition, because they stand a chance of going to heaven, and he of going to hell.

Indeed these four stanzas may be spared, without hurting the sense at all. After "brave the torrent's roar," it goes on very well. "Go, wiser ye," &c.; and the whole was before rather spun out and weakly.

AGIS, DODSLEY'S MISCELLANY, ETC.

[To Thomas Wharton]

Cambridge, March 8, 1758.

It is indeed for want of spirits, as you suspect, that my studies lie among the Cathedrals, and the Tombs, and the Ruins. To think, though to little purpose, has been the chief amusement of my days; and when I would not, or cannot think, I dream. At present I find myself able to write a Catalogue, or to read the Peerage book, or Miller's Gardening Dictionary, and am thankful that there are such employments and such authors in the world. Some people, who hold me cheap for this, are doing perhaps what is not half so well worth while. As to posterity, I may ask, (with somebody whom I have forgot) what has it ever done to oblige me?

To make a transition from myself to as poor a subject, the Tragedy of Agis; I cry to think that it should be by the author of Douglas: Why, it is all modern Greek; the story is an antique statue, painted white and red, frized, and dressed in a negligée made by a Yorkshire mantua-maker. Then here is the Miscellany (Mr. Dodsley has sent me the whole set gilt and lettered, I thank him). Why, the two last volumes are worse than the four first; particularly Dr. Akenside is in a deplorable way. What signifies Learning and the Antients, (Mason will say triumphantly) why should people read Greek to lose their imagination, their ear, and their mother tongue? But then there is Mr. Shenstone, who trusts to nature and simple sentiment, why does he do no better? He goes hopping along his own gravel-walks, and never deviates from the beaten paths for fear of being lost.

I have read Dr. Swift, and am disappointed. There is nothing of the negotiations that I have not seen better in M. de Torcy before. The manner is careless, and has little to distinguish it from common writers. I met with nothing to please me but the spiteful characters of the opposite party and its leaders. I expected much more secret history.

THE RELIGION OF THE GAULS

[To William Mason, from Cambridge, March 24, 1758]

... You do not seem to discover that Mons. Mallet is but a very small scholar, except in the erudition of the Goths. There are, *à propos*, two Dissertations on the Religion and Opinions of the Gauls, published in the Mémoires de l'Acad. des Belles Lettres et des Inscriptions, vol. xxiv. 4to, one by the Abbé Fénel, in which he would shew that, about Tiberius' and Claudius' times the Druids, persecuted and dispersed by the Romans, probably retired into Germany, and propagated their doctrines there. This is to account for some similitude to the Gaulish notions which the religion of Germany seems to bear, as Tacitus has described it, whereas Julius Cæsar makes them extremely different, who lived before this supposed dispersion of the Druids; the other, by Monsieur Freret, is as to shew the reverse of all this,—that there was no such dispersion, no such similitude, and that, if Cæsar and Tacitus disagree, it is because the first knew nothing but of those nations that bordered on the Rhine, and the other was acquainted with all Germany. I do not know whether these will furnish you with any new matter, but they are well enough written and easily read. I told you before, that, in a time of dearth, I would venture to borrow from the Edda without entering too minutely on particulars; but, if I did so, I would make each image so clear, that it might be fully understood by itself, for in this obscure mythology we must not hint at things, as we do with the Greek fables, that every body is supposed to know at school. However, on second thoughts, I think it would be still better to graft any wild picturesque fable, absolutely of one's own invention, upon the Druid stock; I mean upon those half-dozen of old fancies that are known to have made their system: this will give you more freedom and latitude, and will leave no hold for the critics to fasten on.

Pray, when did I pretend to finish, or even insert passages into other people's works? As if it were equally easy to pick holes and to mend them. All I can say is, that your Elegy must not end with the worst line in it; it is flat, it is prose; whereas that above all ought to sparkle, or at least to shine. If the sentiment must stand, twirl it a little into an apophthegm, stick a flower in it, gild it with a costly expression; let it strike the fancy, the ear, or the heart, and I am satisfied.

Hodges is a sad fellow; so is Dr. Akenside, and Mr. Shenstone, our friends and companions. Your story of Garrick is a good one; pray is it true, and what came of it? Did the tragic poet call a guard? It was I that hindered Mr. Brown from sending the pamphlet. It is nonsense, and that nonsense all stolen from Dr. Stukeley's book about Abury and Stonehenge; yet if you will have it, you may. . . .

MATERIALISM AND SHAFTESBURY

[*To Richard Stonehewer*]

Cambridge, August 18, 1758.

I am as sorry as you seem to be, that our acquaintance harped so much on the subject of materialism, when I saw him with you in town, because it was plain to which side of the long-debated question he inclined. That we are indeed mechanical and dependent beings, I need no other proof than my own feelings; and from the same feelings I learn, with equal conviction, that we are not *merely* such: that there is a power within that struggles against the force and bias of that mechanism, commands its motion, and, by frequent practice, reduces it to that ready obedience which we call *Habit;* and all this in conformity to a preconceived opinion (no matter whether right or wrong), to that least material of all agents, a Thought. I have known many in his case who, while they thought they were conquering an old prejudice, did not perceive they were under the influence of one far more dangerous; one that furnishes us with a ready apology for all our worst actions, and opens to us a full license for doing whatever we please; and yet these very people were not at all the more indulgent to other men (as they naturally should have been); their indignation to such as offended them, their desire of revenge on anybody that hurt them was nothing mitigated: in short, the truth is, they wished to be persuaded of that opinion for the sake of its convenience, but were not so in their heart; and they would have been glad (as they ought in common prudence) that nobody else should think the same, for fear of the mischief that might ensue to themselves. His French author I never saw, but have read fifty in the same strain, and shall read no more. I can be wretched enough without them. They put me in mind of the Greek Sophist that got immortal honour by discoursing so feelingly on the miseries of our condition, that fifty of his audience went home and hanged themselves; yet he lived himself (I suppose) many years after in very good plight.

You say you cannot conceive how Lord Shaftesbury came to be a Philosopher in vogue; I will tell you: First, he was a Lord; 2dly, he was as vain as any of his readers; 3dly, men are very prone to believe what they do not understand; 4thly, they will believe anything at all, provided they are under no obligation to believe it; 5thly, they love to take a new road, even when that road leads nowhere; 6thly, he was reckoned a fine writer, and seemed always to mean more than he said. Would you have any more reasons? An interval of about forty years has pretty well destroyed the charm. A dead Lord ranks but with Commoners: Vanity is no longer interested in the matter, for the new road has become an old one. The mode of free-thinking is like that of Ruffs and Farthingales, and has given place to the mode of not thinking at all; once it was reckoned graceful, half to discover and half conceal the mind, but now we have been long accustomed to see it quite naked: primness and affectation of style, like the good breeding of Queen Anne's Court, has turned to hoydening and rude familiarity.

OBSERVATION AND MEMORY

[*To Willam Palgrave*]

Stoke, September 6, 1758.

I do not know how to make you amends, having neither rock, ruin, or precipice near me to send you; they do not grow in the South: but only say the word, if you would have a compact neat box of red brick with sash windows, or a grotto made of flints and shell-work, or a walnut-tree with three mole-hills under it, stuck with honey-suckles round a basin of gold-fishes, and you shall be satisfied; they shall come by the Edinburgh coach.

In the meantime I congratulate you on your new acquaintance with the *savage*, the *rude*, and the *tremendous*. Pray, tell me, is it anything like what you had read in your book, or seen in two-shilling prints? Do not you think a man may be the wiser (I had almost said the better) for going a hundred or two of miles; and that the mind has more room in it than most people seem to think, if you will but furnish the apartments?

I almost envy your last month, being in a very insipid situation myself; and desire you would not fail to send me some furniture for my Gothic apartment, which is very cold at present. It will be the easier task, as you have nothing to do but transcribe your little red books, if they are not rubbed out; for I conclude you have not trusted everything to memory, which is ten times worse than a lead pencil: half a word fixed upon or near the spot, is worth a cartload of recollection. When we trust to the picture that objects draw of themselves on our mind, we deceive ourselves; without accurate and particular observation, it is but ill-drawn at first, the outlines are soon blurred, the colours every day grow fainter; and at last, when we would produce it to anybody, we are forced to supply its defects with a few strokes of our own imagination. God forgive me, I suppose I have done so myself before now, and misled many a good body that put their trust in me. . . .

MASON'S CARACTACUS

[*To William Mason*]

Stoke, November 9, 1758.

. . . While I am writing, your second packet is just arrived. I can only tell you in gross that there seem to me certain passages altered, which might as well have been let alone; and that I shall not be easily reconciled to Mador's own song. I must not have my fancy raised to that agreeable pitch of heathenism and wild magical enthusiasm, and then have you let me drop into moral philosophy and cold good sense. I remember you insulted me when I saw you last, and affected to call that which delighted my imagination nonsense. Now I insist that sense is nothing in poetry but according to the dress she wears, and the scene she appears in. If you should lead me into a superb Gothic building with a thousand clustered pillars, each of them half a mile high, the walls all covered with fretwork, and the windows full of red and blue saints, that had neither head nor tail, and I should find the Venus of Medici in person perked up in a long niche over the high altar, as naked as ever she was born, do you think it would raise or damp my devotions? I say that Mador must be entirely a Briton, and that his pre-eminence among his companions must be shewn by superior wildness, more barbaric fancy, and a more striking and deeper harmony, both of words and numbers. If British antiquity be too narrow, this is the place for invention; and if it be pure invention, so much the clearer must the expression be, and so much the stronger and richer the imagery — there's for you now. . . .

[*To William Mason, from Cambridge, probably December* 1 *or* 2, 1758]

Ode, p. 32. — "Whom Camber bore." I suppose you say "whom" because the harp is treated as a person; but there is an ambiguity in it; and I should read "that Camber bore." There is a specimen of nice criticism for you!

I much approve the six last lines of this stanza; it is a noble image, and well expressed to the fancy and to the ear.

I. 2. — A rill has no tide of waters to "tumble down amain." I am sorry to observe this just in a place where I see the difficulty of rhyming. I object nothing to the "Symphony of ringdoves and poplars," but that it is an idea borrowed from yourself; and I would not have you seem to repeat your own inventions.

I conceive the four last lines to be allegorical, alluding to the brutal ferocity of the natives, which by the power of music was softened into civility. It should not, therefore, be the "wolf-dog," but the "wolf" itself, that bays the trembling moon; it is the wolf that thins the flocks, and not the dog, who is their guardian.

I. 3. — I read "The Fairy Fancy." I like all

this extremely, and particularly the ample plumes of Inspiration, that

> "Beat on the breathless bosom of the air."

Yet, if I were foolish, I could find fault with this verse, as others will do. But what I do not conceive is, how such wings as those of Inspiration should be mistaken for the wings of Sleep, who (as you yourself tell me presently) "sinks softly down the skies"; besides, is not "her" false English? The nominative case is "she."

II. 3.— This belongs to the second epode. Does the swart-star (that is, Sirius) shine from the north? I believe not. But Dr. Long will tell you.

[*To William Mason, from London, January* 18, 1759]

... I send you in short my opinion of Caractacus, so far, I mean, as I have seen of it; I shall only tell you further, that I am charmed with the idea you give me of your fourth Ode; it is excellently introduced, and the specimen you send me even sublime. I am wrapped in it; but the last line of the stanza falls off, and must be changed, "Courage was in his van," etc., for it is ordinary when compared with the rest; to be sure, the immortality of the soul and the happiness of dying in battle are Druid doctrines; you may dress them at pleasure, so they do but look wild and British.

I have little to say from hence but that Cleone has succeeded very well at Covent Garden, and that people who despised it in manuscript went to see it, and confess — they cried so. For fear of crying too I did not go. Poor Smart is not dead, as was said, and *Merope* is acted for his benefit this week, with a new farce, *The Guardian*. Here is a very agreeable opera of Cocchi's, the *Cyrus*, which gave me some pleasure; do you know I like both Whitehead's Odes in great measure, but nobody else does. . . .

II. 2.— These are my favourite stanzas. I am satisfied, both mind and ear, and dare not murmur. If Mador would sing as well in the first chorus, I should cease to plague you. Only,—

"Rise at her art's command"

is harsh, and says no more than

"Arise at her command,"

or

"Are born at her command."

II. 3.— I told you of the swart-star before. At the end I read,

"Till Destiny prepare a shrine of purer clay."

Afterwards read, "Resume no more thy strain."

You will say I have no notion of *tout-ensembles*, if I do not tell you that I like the scheme of this ode at least as well as the execution.

P. 2.— I liked the opening as it was originally better than I do now, though I never thoroughly understood " how blank he frowns." And as to " black stream," it gives me the idea of a river of mud. I should read " dark stream," imagining it takes its hue only from the rocks and trees that overhang it. " These cliffs, these yawning," etc., comes in very well where it stood at first, and you have only removed it to another place where, by being somewhat more diffused, it appears weaker. You have introduced no new image in your new beginning but one, " utters deep wailings," which is very well : but as to a " trickling runlet," I never heard of such a thing, unless it were a runlet of brandy.

Yet I have no objection at all to the reflection Didius makes on the power objects of the sight have over the soul; it is in its place, and might even be longer, but then it should be more choicely and more feelingly expressed. He must not talk of dells and streams only, but of something more striking, and more corresponding to the scene before him. Intellect is a word of science, and therefore is inferior to any more common word.

P. 3. — For the same reason I reject "philosophy," and read "studious they measure, save when contemplation," etc., and here you omit two lines, relating to astronomy, for no cause that I discern.

P. 4. — What is your quarrel to "shallops"? I like "Go bid thine eagles soar," perhaps from obstinacy, for I know you have met with some wise gentleman who says it is a false thought, and informs you that these were not real eagles, but made of metal or wood, painted. The word "seers," comes over too often: here, besides, it sounds ill. Elidurus need not be so fierce. "Dost thou insult us, Roman?" was better before. Sure "plan'd" is a nasty stiff word.

P. 6. — It must be Cæsar and Fate; the name of Claudius carries contempt with it.

P. 7. — "Brother, I spurn it," — better than "I scorn it." "Misjudging Boy!" is weakly. He calls him coward because such a reproach was most likely to sting him. "I'll do the deed myself," is bolder, more resolute, more hearty, than the alteration. "Lead forth the saintly," etc., better, shorter, and more lively at first. What have I to do with "purple robes" and "arraignments"? — like a trial at York assizes.

P. 8. — "Try, if 'twill bring her deluging," etc., better so, only I do not like "strait justice": "modest mounds" is far worse.

P. 9.—"Do this and prosper, but pray thee," etc. Oh! how much superior to the cold lines for which you would omit them. It is not you but somebody else that has been busy here and elsewhere. "Come from their caves." I read, "Are issuing from their caves. Hearest thou yon signal?" and put "awful" where it was before. "I'll wait the closing," etc. Leave it as it was. "Do thou as likes thee best, betray, or aid me": it is shorter and more sulky. Elidurus too must not go off in silence; and what can he say better?

P. 10.—I do not dislike the idea of this ceremony, but the execution of it is careless and hasty. The reply of the semi-chorus is stolen from Dryden's Œdipus, which, perhaps, you never saw, nor I since I was a boy, at which time it left an impression on my fancy. Pray look at it. "This dread ground" breaks my teeth. "Be it worm, or aske, or toad": these are things for fairies to make war upon but not Druids, at least they must not name them. An *aske* is something I never heard of. "Full five fathom under ground." Consider, five fathom is but thirty feet; many a cellar lies deeper. I read, "Gender'd by the autumnal moon"; by its light I mean. "Conjoined" is a bad word. "Supernal art profound" is negligent. Indeed I do not understand the image, how the snakes in copulation should heave their egg to the sky; you will say it is an old British fancy. I know it of old; but then it must be made picturesque, and look almost as if it were true.

P. 13.—"Befit such station." The verse wants a syllable. "Even in the breast of Mona," read "the heart of Mona." "Catches fresh grace"; the simile is good, but not this expression. The Tower is more majestic, more venerable, not more graceful. I read,

> "He looks as doth the Tower
> After the conflict of Heaven's angry bolts;
> Its nodding walls, its shatter'd battlements,
> Frown with a dignity unmark'd before,
> Ev'n in its prime of strength."

P. 13.—I do not desire he should return the Druid's salute so politely. Let him enter with that reflection, "This holy place," etc., and not stand upon ceremony. It required no alteration, only I hate the word "vegetate," and would read,

> "Tell me, Druid,
> Is it not better to be such as these
> Than be the thing I am?"

I read, too, "Nor show a Prætor's edict," etc., and "pestilent glare," as they were before. Add, too, "See to the altar's base the victims led," etc. And then, whether they were bulls or men, it is all one. I must repeat again, that the word "Seers" is repeated for ever.

P. 15.—"I know it, rev'rend Fathers," etc. This speech is sacred with me, and an example of dramatic poetry. Touch not a hair of its head, as you love your honour.

P. 16.—I had rather some of these personages, "Resignation, Peace, Revenge, Slaughter, Ambition," were stript of their allegorical garb. A little simplicity here in the expression would better prepare the high and fantastic strain, and all the unimaginable harpings that follow. I admire all from "Eager to snatch thee," etc., down to the first epode of the chorus. You give these Miltonic stanzas up so easily that I begin to waver about Mador's song. If you have written it, and it turn out the finest thing in the world, I rejoice, and say no more. Let it come though it were in the middle of a sermon; but if not, I do confess, at last, that the chorus may break off, and do very well without a word more. Do not be angry at the trouble I have given you; and now I have found the reason why I could not be pleased with Mador's philosophic song. The true lyric style, with all its flights of fancy, ornaments, and heightening of expression, and harmony of sound, is in its nature superior to every other style; which is just the cause why it could not be borne in a work of great length, no more than the eye could bear to see all this scene that we constantly gaze upon, — the verdure of the fields and woods, the azure of the sea and skies, turned into one dazzling expanse of gems. The epic, therefore, assumed a style of graver colours, and only stuck on a diamond (borrowed from her sister) here and there, where it best became her. When we pass from the diction that suits this kind of writing to that which belongs to the former, it appears natural, and delights us; but to pass on a sudden from the lyric glare to the epic solemnity (if I may be allowed to talk nonsense) has a very different effect. We seem to drop from verse into mere prose, from light into darkness. Another thing is, the pauses proper to one and the other are not at all the same; the ear therefore loses by the change. Do you think if Mingotti stopped in the middle of her best air, and only repeated the remaining verses (though the best Metastasio ever wrote), that they would not appear very cold to you, and very heavy?

P. 24. — " Boldly dare " is tautology.

P. 27. — " Brigantum ": there was no such place.

P. 28. — " The sacred hares." You might as well say " the sacred hogs."

P. 29. — There is an affectation in so often using the old phrase of " or ere " for " before."

P. 30. — " Rack " is the course of the clouds,

"wreck" is ruin and destruction. Which do you mean? I am not yet entirely satisfied with the conclusion of this fine allegory. "That blest prize redeem'd" is flatly expressed; and her sticking the pages over the arch of her bower is an idea a little burlesque; besides, are we sure the whole is not rather too long for the place it is in, where all the interests of the scene stand still for it? And this is still drawn out further by the lines you have here put into the mouth of Caractacus. Do not mistake me; I admire part of it, and approve almost all; but consider the time and place.

P. 31. — "Pensive Pilgrim." Why not? There is an impropriety in "wakeful wanderer." I have told you my thoughts of this chorus already; the whole scheme is excellent, the 2d strophe and antistrophe divine. Money (I know) is your motive, and of that I wash my hands. Fame is your second consideration; of that I am not the dispenser, but if your own approbation (for every one is a little conscious of his own talents) and mine have any weight with you, you will write an ode or two every year, till you are turned of fifty, not for the world, but for us two only; we will now and then give a little glimpse of them, but no copies.

P. 37. — I do not like "maidenhood."

P. 38. — Why not "smoke in vain" as before? The word "meek" is too often repeated.

P. 42. — The only reason why you have altered my favourite speech is, that "surging and plunging," "main and domain," come too near each other; but could not you correct these without spoiling all? I read

> "Cast his broad eye upon the wild of ocean,
> And calm'd it with a glance; then, plunging deep
> His mighty arm, pluck'd from its dark domain," etc.

Pray have done with your "piled stores and coral floors."

P. 43. — "The dies of Fate," that is, "the dice of Fate." Find out another word.

P. 44. — I cannot say I think this scene improved: I had no objection before, but to "harm a poor wretch like me"; and what you have inserted is to me inferior to what it was meant to replace, except p. 47, "And why this silence," which is very well; the end of the scene is one of my favourite passages.

P. 49. — Why scratch out, "Thou, gallant boy"? I do not know to what other scene you have transferred these rites of lustration, but methinks they did very well here. Arviragus's account of himself I always was highly pleased with.

P. 51. — "Fervid" is a bad word.

[*To William Mason, from Cambridge, March* 1, 1759]

... I did not remember ever to have seen the joint criticism from Prior Park that you speak of, so little impression did it make; nor should I believe now that I had ever seen it, did I not recollect what a prejudice the parsons expressed to human sacrifice, which is quite agreeable to my way of thinking; since Caractacus convinced me of the propriety of the thing, it is certain that their fancies did in no sort influence me in the use of my tomahawk. Now you must know I do not much admire the chorus of the rocking-stone, nor yet much disapprove it; it is grave and solemn, and may pass. I insist, however, that "deigns" (though it be a rhyme) should be "deign'st," and "fills" "fill'st," and "bids" "bid'st." Do not blame me, but the English tongue. The beginning of the antistrophe is good. I do not like

"meandring way
Where Vice and Folly stray,"

nor the word "sprite." The beginning too of the epode is well; but you have used the epithet "pale" before in a sense somewhat similar, and I do not love repetitions. The line

"Or magic numbers"

interrupts the run of the stanza, and lets the

measure drop too short. There is no beauty in repeating "ponderous sphere." The two last lines are the best.

The sense of your simile about the "distant thunder" is not clear, nor well expressed; besides, it implies too strong a confession of guilt.

The stanza you sent me for the second Ode is very rude; and neither the idea nor verses touch me much. It is not the gout that makes me thus difficult. Finish but your Death-song as well as you imagined and begun it, and mind if I won't be more pleased than anybody. ... Did I tell you how well I liked Whitehead's two Odes? They are far better than anything he ever wrote. ...

STAINED GLASS

[To Thomas Wharton, from London, November 28, 1759]

... I have had an enquiry from Mr. Jonathan about painted glass, and have given him such information, as I could procure. The manufacture at York seems to be the thing for your purpose, but the name of the Person I cannot learn. He at Worcester sells it for two shillings a pound (for it is sold by weight). I approve very well of the canopy work border on the sides of each light descending to the bottom, provided it do not darken the window too much, and take up so much of the twenty inches space, as to make the plain glass in the middle appear over narrow. But I have been more used to see the whole top of colour'd glass (from where the arch begins to turn), the gloom above contributing much to the beauty of the clear view below. I cannot decide: the first is more Gothic and more uncommon, the latter more convenient and more cheerful. Green glass is not classical, nor ever seen in a real Church window, but where there is History painted, and there the Green is remarkably bad. I propose, the rich amethyst-purple instead of it. The mosaic pattern can hardly come amiss, only do not let too much yellow and scarlet come together. If I could describe the mosaic at Mr. W[alpole']s it would be of no use to you, because it is not merely made of squares put together, but painted in a pattern by Price, and shaded. It is as if little Balaustines, or Pomegranate-flowers, were set four together, and formed a lozenge. These are of a golden yellow with a white Pearl at the junctions, and the spaces inclosed by them are scarlet, or blue. This repeated makes a Diaper-work, and fills the whole top of the window. . . .

FROISSART

[To Thomas Wharton]

LONDON, Thursday, January 23, 1760.

DEAR DOCTOR — I am much obliged to you for your antique news: Froissard is a favourite book of mine (tho' I have not attentively read him, but only dip'd here and there) and it is strange to me that people who would give thousands for a dozen Portraits (Originals of that time) to furnish a gallery, should never cast an eye on so many moving pictures of the life, actions, manners, and thoughts of their ancestors done on the spot, and in strong tho' simple colours. In the succeeding century Froissard (I find) was read with great satisfaction by everybody, that could read; and on the same footing with King Arthur, Sir Tristram, and Archbishop Turpin: not because they thought him a fabulous Writer, but because they took them all for true and authentic Historians. To so little purpose was it in that age for a Man to be at the pains of writing truth! Pray, are you come to the four Irish Kings, that went to school to K. Richard the 2d.'s Master of the Ceremonies; and the Man who informed Froissard of all he had seen in St. Patrick's Purgatory? . . .

OSSIAN

[To Horace Walpole, probably from London, before April 4, 1760]

I am so charmed with the two specimens of Erse poetry, that I cannot help giving you the trouble to enquire a little farther about them, and should wish to see a few lines of the original, that I may form some slight idea of the language, the measures, and the rhythm.

Is there anything known of the author or authors, and of what antiquity are they supposed to be? Is there any more to be had of equal beauty, or at all approaching to it? I have been often told that the Poem called Hardycanute (which I always admired and still admire) was the work of somebody that lived a few years ago. This I do not at all believe, though it has evidently been retouched in places by some modern hand: but however, I am authorized by this report to ask, whether the two Poems in question are certainly antique and genuine. I make this enquiry in quality of an antiquary, and am not otherwise concerned about it: for, if I were sure that any one now living in Scotland had written them to divert himself, and laugh at the credulity of the world, I would undertake a journey into the Highlands only for the pleasure of seeing him.

FREDERICK THE GREAT, STERNE, ETC.

[To Thomas Wharton, from London, April 22, 1760]

... The town are reading the K. of Prussia's poetry, (Le Philosophe sans Souci) and I have done, like the town. They do not seem so sick of it, as I am. It is all the scum of Voltaire and Lord Bolingbroke, the *Crambe recocta* of our worst Freethinkers, toss'd up in German-French rhyme. Tristram Shandy is still a greater object of admiration, the Man as well as the Book. One is invited to dinner, where he dines, a fortnight beforehand. His portrait is done by Reynolds, and now engraving. Dodsley gives £700 for a second edition, and two new volumes not yet written; and to-morrow will come out two Volumes of Sermons by him. Your friend, Mr. Hall has printed two Lyric Epistles, one to my Cousin Shandy on his coming to Town, the other to the grown gentlewomen, the Misses of York: they seem to me to be absolute madness. These are the best lines in them: —

> I'll tell you a story of Elijah—
> Close by a Mob of Children stood,
> Commenting on his sober mood, &c.:
> And backed them (their opinions) like such sort of folks
> With a few stones and a few jokes:
> Till, weary of their pelting and their prattle,

> He ordered out his Bears to battle.
> It was delightful fun
> To see them run
> And eat up the young Cattle.

The 7th volume of Buffon is come over: do you choose to have it?

THE ODES TO OBSCURITY AND OBLIVION

[To William Mason, from London, June 7, 1760]

... I have sent Musæus to Mr. Fraser, scratched here and there; and with it I desired him to inclose a bloody satire, written against no less persons than you and me by name. I concluded at first it was Mr. Pottinger, because he is your friend and my humble servant; but then I thought he knew the world too well to call us the favourite minions of taste and of fashion, especially as to Odes, for to them his abuse is confined. So it is not Secretary Pottinger, but Mr. Colman, nephew to my Lady Bath, author of "The Connoisseur" a member of some of the inns of court, and a particular acquaintance of Mr. Garrick's. What have you done to him? For I never heard his name before? He makes very tolerable fun with me, where I understand him, which is not everywhere, but seems more angry with you. Lest people should not understand the humour of the thing (which indeed to do they must have our lyricisms at their fingers' ends), he writes letters in Lloyd's Evening Post to tell them who and what it was that he meant, and says that it is like to produce a great *combustion* in the literary world; so if you have any mind to *combustle* about it well and good; for me, I am neither so literary nor so *combustible*. . . .

OSSIAN, THE TWO ODES, TRISTRAM SHANDY

[*To Thomas Wharton, probably from London, June,* 1760]

. . . If you have seen Stonehewer he has probably told you of my old Scotch (or rather Irish) poetry. I am gone mad about them. They are said to be translations (literal and in prose) from the *Erse*-tongue, done by one Macpherson, a young Clergyman in the High-lands. He means to publish a Collection he has of these specimens of antiquity, if it be antiquity: but what plagues me is, I cannot come at any certainty on that head. I was so struck, so *extasié* with their infinite beauty, that I writ into Scotland to make a thousand enquiries. The letters I have in return are ill-wrote, ill-reasoned, unsatisfactory, calculated (one would imagine) to deceive one, and yet not cunning enough to do it cleverly. In short, the whole external evidence would make one believe these fragments (for so he calls them, tho' nothing can be more entire) counterfeit: but the internal is so strong on the other side, that I am resolved to believe them genuine, spite of the Devil and the Kirk. It is impossible to convince me, that they were invented by the same Man, that writes me these letters. On the other hand it is almost as hard to suppose, if they are original, that he should be able to translate them so admirably. What can one do? Since Stonehewer went, I have received another of a very different and inferior kind (being merely descriptive) much more modern than the former (he says) yet very old too; this too in its way is extremely fine. In short this Man is the very Demon of poetry, or he has lighted on a treasure hid for ages. The Welsh Poets are also coming to light: I have seen a Discourse in MS. about them (by one Mr. Evans, a Clergyman) with specimens of their writings. This is in Latin, and though it don't approach the other, there are fine scraps among it.

You will think I am grown mighty poetical of a sudden; you would think so still more, if you knew, there was a Satire printed against me and Mason jointly. It is call'd *Two Odes:* the one is inscribed to Obscurity (that is me) the other to Oblivion. It tells me what I never heard before, for (speaking of himself) the Author says, tho' he has,

> "Nor the Pride, nor Self-Opinion,
>   That possess the happy Pair,
> Each of Taste the fav'rite Minion,
>   Prancing thro' the desert air:
> Yet shall he mount, with classic housings grac'd,
>   By help mechanic of equestrian block;
> And all unheedful of the Critic's mock
>   Spur his light Courser o'er the bounds of Taste."

The writer is a Mr. Coleman, who publish'd the *Connoisseur*, nephew to the late Lady Bath, and a Friend of Garrick's. I believe his Odes sell no more than mine did, for I saw a heap of them lie in a Bookseller's window, who recommended them to me as a very pretty thing.

If I did not mention Tristram to you, it was because I thought I had done so before. There is much good fun in it, and humour sometimes hit and sometimes mist. I agree with your opinion of it, and shall see the two future volumes with pleasure. Have you read his Sermons (with his own comic figure at the head of them)? They are in the style, I think, most proper for the pulpit, and shew a very strong imagination and a sensible heart: but you see him often tottering on the verge of laughter, and ready to throw his periwig in the face of his audience. . . .

D'ALEMBERT AND OSSIAN

[To Richard Stonehewer, from London, June 29, 1760]

I too was reading M. D'Alembert, and (like you) am totally disappointed in his Elements. I could only taste a little of the first course: it was dry as a stick, hard as a stone, and cold as a cucumber. But then the letter to Rousseau is like himself; and the "Discourses on Elocution," and on the "Liberty of Music," are divine. He has added to his translations from Tacitus; and (what is remarkable) though that author's manner more nearly resembles the best French writers of the present age, than anything, he totally fails in the attempt. Is it his fault, or that of the language?

I have received another Scotch packet with a third specimen, inferior in kind (because it is merely description), but yet full of nature and noble wild imagination. Five Bards pass the night at the Castle of a Chief (himself a principal Bard); each goes out in his turn to observe the face of things, and returns with an extempore picture of the changes he has seen; it is an October night (the harvest month of the Highlands). This is the whole plan; yet there is a contrivance, and a preparation of ideas, that you would not expect. The oddest thing is, that every one of them sees Ghosts (more or less). The idea, that struck and surprised me most, is the following. One of them (describing a storm of wind and rain) says

> "Ghosts ride on the tempest to-night:
> Sweet is their voice between the gusts of wind;
> *Their songs are of other worlds!*"

Did you never observe (*while rocking winds are piping loud*) that pause, as the gust is recollecting itself, and rising upon the ear in a shrill and plaintive note, like the swell of an Æolian harp? I do assure you there is nothing in the world so like the voice of a spirit. Thomson had an ear sometimes: he was not deaf to this; and has described it gloriously, but given it another different turn, and of more horror. I cannot repeat the lines: it is in his "Winter." There is another very fine picture in one of them. It describes the breaking of the clouds after the storm, before it is settled into a calm, and when the moon is seen by short intervals.

> "The waves are tumbling on the lake,
> And lash the rocky sides.
> The boat is brim-full in the cove,
> The oars on the rocking tide.
> Sad sits a maid beneath a cliff,
> And eyes the rolling stream:
> Her lover promised to come,
> She saw his boat (when it was evening) on the lake;
> *Are these his groans in the gale?*
> *Is this his broken boat on the shore?*"

OSSIAN, ETC.

[*To William Mason, from Cambridge, August* 7, 1760]

... The Erse Fragments have been published five weeks ago in Scotland, though I had them not (by a mistake) till last week. As you tell me new things do not soon reach you at Aston, I inclose what I can; the rest shall follow when you tell me whether you have not got it already. I send the two which I had before, for Mr. Wood, because he has not the affectation of not admiring. I continue to think them genuine, though my reasons for believing the contrary are rather stronger than ever: but I will have them antique, for I never knew a Scotchman of my own time that could read, much less write, poetry; and such poetry too! I have one (from Mr. Macpherson) which he has not printed: it is mere description, but excellent, too, in its kind. If you are good, and will learn to admire, I will transcribe it. Pray send to Sheffield for the last *Monthly Review*: there is a deal of stuff about us and Mr. Colman. It says one of us, at least, has always borne his faculties meekly. I leave you to guess which that is: I think I know. You oaf, you must be meek, must you? And see what you get by it! ...

A NOTE. — Having made many enquiries about the authenticity of these Fragments, I have got a letter from Mr. David Hume, the historian, which is more satisfactory than anything I have yet met with on that subject: he says, —

"Certain it is that these poems are in everybody's mouth in the Highlands — have been handed down from father to son — and are of an age beyond all memory and tradition. Adam Smith, the celebrated Professor in Glasgow, told me that the piper of the Argyleshire militia repeated to him all those which Mr. Macpherson has translated, and many more of equal beauty. Major Mackay (Lord Rae's brother) told me that he remembers them perfectly well; as likewise did the Laird of Macfarline (the greatest antiquarian we have in this country), and who insists strongly on the historical truth, as well as the poetical beauty, of these productions. I could add the Laird and Lady Macleod, with many more that live in different parts of the Highlands, very remote from each other, and could only be acquainted with what had become (in a manner) national works. There is a country-surgeon in Lochaber, who has by heart the entire epic poem mentioned by Mr. Macpherson in his Preface, and, as he is old, is perhaps the only person living that knows it all, and has never committed it to writing. We are in the more haste to recover a monument which will certainly be regarded as a curiosity in the republic of letters. We have therefore set about a subscription of a guinea or two guineas a-piece in order to enable Mr. Macpherson to undertake a mission into the Highlands to recover this poem and other fragments of antiquity."

I forgot to mention to you that the names of Fingal, Ossian, Oscar, &c., are still given in the Highlands to large mastiffs, as we give to ours the names of Cæsar, Pompey, Hector, &c.

[*To Dr. Clarke, from Cambridge, August 12, 1760*]

. . . Have you seen the Erse Fragments since they were printed? I am more puzzled than ever about their antiquity, though I still incline (against everybody's opinion) to believe them old. Those you have already seen are the best; though there are some others that are excellent too.

OSSIAN, GOTHIC ARCHITECTURE

[*To Horace Walpole, from Cambridge, September 2, 1760*]

. . . What do you think of the Erse Poems now they are come out? I suppose your suspicions are augmented: yet (upon some further inquiries I have made) Mr. David Hume (the historian) writes word that "their authenticity is beyond all question; that Adam Smith, the celebrated Professor at Glasgow, has assured him (who doubted too) that he had heard the *Piper of the Argyleshire militia* repeat all these and many more of equal beauty. That Major Mackay, the Laird and Lady of Macleod, and the Laird of Macfarline, the greatest antiquarian in all their country, and others, who live in the Highlands very remote from each other, remember them perfectly well, and could not be acquainted with them if they were not spread into every one's mouth there, and become in a manner national works." This is certainly the only proof, that works preserved merely by tradition, and not in manuscript, will admit of.

I beg leave to differ as to the era of Gothic perfection. There is nothing finer than the nave of York Minster (in a great and simple style), or than the choir of the same church (in the rich and filigraine workmanship). Both these are of Edward the Third's reign, the first in the beginning, and the latter in the end of it. The Lady Chapel (now Trinity Church) at Ely, and the lantern tower in the same Cathedral, are noble works of the same time. I mention these as great things; but if we must take our idea from little ones, the Chapel of Bishop West (also at Ely), who died in 1533, 24 Henry VIII. surpasses all other things of the kind.

[*To Thomas Wharton, from London, October 21, 1760*]

. . . There is a second edition of the Scotch Fragments, yet very few admire them, and almost all take them for fictions. I have a letter from D. Hume, the Historian, that asserts them to be genuine, and cites the names of several people (that know both languages) who have heard them current in the mouths of Pipers and other illiterate persons in various and distant parts of the Highlands. There is a subscription for Mr. Macpherson, which will enable him to undertake a mission among the Mountaineers, and pick up all the scattered remnants of old poetry. He is certainly an admirable Judge; if his *learned* Friends do not pervert or over-rule his taste.

MASON'S ELEGY ON LADY COVENTRY

[*To William Mason*]

LONDON, at Mr. Jauncey's, not Jenour's, December 10, 1760.

DEAR MASON — It is not good to give copies of a thing before you have given it the last hand.

If you would send it to Lord H[oldernesse] you might have spared that to Lady M. C.; they have both shewed it to particular friends, and so it is half published before it is finished. I begin again from the beginning: —

"Ah, mark," is rather languid. I would read "Heard ye."

V. 3. I read, "and now with rising knell," to avoid two "the's."

V. 10. I read, "since now that bloom," &c.

V. 11, 12, are altered for the better, and so are the following; but for "liquid lightning," Lord J. Cavendish says there is a dram which goes by that name; and T. G. adds, that the words are stolen from a sonnet of the late Prince of Wales. What if we read "liquid radiance," and change the word "radiant" soon after.

V. 18. Read, "that o'er her form," &c.

V. 23. "Cease, cease, luxuriant muse." Though mended, it is still weakly. I do not much care for any muse at all here.

V. 26. "Mould'ring" is better than "clay-cold"; somewhat else might be better perhaps than either.

V. 35. "Whirl you in her wild career." This image does not come in so well here between two real happinesses. The word "lead" before it, as there is no epithet left to "purple," is a little faint.

"Of her choicest stores an ampler share," seems to me prosaic.

"Zenith-height" is harsh to the ear and too scientific.

I take it the interrogation point comes after "fresh delight"; and there the sense ends. If so, the question is too long in asking, and leaves a sort of obscurity.

V. 46. I understand, but cannot read, this line. Does "tho' soon" belong to "lead her hence," or to "the steps were slow"? I take it to the latter; and if so, it is hardly grammar; if to the former, the end of the line appears very naked without it.

V. 55. "Rouse, then — his voice pursue." I do not like this broken line.

V. 74. "Firm as the sons," that is, "as firmly as." The adjective used for the adverb here gives it some obscurity, and has the appearance of a contradiction.

V. 76. A less metaphorical line would become this place better.

V. 80. This, though a good line, would be better too if it were more simple, for the same figure is amplified in the following stanza, and there is no occasion for anticipating it here.

V. 85. "And why?" I do not understand. You mean, I imagine, that the warrior must not expect to establish his fame as a hero while he is yet alive; but how does "living fame" signify this? The construction too, is not good; if you mean, with regard to Fame, while he yet lives, Fate denies him that. The next line is a bold expression of Shakespeare. The third, "ere from her trump — heaven breathed," is not good.

V. 89. "Is it the grasp?" You will call me a coxcomb if I remind you, that this stanza in the turn of it is too like a stanza of "another body's."

V. 98. "Truth ne'er can sanctify," is an indifferent line. Both Mr. Brown and I have some doubt about the justness of this sentiment. A kingdom is purchased, we think, too dear with the life of any man; and this no less if there "be a life hereafter" than if there be none.

V. 102. We say the juice of the grape "mantles," but not the grape.

V. 107. "By earth's poor pittance"; will not do; the end is very well, but the whole is rather too long, and I would wish it reduced a little in the latter part. . . .

LA NOUVELLE HÉLOÏSE, ETC.

[*To William Mason, from London, January 22, 1761*]

I cannot pity you; *au contraire*, I wish I had been at Aston when I was foolish enough to go through the six volumes of the Nouvelle Heloïse. All that I can say for myself is, that I was confined at home for three weeks by a severe cold, and had nothing better to do. There is no one event in it that might not happen any day of the week (separately taken), in any private family: yet these events are so put together that the series of them are more absurd and more improbable than Amadis de Gaul. The *dramatis personæ* (as the author says) are all of them good characters; I am sorry to hear it, for had they been all hanged at the end of the third volume nobody (I believe) would have cared. In short, I went on and on in hopes of finding some wonderful *dénouement* that would set all right, and bring something like nature and interest out of absurdity and insipidity; no such thing, it grows worse and worse, and (if it be Rousseau, which is not doubted) is the strongest instance I ever saw that a very extraordinary man may entirely mistake his own talents. By the motto and preface it appears to be his own story, or something similar to it.

The Opera House is crowded this year like any ordinary theatre. Elisi is finer than anything that has been here in your memory, yet, as I suspect, has been finer than he is. He appears to be near forty, a little pot-bellied and thick-shouldered, otherwise no bad figure; his action proper, and not ungraceful. We have heard nothing, since I remember operas, but eternal passages, divisions, and flights of execution; of these he has absolutely none, whether merely from judgment, or a little from age, I will not affirm. His point is expression, and to that all the graces and ornaments he inserts (which are few and short), are evidently directed. He goes higher (they say) than Farinelli, but then this celestial note you do not hear above once in a whole opera, and he falls from this altitude at once to the mellowest, softest, strongest tones (about the middle of his compass) that can be heard. The Mattei (I assure you) is much improved by his example, and by her great success this winter. But then the Burlettas and the Paganina. I have not been so pleased with anything these many years; she too is fat and about forty, yet handsome withal, and has a face that speaks the language of all nations. She has not the invention, the fire, and the variety of action, that the Spiletta had; yet she is light, agile, ever in motion, and above all graceful; but then her voice, her ear, her taste in singing: Good God! — as Mr. Richardson the painter says. Pray ask my Lord, for I think I have seen him there once or twice, as much pleased as I was.

I have long thought of reading Jeremy Taylor, for I am persuaded that chopping logic in the pulpit, as our divines have done ever since the Revolution, is not the thing; but that imagination and warmth of expression are in their place there as much as on the stage, moderated however, and chastised a little by the purity and severity of religion. . . .

GOTHIC DESIGN

[*To Thomas Wharton, from London, September 8, 1761*]

DEAR DOCTOR — I am just come to Town, where I shall stay six weeks or more, and (if you will send your dimensions) will look out for papers at the shops. I own I never yet saw any Gothic papers to my fancy. There is one fault, that is in the nature of the thing, and cannot be avoided. The great beauty of all Gothic designs is the variety of perspectives they occasion. This a Painter may represent on the walls of a room in some measure; but not a Designer of Papers, where, what is represented on one breadth, must be exactly repeated on another, both in the light and shade, and in the dimensions. This we cannot help; but they do not even do what they might: they neglect Hollar, to copy Mr. Halfpenny's architecture, so that all they do is more like a goose-pie than a cathedral. You seem to suppose, that they do Gothic papers in colours, but I never saw any but such as were to look like Stucco: nor indeed do I conceive that they could have any effect or meaning. Lastly, I never saw anything of gilding, such as you mention, on paper, but we shall see. Only pray leave as little to my judgment as possible. . . .

FINGAL

[To Thomas Wharton, from Cambridge, January, 1762]

. . . The Heloïse cruelly disappointed me, but it has its partisans, among which are Mason and Mr. Hurd. For me, I admire nothing but Fingal (I conclude you have read it: if not Stonehewer can lend it to you), yet I remain still in doubt about the authenticity of those poems, though inclining rather to believe them genuine in spite of the World. Whether they are the inventions of antiquity, or of a modern Scotchman, either case is to me alike unaccountable. Je m'y pers. . . .

WHITEHEAD'S WORKS, ETC.

[To William Mason, from Cambridge, March 17, 1762]

The laureate has honoured me (as a friend of yours, for I know no other reason) with his new play and his "Charge to the Poets": the first very middling; the second I am pleased with, chiefly with the sense, and sometimes with the verse and expression; and yet the best thing he ever wrote was that "Elegy against Friendship" you once shewed me, where the sense was detestable; so that you see it is not at all necessary a poet should be a good sort of man — no, not even in his writings. Bob Lloyd has published his works in a just quarto volume, containing, among other things, a Latin translation of my Elegy; an epistle in which is a very serious compliment to me by name, particularly on my Pindaric accomplishments; and the very two odes you saw before, in which we were abused, and a note to say they were written in concert with his friend Mr. Colman; so little value have poets for themselves, especially when they would make up a just volume. Mr. Delap is here, and has brought his cub to Trinity. He has picked up again purely since his misfortune, and is fat and well, all but a few bowels. He says Mrs. Pritchard spoilt his *Hecuba* with sobbing so much, and that she was really so moved that she fell in fits behind the scenes. I much like Dr. Lowth's Grammar; it is concise, clear, and elegant. He has selected his solecisms from all the best writers of our tongue. I hear Mr. Hurd is seriously writing against Fingal, by the instigation of the devil and the bishop. Can it be true? I have exhausted all my literary news, and I have no other. . . .

MASON'S ELEGY ON LADY COVENTRY

[*To William Mason, from Cambridge, December* 21, 1762]

. . . We have received your poetical packet and delivered them to the several parties. The sentiments we do not remark, as we can find nothing within ourselves congenial to them: for the expression, we hint (but in a low, timid voice) that there is a want of strength and spirit; in short, they are nothing like the choruses in *Elfrida*, only the lines that relate to Lady C——'s beauty have made a deep impression upon us; we get them by heart and apply them to our sempstresses and bedmakers. This is (I think) the sum and substance of our reflections here; only Mrs. Rutherford observes that there is great delicacy and tenderness in the manner of treating so frail a character as that of Lady C——, and that you have found a way to reconcile contempt and compassion: these might not be her words, but this was the sense of them; I don't believe she had it from the doctor. . . .

THE CHAPEL OF ST. SEPULCHRE, YORK

[*To James Brown*]

Aston, January 15, 1763.

DEAR SIR — I send you with this a drawing of the ruin you were so much pleased with when you saw it at York. I take it certainly to have been the chapel of St. Sepulchre, founded by Archbishop Roger, of which Dugdale has given us the original *charta fundationis*; but, as this opinion seems to contradict the opinion of Torre, and of Drake too, who follows him, it is necessary to produce authentic authority in proof of my assertion. These two learned antiquaries suppose that the chapel in question joined to the minster. Thus Torre: "Roger (Archbishop) having built against the great church a chapel."

And Drake: "Roger was buried in the cathedral, near the door of St. Sepulchre's chapel, which he himself had founded." — Vide Drake's *Ebor.*, p. 478, p. 421. From these accounts we should be led to conclude that this chapel was as much and as close an appendage to the minster as the chapter-house is; but the original records, on which they found this opinion, may I think be construed very differently.

Archbishop Roger himself, in his *charta fundationis*, describes its situation thus: — "capellam quam juxta majorem ecclesiam extruximus." "Juxta" is surely "near" only, not "adjoining"; and this ruin is near enough. In the extract of this archbishop's life, from an ancient MS. which Dugdale also gives us, we find these words, " Condidit etiam Capellam Sancti Sepulchri ad januam ipsius Palatii ex parte boreali juxta eccl'am S. Petri." The ruin in question might very probably be connected with the palace gate by a cloister, of which on one side there are a string of arches remaining; and on the outside of the minster, over the little gate next the tomb, there are also vestiges of the roof of a cloister, which I imagine went aside the palace gateway, and connected the three buildings; vide plan. But between this little gate and the palace gate (which still remains) it is very evident there was no room for anything but a cloister, for I do not think they are twenty yards asunder.

The last and only further account I can find of the situation is from the same Life, where it is said the canons of St. Peter, "graviter murmurabant super situ dictæ capellæ eo quod nimis adhæsit matrici ecclesiæ."

This I think need not be translated literally; the word "nimis" leads one to a metaphorical sense. The priests of St. Sepulchre were too near neighbours to St. Peter's canons, and were troublesome to them; accordingly we find the archbishop, to quiet matters, ordered that the saint of his chapel should make them a recompense, which is in this extract stated.

To these arguments I would add, that Archbishop Roger's donation was very great (as we find in Drake) to this chapel; and from the number of persons maintained in its service, I question not but there was a large convent built round it, of which there are plainly the foundations still to be seen; and what puts the matter out of all doubt that this building was separate and entire, though indeed near to the minster, is the following fact, viz. that the tithes of the chapel and chapel itself were sold to one Webster, anno 42 Elizabeth: "Capella vocat. St. Sepulcre's Chapell prope Eccles. Cath. Ebor. cum decimis ejusdem. W. Webster. Ap. 4, anno 4[2] Eliz." — Rolls. Chap. Thus you see the "juxta" and "prope" are clearly on my side; the "nimis adhæsit" is equivocal. I conclude with a rude draught of the platform according to my idea, but without any mensuration, and merely to explain what has been said. I am with the greatest respect and deference to your sagacity, yours, &c. &c. &c.

P. S. — I ought to mention to you, that in

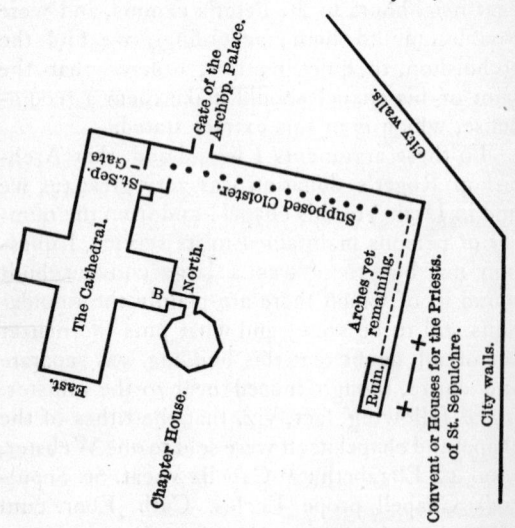

the transept (I think you call it) of the church, namely, at B, there is at the top over the large pillars, a range of stonework like the windows in the ruin, viz. three pointed arches under a circular one, but of a clumsy proportion. This part I think you said was the oldest in the minster. Johnny Ludlam found this out. Perhaps it contradicts all I have been saying, and proves the building much older than Archbishop Roger.

[To William Mason, from Cambridge, February 8, 1763]

I am obliged to you for your drawing, and very learned dissertation annexed. You have made out your point with a great degree of probability (for though the "nimis adhæsit" might startle one, yet the sale of the tithes and chapel to Webster seems to set all right again), and I do believe the building in question was the chapel of St. Sepulchre; but then that the ruin now standing was the individual chapel, as erected by Archbishop Roger, I can by no means think. I found myself merely on the style and taste of architecture. The vaults under the choir are still in being, and were undoubtedly built by this very archbishop. They are truly Saxon, only that the arches are pointed, though very obtusely. It is the south transept (not the north) that is the oldest part of the minster now above ground. It is said to have been begun by Geoffrey Plantagenet, who died about thirty years after Roger, and left it unfinished. His successor, Walter Grey, completed it; so we do not exactly know to which of these two prelates we are to ascribe any certain part of it. Grey lived a long time, and was archbishop from 1216 to 1255 (39mo Hen. III.); and in this reign it was that the beauty of the Gothic architecture began to appear. The chapter-house is in all probability his work, and (I should suppose) built in his latter days, whereas what he did of the south transept might be performed soon after his accession. It is in the second order of this building that the round arches appear, including a row of pointed ones (which you mention, and which I also observed), similar to those in St. Sepulchre's Chapel, though far inferior in the proportions and neatness of workmanship. The same thing is repeated in the north transept, but this is only an imitation of the other, done for the sake of regularity, for this part of the building is no older than Archbishop Romaine, who came to the see in 1285, and died 1296.

All the buildings of Henry the Second's time (under whom Roger lived, and died, 1181) are of a clumsy and heavy proportion, with a few rude and awkward ornaments; and this style continues to the beginning of Henry the Third's reign, though with a little improvement, as in the nave of Fountains Abbey, &c. Then all at once come in the tall piqued arches, the light clustered columns, the capital of curling foliage, the fretted tabernacles and vaultings, and a profusion of statues, &c., that constitute the good Gothic style, together with decreasing and flying buttresses and pinnacles on the outside. Nor must you conclude anything from Roger's own tomb, which has, I remember, a wide surbased arch with scalloped ornaments, &c.; for this can be no older than the nave itself, which was built by Archbishop Melton after the year 1315, one hundred and thirty years after our Roger's death. . . .

MASON, OSSIAN, ETC.

[*To James Brown, from Cambridge*]

February 17, 1763.

You will make my best acknowledgments to Mr. Howe, who not content to rank me in the number of his friends, is so polite as to make excuses for having done me that honour.

I *was not born so* far from the sun as to be ignorant of Count Algarotti's name and reputation; nor am I so far advanced in years or in philosophy, as not to feel the warmth of his approbation. The Odes in question, as their motto shews, were meant to be *vocal to the intelligent alone*. How few *they* were in my own country, Mr. Howe can testify; and yet my ambition was terminated by that small circle. I have good reason to be proud, if my voice has reached the ear and apprehension of a stranger distinguished as one of the best judges in Europe.

I am equally pleased with the just applause he bestows on Mr. Mason, and particularly on his *Caractacus*, which is the work of a Man: whereas the *Elfrida* is only that of a boy, a promising boy indeed, and of no common genius: yet this is the popular performance with us, and the other little known in comparison.

Neither Count Algarotti, nor Mr. Howe (I believe) have heard of *Ossian, the Son of Fingal*. If Mr. Howe were not upon the wing, and on his way homewards, I would send it to him in Italy. He would there see, that Imagination dwelt many hundred years ago in all her pomp on the cold and barren mountains of Scotland. The truth (I believe) is that without any respect of climates she reigns in all the nascent societies of men, where the necessities of life force every one to think and act much for himself. Adieu!

ÉMILE

[To Thomas Wharton, from Cambridge, August 5, 1763]

... I doubt you have not read Rousseau's *Émile*; everybody that has children, should read it more than once, for though it abounds with his usual glorious absurdity, though his general scheme of education be an impracticable chimera; yet there are a thousand lights struck out, a thousand important truths better expressed than ever they were before, that may be of service to the wisest man. Particularly I think he has observed children with more attention and knows their meaning and the working of their little passions better than any other writer. As to his religious discussions, which have alarmed the world, and engaged their thoughts more than any other part of his book, I set them all at nought, and wish they had been omitted. ...

THE ARTS IN ENGLAND AND ITALY

[To Count Algarotti]

Cambridge, September 9, 1763.

SIR — I received some time since the unexpected honour of a Letter from you, and the promise of a pleasure, which, till of late I had not the opportunity of enjoying. Forgive me if I make my acknowledgments in my native tongue, as I see it is perfectly familiar to you, and I (though not unacquainted with the writings of Italy) should from disuse speak its language with an ill grace, and with still more constraint to one, who possesses it in all its strength and purity.

I see with great satisfaction your efforts to re-unite the congenial arts of poetry, music, and the dance, which with the assistance of painting and architecture, regulated by taste, and supported by magnificence and power, might form the noblest scene, and bestow the sublimest pleasure, that the imagination can conceive. But who shall realise these delightful visions? There is, I own, one Prince in Europe, that wants neither the will, the spirit, nor the ability: but can he call up Milton from his grave, can he re-animate Marcello, or bid the Barberina or the Sallé move again? Can he (as much a king as he is) govern an Italian *Virtuosa*, destroy her caprice and impertinence, without hurting her talents, or command those unmeaning graces and tricks of voice to be silent, that have gained her the adoration of her own country?

One cause, that so long has hindered, and (I

fear) will hinder that happy union, which you propose, seems to be this: that poetry (which, as you allow, must lead the way, and direct the operation of the subordinate arts) implies at least a liberal education, a degree of literature, and various knowledge, whereas the others (with a few exceptions) are in the hands of slaves and mercenaries, I mean, of people without education, who, though neither destitute of genius, nor insensible to fame, must yet make gain their principal end, and subject themselves to the prevailing taste of those, whose fortune only distinguishes them from the multitude.

I cannot help telling you, that eight or ten years ago, I was a witness to the power of your comic music. — There was a little troop of Buffi, that exhibited a Burletta in London, not in the Opera House, where the audience is chiefly of the better sort, but on one of the common Theatres full of all kinds of people and (I believe) the fuller from that natural aversion we bear to foreigners: their looks and their noise made it evident, they did not come thither to hear; and on similar occasions I have known candles lighted, broken bottles, and pen knives flung on the stage, the benches torn up, the scenes hurried into the street and set on fire. The curtain drew up, the music was of Cocchi, with a few airs of Pergolesi interspersed. The singers were (as usual) deplorable, but there was one girl (she called herself the Niccolina) with little voice and less beauty; but with the utmost justness of ear, the strongest expression of countenance, the most speaking eyes, the greatest vivacity and variety of gesture. Her first appearance instantly fixed their attention; the tumult sunk at once, or if any murmur rose, it was hushed by a general cry for silence. Her first air ravished everybody; they forgot their prejudices, they forgot, that they did not understand a word of the language; they entered into all the humour of the part, made her repeat all her songs, and continued their transports, their laughter, and applause to the end of the piece. Within these three last years the Paganini and Amici have met with almost the same applause once a week from a politer audience on the Opera stage. The truth is, the Opera itself, though supported there at a great expence for so many years, has rather maintained itself by the admiration bestowed on a few particular voices, or the borrowed taste of a few men of condition, that have learned in Italy how to admire, than by any genuine love we bear to the best Italian music: nor have we yet got any style of our own, and this I attribute in great measure to the language, which in spite of its energy, plenty, and the crowd of excellent writers this nation has produced, does yet (I am sorry to say it) retain too much of its barbarous original to adapt itself to musical composition. I by no means wish to have been born anything but an Englishman; yet I should rejoice to exchange tongues with Italy.

Why this nation has made no advances hitherto in painting and sculpture is hard to say. The fact is undeniable, and we have the vanity to apologise for ourselves, as Virgil did for the Romans, *Excudent alii*, &c. It is sure, that architecture had introduced itself in the reign of the unfortunate Charles I. and Inigo Jones has left us some few monuments of his skill, that shew him capable of greater things. Charles had not only a love for the beautiful arts, but some taste in them. The confusion that soon followed, swept away his magnificent collection; the artists were dispersed, or ruined, and the arts disregarded till very lately. The young monarch now on the throne is said to esteem and understand them. I wish he may have the leisure to cultivate and the skill to encourage them with due regard to merit, otherwise it is better to neglect them. You, Sir, have pointed out the true sources, and the best examples to your countrymen. They have nothing to do, but to be what they once were;

and yet perhaps it is more difficult to restore good taste to a nation, that has degenerated, than to introduce it in one, where as yet it has never flourished. You are generous enough to wish, and sanguine enough to foresee, that it shall one day flourish in England. I too must wish, but can hardly extend my hopes so far. It is well for us that you do not see our public exhibitions. — But our artists are yet in their infancy, and therefore I will not absolutely despair.

I owe to Mr. How the honour I have of conversing with Count Algarotti, and it seems as if I meant to indulge myself in the opportunity: but I have done. Sir, I will only add, that I am proud of your approbation, having no relish for any other fame than what is conferred by the few real judges, that are so thinly scattered over the face of the earth. I am, Sir, with great respect, your most obliged humble Servant,

T. GRAY.

A. S. E. Il Conte Fransisco Algarotti,
Ciambellan di S. M. il Ré di Prussia, &c. &c.
Italia, Bolognia.

[*To William Taylor Howe*]

Cambridge, September 10, 1763.

SIR — I ought long since to have made you my acknowledgments for the obliging testimonies of your esteem that you have conferred upon me; but Count Algarotti's books did not come to my hands till the end of July, and since that time I have been prevented by illness from doing any of my duties. I have read them more than once with increasing satisfaction, and should wish mankind had eyes to descry the genuine sources of their own pleasures, and judgment to know the extent, that nature has prescribed to them: if this were the case, it would be their interest to appoint Count Algarotti their "Arbiter Elegantiarum." He is highly civil to our nation, but there is one little point, in which he does not do us justice. I am the more solicitous about it, because it relates to the only taste we can call our own, the only proof of our original talent in matter of pleasure; I mean, our skill in gardening, and laying out grounds. That the Chinese have this beautiful art in high perfection, seems very probable from the *Jesuits' Letters*, and more from Chambers's little discourse published some few years ago. But it is very certain, we copied nothing from them, nor had anything but nature our model. It is not forty years, since the art was born among us; and it is sure, that there was nothing in Europe like it, and as sure, we then had no information on this head from China at all.

I shall rejoice to see you in England, and talk over these and many other matters with you at leisure. Do not despair of your health, because you have not found all the effects you had promised yourself from a finer climate. I have known people, who have experienced the same thing, and yet at their return have lost all their complaints as by miracle. — I am, S^r, your obliged humble Servant,

T. GRAY.

P.S. — I have answered C. Algarotti, whose letter I conveyed to Mr. Mason, whether he has received his books, I have not yet heard. Mr. Brown charges me with his best compliments.

ALGAROTTI, PERGOLESI, ETC.

[To William Mason, from Cambridge, 1763]

DEAR MASON — As I have no more received my little thing than you have yours, though they were sent by the *Beverley*, Captain Allen, I have returned no answer yet; but I must soon, and that in plain English, and so should you too. In the meantime I borrowed and read them. That on the Opera is a good clever dissertation, dedicated to Guglielmo Pitt; the other (*Il Congresso di Citera*), in poetical prose, describes the negociation of three ambassadresses sent by England, France, and Italy to the Court of Cupid, to lay before him the state of his empire in the three nations; and is not contemptible neither in its kind; so pray be civil to the count and Signor Howe. . . .

I like your Sonnet better than most dedications; it is simple and natural. The best line in it is: —

"So, to deceive my solitary days," &c.

There are an expression or two that *break the repose of* it by looking common and overworn: "sequestered shade," "woodbine sprays," "selected lays"; I dare not mention "lettered ease." "Life's vain vision" does not pronounce well. Bating these, it looks in earnest, and as if you could live at Aston, which is not true; but that is not my affair.

I have got a mass of Pergolesi, which is all divinity; but it was lent me, or you should have it by all means. Send for six lessons for the pianoforte or harpsichord of Carlo Bach, not the Opera Bach, but his brother. To my fancy they are charming, and in the best Italian style. Mr. Neville and the old musicians here do not like them, but to me they speak not only music, but passion. I cannot play them, though they are not hard; yet I make a smattering that serves " to deceive my solitary days"; and I figure to myself that I hear you touch them triumphantly. . . .

[*To William Taylor Howe, from London, November,* 1763]

. . . I saw and read the beginning of this year, the *Congresso di Citéra*, and was excessively pleased in spite of prejudice, for I am naturally no friend to allegory, nor to poetical prose. Entre nous, what gives me the least pleasure of any of his writings, that I have seen, is the *Newtoniasm*. It is so direct an imitation of Fontenelle, a writer not easy to imitate, and least of all in the Italian tongue, whose character and graces are of a higher style, and never adapt themselves easily to the elegant *badinage* and *légèreté* of conversation, that sets so well on the French. But this is a secret between us.

I am glad to hear, he thinks of revisiting England; though I am a little ashamed of my country at this present. Our late acquired glory does not set becomingly upon us; and even the Author of it, that *Restitutor d'Inghilterra*, is doing God knows what! If he should deign to follow the track of vulgar Ministers, and regain his power by ways injurious to his fame, whom can we trust hereafter? M. de Nivernois on his return to France says (I hear) of England, "Quel Roy, quel Peuple, quelle Societé!" And so say I. . . .

VOLTAIRE, ROUSSEAU, ETC.

[To Thomas Wharton, from Cambridge, July 10, 1764]

. . . Two more volumes of Buffon are come over: I mention them in case you choose to have them. I know of nothing else, except half a dozen new works of that inexhaustible, eternal, entertaining scribbler Voltaire, who at last (I fear) will go to heaven, for to him entirely it is owing, that the king of France and his council have review'd and set aside the decision of the parliament of Thoulouse in the affair of Calas. The poor man, 'tis true, has been broke on the wheel long ago; but his widow and wretched family may have some reparation, and his murtherers may smart a little for it. You see a scribbler may be of some use in the world! . . .

[To William Mason, from Cambridge, November, 1764]

. . . I read and liked the Epigram as it was printed, and do insist it is better without the last lines, not that the thought is amiss, but because the same rhyme is repeated, and the sting is not in the epigrammatic style; I mean, not easy and familiar. In a satire it might do very well. Mr. Churchill is dead indeed, drowned in a butt of claret, which was tapped on the meeting of the

Friends at Boulogne. He made an excellent end, as his executor Humphrey Cotes testifies. I did not write any of the elegies, being busy in writing the *Temple of Tragedy*. Send for it forthwith, for you are highly interested in it. If I had not owned the thing, perhaps you might have gone and taken it for the Reverend Mr. Langhorne's. It is divine. I have not read the *Philosophic Dictionary*. I can stay with great patience for anything that comes from Voltaire. They tell me it is frippery, and blasphemy, and wit. I could have forgiven myself if I had not read Rousseau's *Letters*. Always excepting the *Contract Social*, it is the dullest performance he ever published. It is a weak attempt to separate the miracles from the morality of the Gospel. The latter he would have you think he believes was sent from God, and the former he very explicitly takes for an imposture. This is in order to prove the cruelty and injustice of the State of Geneva in burning his *Émile*. The latter part of his book is to shew the abuses that have crept into the constitution of his country, which point (if you are concerned about it) he makes out very well, and his intention in this is plainly to raise a tumult in the city, and to be revenged on the *Petit Conseil*, who condemned his writings to the flames. . . .

THE CASTLE OF OTRANTO, ROUSSEAU, ETC.

[*To Horace Walpole, from Cambridge*]

Sunday, December 30, 1764.

I HAVE received the *Castle of Otranto*, and return you my thanks for it. It engages our attention here, makes some of us cry a little, and all in general afraid to go to bed o' nights. We take it for a translation, and should believe it to be a true story, if it were not for St. Nicholas.

When your pen was in your hand you might have been a little more communicative, for though disposed enough to believe the opposition rather consumptive, I am entirely ignorant of all the symptoms. Your canonical book I have been reading with great satisfaction. He speaketh as one having authority. If Englishmen have any feeling left, methinks they must feel now; and if the Ministry have any feeling (whom nobody will suspect of insensibility) they must cut off the author's ears, for it is in all the forms a most wicked libel. Is the old man and the lawyer put on, or is it real? or has some real lawyer furnished a good part of the materials, and another person employed them? This I guess; for there is an uncouthness of diction in the beginning which is not supported throughout, though it now and then occurs again, as if the writer was weary of supporting the character he had assumed, when the subject had warmed him, beyond dissimulation.

Rousseau's *Letters* I am reading heavily, heavily! He justifies himself, till he convinces me that he deserved to be burnt, at least that his book did. I am not got through him, and you never will. Voltaire I detest, and have not seen his book: I shall in good time. You surprise me, when you talk of going in February. Pray, does all the minority go too? I hope you have a reason. *Desperare de republica* is a deadly sin in politics. . . .

AN ITINERARY OF FRANCE AND ITALY

[*To William Palgrave, probably from Cambridge*]

March, 1765.

MY instructions, of which you are so desirous, are twofold: the first part relates to what is past, and that will be rather diffuse: the second, to what is to come; and that we shall treat more succinctly, and with all due brevity.

First, when you come to Paris you will not fail to visit the cloister of the Chartreuse, where Le

Sueur (in the history of St. Bruno) has almost equalled Raphael. Then your Gothic inclinations will naturally lead you to the Sainte Chapelle built by St. Louis: in the treasury is preserved one of the noblest gems of the Augustan age. When you take a trip into the country, there is a fine old chapel at Vincennes with admirable painted windows; and at Fontainbleau, the remains of Francis the First's magnificence might give you some pleasure. In your way to Lyons you will take notice of the view over the Saone, from about Tournus and Macon. Fail not to walk a few miles along the banks of the Rhone, down the river. I would certainly make a little journey to the Grande Chartreuse, up the mountains: at your return out of Italy this will have little effect. At Turin you will visit the Capuchins' convent just without the city, and the Superga at no great distance, for the sake of the views. At Genoa observe the Terreno of the Palace Brignoli, as a model of an apartment elegantly disposed in a hot climate. At Parma you will adore the great Madonna and St. Jerome, once at St. Antonio Abbate, but now (I am told) in the Ducal Palace. In the Madonna della Steccata observe the Moses breaking the tables, a chiaroscuro figure of the Parmeggiano at too great a height, and ill-lighted, but immense. At the Capuchins, the great Pietá of Annib. Carracci; in the Villa Ducale, the room painted by Carlo Cignani; and the last works of Agostino Caracci at Modena. I know not what remains now, the flower of the collection is gone to Dresden. Bologna is too vast a subject for me to treat: the palaces and churches are open; you have nothing to do but to see them all. In coming down the Appennine you will see (if the sun shines) all Tuscany before you. And so I have brought you to Florence, where to be sure there is nothing worth seeing. Secondly,

1. Vide, quodcunque videndum est.

2. Quodcunque ego non vidi, id tu vide.

3. Quodcunque videris, scribe & describe; memoria ne fide.

4. Scribendo nil admirare; & cum pictor non sis, verbis omnia depinge.

5. Tritam viatorum compitam calca, & cum poteris, desere.

6. Eme, quodcunque emendum est; I do not mean pictures, medals, gems, drawings, &c., only; but clothes, stockings, shoes, handkerchiefs, little moveables; everything you may want all your life long: but have a care of the custom house.

Pray, present my most respectful compliments

to Mr. Weddell. I conclude when the winter is over, and you have seen Rome and Naples, you will strike out of the beaten path of English travellers, and see a little of the country, throw yourselves into the bosom of the Appennine, survey the horrid lake of Amsanctus (look in Cluver's Italy), catch the breezes on the coast of Taranto and Salerno, expatiate to the very toe of the continent, perhaps strike over the Faro of Messina, and having measured the gigantic columns of Girgenti, and the tremendous caverns of Syracusa, refresh yourselves amidst the fragrant vale of Enna. Oh! che bel riposo! Addio.

A SONNET BY MASON

[To William Mason, from Cambridge, in the spring of 1765]

. . . I hope in God the dedicatorial sonnet has not staid for me. I object nothing to the second line, but like it the better for Milton, and with him too I would read *in penult.* (give me a shilling) "his ghastly smile," &c. But if you won't put it in, then read "wonted smile," and a little before "secure from envy." I see nothing to alter. What I said was the best line is the best line still. Do come hither, and I will read and criticise "your amorous ditties all a winter's day." . . .

BENTHAM'S GOTHIC ARCHITECTURE

[To James Bentham, from Cambridge]

About the year 1765.

TO THE REV. MR. BENTHAM — Mr. Gray returns the papers and prints to Mr. Bentham, with many thanks for the sight of them.

Concludes he has laid aside his intention of publishing the first four sections of his Introduction, that contain the settlement and progress of Christianity among the Saxons; as (however curious and instructive of themselves) they certainly have too slight a connection with the subject in hand to make a part of the present work.

Has received much entertainment and information from his remarks on the state of Architecture among the Saxons, and thinks he has proved his point against the authority of Stow and Somner. The words of Eddius, Richard of Hexham, &c., must be everywhere cited in the original tongue, as the most accurate translation is in these cases not to be trusted; this Mr. B. has indeed commonly done in the MSS., but not everywhere.

P. 31. He says, the instances Sir C. Wren brings, were, *some of them at least*, undoubtedly erected after the Conquest. Sure they were all so without exception.

There is much probability in what he asserts with respect to the *New Norman Mode* of building; though this is not, nor perhaps can be, made out with so much precision as the former point.

P. 35. Here, where the Author is giving a compendious view of the peculiarities that distinguish the Saxon style, it might be mentioned, that they had no tabernacles (or niches and canopies), nor any statues to adorn their buildings on the outside, which are the principal grace of what is called Gothic; the only exception that I can recollect, is a little figure of Bishop Herebert Losing over the north transept door at Norwich, which appears to be of that time: but this is rather a mezzo-relievo than a statue, and it is well known that they used reliefs sometimes with profusion, as in the Saxon gateway of the Abbey at Bury, the gate of the Temple Church at London, and the two gates at Ely, &c.

The want of pinnacles and of tracery in the vaults, are afterwards mentioned, but may as well be placed here too (in short) among the other characteristics.

Escutcheons of arms are hardly (if ever) seen

in these fabrics, which are the most frequent of all decorations in after-times.

P. 34. Besides the chevron-work (or zig-zag moulding), so common, which is here mentioned, there is also,

The *Billeted-moulding*, as if a cylinder should be cut into small pieces of equal length, and these stuck on alternately round the face of the arches, as in the choir at Peterborough, and at St. Cross, &c.

The *Nail-head*, resembling the heads of great nails driven in at regular distances, as in the nave of old St. Paul's, and the great tower of Hereford, &c.

The *Nebule*, a projection terminated by an undulating line as under the upper range of windows, on the outside of Peterborough.

Then to adorn their vast massive columns there was the *spiral-grove* winding round the shafts, and the *net*, or *lozenge-work*, overspreading them, both of which appear at Durham, and the first in the undercroft at Canterbury.

These few things are mentioned only, because Mr. Bentham's work is so nearly complete in this part, that one would wish it were quite so. His own observation may doubtless suggest to him many more peculiarities, which, however minute in appearance, are not contemptible, because they directly belong to his subject, and contribute to ascertain the age of an edifice at first sight. The great deficiency is from Henry VIth's time to the Reformation, when the art was indeed at its height.

P. 36. At York, under the choir, remains much of the old work, built by Archbishop Roger, of Bishop's-bridge, in Henry IId's reign; the arches are but just pointed, and rise on short round pillars, whose capitals are adorned with animals and foliage.

P. 37. Possibly the pointed arch might take its rise from those arcades we see in the early Norman (or Saxon) buildings on walls, where the wide semi-circular arches cross and intersect each other, and form thereby at their intersection exactly a narrow and sharp-pointed arch. In the wall south of the choir at St. Cross, is a facing of such wide, round, interlaced arches by way of ornament to a flat vacant space; only so much of it as lies between the legs of the two neighbouring arches, where they cross each other, is pierced through the fabric, and forms a little range of long pointed windows. It is of King Stephen's time.

P. 43. As Mr. B. has thought it proper to make a compliment to the *present set of governors* in their respective churches, it were to be wished he would insert a little reflection on the rage of repairing, beautifying, whitewashing, painting, and gilding, and above all, the mixture of Greek (or Roman) ornaments in Gothic edifices. This well-meant fury has been, and will be little less fatal to our ancient magnificent edifices, than the Reformation and the civil wars.

Mr. G. would wish to be told (at Mr. Bentham's leisure) whether over the great pointed arches, on which the western tower at Ely rises, anything like a semicircular curve appears in the stone work? And whether the screen (or roodloft) with some part of the south-cross, may not possibly be a part of the more ancient church built by Abbot Simeon and Fitz-Gilbert.

AN EPITAPH BY MASON

[To William Mason]

Old Park, Sunday, July 19, 1767.

DEAR MASON — I come forthwith to the epitaph which you have had the charity to write at the Archbishop's request. It will certainly do (for it is both touching and new), but yet will require much finishing. I like not the first three lines: it is the party most nearly concerned, at least some one closely connected, and bearing a part of the loss, that is usually supposed to speak on these occasions, but these lines appear to be written by the chaplain, and have an air of flattery to his patron. All that is good in them is better expressed in the four last verses: "where the cold ashes," &c. These five verses are well, except the word "benignant," and the thought (which is not clear to me, besides that it is somewhat *hardly* expressed) of "when beauty only blooms," &c. In gems that want colour and perfection, *a foil* is put under them to add to their lustre. In others, as in diamonds, the foil is black; and in this sense, when a pretty woman chooses to appear in public with a homely one, we say she uses her *as a foil*. This puzzles me, as you neither mean that beauty sets off virtue by its contrast and opposition to it, nor that her virtue was so imperfect as to stand in need of beauty to heighten its lustre. For the rest I read, "that sweetest harmony of soul," &c.; "such was the maid," &c. All this to the end I much approve, except "crowned with truth," and "lightens all their load." The first is not precise; in the latter you say too much. "Spreads his child," too, is not the word. When you have corrected all these faults it will be excellent.

[*From Old Park, August 9, 1767*]

. . . I exceedingly approve the epitaph in its present shape. Even what I best liked before is altered for the better. The various readings I do not mind, only, perhaps, I should read the 2d line:

"Grace that with tenderness and sense combined,
   To form," &c.

for I hate "sentiment" in verse. I will say nothing to "taste" and "truth," for perhaps the Archbishop may fancy they are fine things; but, to my palate, they are wormwood. All the rest is just as it should be, and what he ought to admire. . . .

BEATTIE, FERGUSON'S ESSAY

[*To James Beattie*]

Old Park, near Darlington, Durham, August 12, 1767.

I received from Mr. Williamson, that very obliging mark you were pleased to give me of your remembrance. Had I not entertained some slight hopes of revisiting Scotland this summer, and consequently of seeing you at Aberdeen, I had sooner acknowledged, by letter, the favour you have done me. Those hopes are now at an end; but I do not therefore despair of seeing again a country that has given me so much pleasure;

nor of telling you, in person, how much I esteem you and (as you choose to call them) your amusements: the specimen of them, which you were so good as to send me, I think excellent; the sentiments are such as a melancholy imagination naturally suggests in solitude and silence, and that (though light and business may suspend or banish them at times) return with but so much the greater force upon a feeling heart: the diction is elegant and unconstrained; not loaded with epithets and figures, nor flagging into prose; the versification is easy and harmonious. My only objection is . . .

You see, Sir, I take the liberty you indulged me in when I first saw you; and therefore I make no excuses for it, but desire you would take your revenge on me in kind.

I have read over (but too hastily) Mr. Ferguson's book. There are uncommon strains of eloquence in it: and I was surprised to find not one single idiom of his country (I think) in the whole work. He has not the fault you mention. His application to the heart is frequent, and often successful. His love of Montesquieu and Tacitus has led him into a manner of writing too short-winded and sententious; which those great men, had they lived in better times and under a better government, would have avoided.

AN ODE BY BEATTIE

[*To James Beattie, from Cambridge, December 24, 1767*]

... I have read, with much pleasure, an Ode of yours (in which you have done me the honour to adopt a measure that I have used) on Lord Hay's birth-day. Though I do not love panegyric, I cannot but applaud this, for there is nothing mean in it. The diction is easy and noble, the texture of the thoughts lyric, and the versification harmonious. The few expressions I object to are ... These, indeed, are minutiæ; but they weigh for something, as half a grain makes a difference in the value of a diamond.

ALGAROTTI'S WORKS

[*To William Taylor Howe*]

Cambridge, Pembroke College,
January 12, 1768.

SIR — You perceive by Mr. Brown's letter, that I passed all the summer in the North of England, went from thence to London, and did not arrive here till the middle of December, where I found your parcel. Since that time I have been generally confined to my room, and besides I was willing to go through the eight volumes, before I returned you an answer. This must be my excuse to you, for only doing now, what in mere civility I ought to have done long ago. First I must condole with you, that so neat an edition should swarm in almost every page with errors of the press, not only in notes and citations from Greek, French, and English authors, but in the Italian text itself, greatly to the disreputation of the Leghorn publishers. This is the only reason (I think), that could make an edition in England necessary. But I doubt you would not find the matter much mended here; our presses, as they improve in beauty, declining daily in accuracy; besides you would find the expense very considerable, and the sale in no proportion to it, as in reality, it is but few people in England, that read currently and with pleasure the Italian tongue; and the fine old editions of their capital writers are sold in London for a lower price, than they bear in Italy. An English translation I can by no means advise. The justness of thought and good sense might remain; but the graces of elocution (which make a great part of Algarotti's merit) would be entirely lost, and that merely from the very different genius and complexion of the two languages.

I rather think these volumes should be handsomely bound, before they are put into the library: they bind very neatly here; and if you approve it, Mr. Brown will order it to be done. Doubtless there can be no impropriety in making the same present to the University, nor need you at all to fear for the reputation of your friend: he has merit enough to recommend him in any country, a tincture of various sorts of knowledge; an acquaintance with all the beautiful arts; an easy command, a precision, warmth, and richness of expression, and a judgment, that is rarely mistaken, on any subject to which he applies it. Of the dialogues I have formerly told you my thoughts. The essays and letters (many of them entirely new to me) *on the arts*, are curious and entertaining; those on other subjects (even where the thoughts are not new to me, but borrowed from his various reading and conversation) often better put, and better expressed than in the originals. I rejoice, when I see Machiavel defended or illustrated, who to me appears one of the wisest men that any nation in any age has produced. Most of the other discourses military or political are well worth reading, though that on Kouli-Khan was a mere jeu-d'esprit, a sort of historical exercise. The letters from Russia I have read before with pleasure, particularly the narrative of Munich's and Lascy's campaigns. The detached thoughts are often new and just; but there should have been a revisal of them, as they are often to be found in his letters repeated in the very same words. Some too of the familiar letters might have been spared. The *Congress of Cythera* I had seen, and liked before, the *Giudicio d'Amore* is an addition rather inferior to it. The verses are not equal to the prose, but they are above mediocrity. . . .

WALPOLE'S HISTORIC DOUBTS

[*To Horace Walpole*]

Pembroke College, February 14, 1768.

I received the book you were so good to send me, and have read it again (indeed I could hardly be said to have read it before) with attention and with pleasure. Your second edition is so rapid in its progress, that it will now hardly answer any purpose to tell you either my own objections, or those of other people. Certain it is, that you are universally read here; but what *we* think is not so easy to come at. We stay as usual to see the success, to learn the judgment of the town, to be directed in our opinions by those of more competent judges. If they like you, we shall; if any one of name write against you, we give you up; for we are modest and diffident of ourselves, and not without reason. History in particular is not our *forte;* for (the truth is) we read only modern books and pamphlets of the day. I have heard it objected, that you raise doubts and difficulties, and do not satisfy them by telling us what is really the case. I have heard you charged with disrespect to the King of Prussia; and above all to King William, and the Revolution. These are seriously the most sensible things I have heard said, and all that I recollect. If you please to justify yourself, you may.

My own objections are little more essential: they relate chiefly to inaccuracies of style, which either debase the expression or obscure the meaning. I could point out several small particulars of this kind, and will do so, if you think it can serve any purpose after publication. When I hear you read, they often escape me, partly because I am attending to the subject, and partly because from habit I understand you where a stranger might often be at a loss.

As to your arguments, most of the principal parts are made out with a clearness and evidence that no one would expect, where materials are so scarce. Yet I still suspect Richard of the murder of Henry VI. The chronicler of Croyland charges it full on him, though without a name or any mention of circumstances. The interests of Edward were the interests of Richard too, though the throne were not then in view; and that Henry still stood in their way, they might well imagine, because, though deposed and imprisoned once before, he had regained his liberty and his crown; and was still adored by the people. I should think, from the word *tyranni*, the passage was written after Richard had assumed the crown: but, if it was earlier, does not the bare imputation imply very early suspicions, at least of Richard's bloody nature, especially in the mouth of a person that was no enemy to the House of York, nor friend to that of Beaufort?

That the Duchess of Burgundy, to try the temper of the nation, should set up a false Pretender to the Throne (when she had the true Duke of York in her hands), and that the queen-mother (knowing her son was alive) should countenance that design, is a piece of policy utterly incomprehensible; being the most likely means to ruin their own scheme, and throw a just suspicion of fraud and falsehood on the cause of truth, which Henry could not fail to seize and turn to his advantage. Mr. Hume's first query, as far as relates to the queen-mother, will still have some weight. Is it probable she should give her eldest daughter to Henry, and invite him to claim the crown, unless she had been sure that her sons were then dead? As to her seeming consent to the match between Elizabeth and Richard, she and her daughters were in his power, which appeared now well fixed; his enemies' designs within the kingdom being everywhere defeated, and Henry unable to raise any considerable force abroad. She was timorous and hopeless; or she might dissemble, in order to cover her secret dealings with Richmond: and if this were the case, she hazarded little, supposing Richard to dissemble too, and never to have thought seriously of marrying his niece.

Another unaccountable thing is, that Richard, a prince of the House of York, undoubtedly brave, clear-sighted, artful, attentive to business; of boundless generosity, as appears from his grants; just and merciful, as his laws and his pardons seem to testify; having subdued the Queen and her hated faction, and been called first to the protectorship and then to the crown by the nobility and by the parliament; with the common people to friend (as Carte often asserts), and having nothing against him but the illegitimate family of his brother Edward, and the attainted House of Clarence (both of them within his power);— that such a man should see within a few months Buckingham, his best friend, and almost all the southern and western counties in one day in arms against him; that having seen all these insurrections come to nothing, he should march with a gallant army against a handful of needy adventurers, led by a fugitive, who had not the shadow of a title, nor any virtues to recommend him, nor any foreign strength to depend on; that he should be betrayed by almost all his troops, and fall a sacrifice; — all this is to me utterly improbable, and I do not ever expect to see it accounted for.

I take this opportunity to tell you, that Algarotti (as I see in the new edition of his works printed at Leghorn) being employed to buy pictures for the King of Poland, purchased among others the famous Holbein that was at Venice. It don't appear that he knew anything of your book: yet he calls it *the consul Meyer and his family*, as if it were then known to be so in that city. A young man here, who is a diligent reader of books, an antiquary, and a painter, informs me, that at the Red Lion Inn at Newmarket is a piece of tapestry containing the very design of your marriage of Henry the Sixth, only with several more figures in it, both men and women; that he would have bought it of the people, but they refused to part with it. Mr. Mason, who is here, desires to present his best respects to you.

He says, that to efface from our annals the history of any tyrant, is to do an essential injury to mankind: but he forgives it, because you have shewn Henry the Seventh to be a greater devil than Richard.

Pray do not be out of humour. When you first commenced an author, you exposed yourself to pit, boxes, and gallery. Any coxcomb in the world may come in and hiss if he pleases; ay, and (what is almost as bad) clap too, and you cannot hinder him. I saw a little squib fired at you in a newspaper by some of the *House of Yorke*, for speaking lightly of chancellors. Adieu! I am ever yours,

T. GRAY.

[*From Cambridge, February 25, 1768*]

... I have looked into Speed and Leslie. It appears very odd that Speed in the speech he makes for P. Warbeck, addressed to James IV. of Scotland, should three times cite the *manuscript proclamation* of Perkin, then in the hands of Sir Robert Cotton; and yet when he gives us the proclamation afterwards (on occasion of the insurrection in Cornwall) he does not cite any such manuscript. In Casley's *Catalogue of the Cotton Library* you may see whether this manuscript proclamation still exists or not: if it does, it may be found at the Museum. Leslie will give you no satisfaction at all: though no subject of England, he could not write freely on this matter, as the title of Mary (his mistress) to the crown of England was derived from that of Henry VII. Accordingly he everywhere treats Perkin as an impostor; yet drops several little expressions inconsistent with that supposition. He has preserved no proclamation: he only puts a short speech into Perkin's mouth, the substance of which is taken by Speed, and translated in the end of his, which is a good deal longer: the whole matter is treated by Leslie very concisely and superficially. I can easily transcribe it, if you please; but I do not see that it could answer any purpose.

Mr. Boswell's book I was going to recommend to you, when I received your letter; it has pleased and moved me strangely, all (I mean) that relates to Paoli. He is a man born two thousand years after his time! The pamphlet proves what I have always maintained, that any fool may write a most valuable book by chance, if he will only tell us what he heard and saw with veracity. Of Mr. Boswell's truth I have not the least suspicion, because I am sure he could invent nothing of this kind. The true title of this part of his work is, a Dialogue between a Green-Goose and a Hero. . . .

Pembroke Hall, March 6, 1768.

Here is Sir William Cornwallis, entitled *Essayes of certaine Paradoxes*. 2d Edit. 1617. Lond.

> King Richard III.
> The French Pockes.
> Nothing.
> Good to be in debt. ⎫ Praised.
> Sadnesse.
> Julian the Apostate's virtues.

The title-page will probably suffice you; but if you would know any more of him, he has read nothing but the common chronicles, and those without attention; for example, speaking of Anne the queen, he says, she was barren, of which Richard had often complained to Rotheram. He extenuates the murder of Henry VI. and his son: the first, he says, might be a malicious insinuation, for that many did suppose he died of mere melancholy and grief: the latter cannot be proved to be the action of Richard (though executed in his presence); and if it were, he did it out of love to his brother Edward. He justifies the death of the Lords at Pomfret, from reasons of state, for his own preservation, the safety of the commonwealth, and the ancient nobility. The execution of Hastings he excuses from necessity, from the dishonesty and sensuality of the man:

what was his crime with respect to Richard, he does not say. Dr. Shaw's Sermon was not by the King's command, but to be imputed to the preacher's own ambition: but if it was by order, *to charge his mother with adultery was a matter of no such great moment, since it is no wonder in that sex.* Of the murder in the Tower he doubts: but if it were by his order, the offence was to God, not to his people; and *how could he demonstrate his love more amply, than to venture his soul for their quiet?* Have you enough, pray? You see it is an idle declamation, the exercise of a school-boy that is to be bred a statesman.

I have looked in Stowe; to be sure there is no proclamation there. Mr. Hume, I suppose, means *Speed*, where it is given, how truly I know not; but that he had seen the original is sure, and seems to quote the very words of it in the beginning of that speech which Perkin makes to James IV. and also just afterwards, where he treats of the Cornish rebellion. Guthrie, you see, has vented himself in the *Critical Review*. His *History* I never saw, nor is it here, nor do I know any one that ever saw it. He is a rascal, but rascals may chance to meet with curious records; and that commission to Sir I. Tyrrell (if it be not a lie) is such; so is the order for Henry the Sixth's funeral. I would by no means take notice of him, write what he would. I am glad you have seen the Manchester Roll.

It is not I that talk of *Phil. de Comines.* It was mentioned to me as a thing that looked like a voluntary omission, but I see you have taken notice of it, in the note to p. 71, though rather too slightly. You have not observed that the same writer says, c. 55, *Richard tua de sa main ou fit tuer en sa presence, quelque lieu apart, ce bon homme le Roi Henry.* Another oversight I think there is at p. 43, where you speak of the *Roll of Parliament,* and the contract with Lady Eleanor Botelar, as things newly come to light. Whereas Speed has given at large the same Roll in his *History.* Adieu! — I am ever yours,

T. GRAY.

THE CHARACTER OF A PHILOSOPHER

[*To Charles von Bonstetten*]

Cambridge, April 12, 1770.

Never did I feel, my dear Bonstetten, to what a tedious length the few short moments of our life may be extended by impatience and expectation, till you had left me; nor ever knew before with so strong a conviction how much this frail body sympathizes with the inquietude of the mind. I am grown old in the compass of less than three weeks, like the Sultan in the Turkish tales, that did but plunge his head into a vessel of water and take it out again, as the standers by affirmed, at the command of a Dervise, and found he had passed many years in captivity, and begot a large family of children. The strength and spirits that now enable me to write to you, are only owing to your last letter a temporary gleam of sunshine. Heaven knows when it may shine again! I did not conceive till now, I own, what it was to lose you, nor felt the solitude and insipidity of my own condition before I possessed the happiness of your friendship. I must cite another Greek writer to you, because it is much to my purpose: he is describing the character of a genius truly inclined to philosophy. " It includes," he says, " qualifications rarely united in one single mind, quickness of apprehension and a retentive memory, vivacity and application, gentleness and magnanimity; to these he adds an invincible love of truth, and consequently of probity and justice. Such a soul," continues he, " will be little inclined to sensual pleasures, and consequently temperate; a stranger to illiberality and avarice; being accustomed to the most extensive views of things, and sublimest contemplations, it will contract an habitual greatness, will look down with a kind of disregard on human life and on death; consequently, will possess the truest fortitude. Such," says he, " is the mind born to govern the rest of mankind." But these very endowments, so necessary to a soul formed for philosophy, are often its ruin, especially when joined to the external advantages of wealth, nobility, strength, and beauty; that is, if it light on a bad soil, and want its proper nurture, which nothing but an excellent education can bestow. In this case he is depraved by the public example, the assemblies of the people, the courts of justice, the theatres, that inspire it with false opinions, terrify it with false infamy, or elevate it with false applause; and remember, that extraordinary vices and extraordinary virtues are equally the produce of a vigorous mind: little souls are alike incapable of the one and the other.

If you have ever met with the portrait sketched out by Plato, you will know it again: for my part, to my sorrow I have had that happiness. I see the principal features, and I foresee the dangers with a trembling anxiety. But enough of this, I return to your letter. It proves at least, that in the midst of your new gaieties I still hold some place in your memory, and, what pleases me above all, it has an air of undissembled sincerity. Go on, my best and amiable friend, to shew me your heart simply and without the shadow of disguise, and leave me to weep over it, as I now do, no matter whether from joy or sorrow.

ISOCRATES

[*To Norton Nicholls, from Cambridge, April 14, 1770*]

. . . It would be strange if I should blame you for reading Isocrates: I did so myself twenty years ago, and in an edition at least as bad as yours. *The Panegyrick*, *The De Pace*, *Areopagitica*, and *Advice to Philip*, are by far the noblest remains we have of this writer, and equal to most things extant in the Greek tongue: but it depends on your judgment to distinguish between his real and occasional opinion of things, as he directly contradicts in one place what he has advanced in another; for example, in the *Panathenaic* and the *De Pace*, &c., on the naval power of Athens: the latter of the two is undoubtedly his own undisguised sentiment. . . .

THE MINSTREL

[*To James Beattie*]

Pembroke Hall, July 2, 1770.

I rejoice to hear that you are restored to a better state of health, to your books, and to your muse once again. That forced dissipation and exercise we are obliged to fly to as a remedy, when this frail machine goes wrong, is often almost as bad as the distemper we would cure; yet I too have been constrained of late to pursue a like regimen, on account of certain pains in the head (a sensation unknown to me before), and of great dejection of spirits. This, Sir, is the only excuse I have to make you for my long silence, and not (as perhaps you may have figured to yourself) any secret reluctance I had to tell you my mind concerning the specimen you so kindly sent me of your new Poem. On the contrary, if I had seen anything of importance to disapprove, I should have hastened to inform you, and never doubted of being forgiven. The truth is, I greatly like all I have seen, and wish to see more. The design is simple, and pregnant with poetical ideas of various kinds, yet seems somehow imperfect at the end. Why may not young Edwin, when necessity has driven him to take up the harp, and assume the profession of a Minstrel, do some great and singular service to his country? (what service I must leave to your invention) such as no General, no Statesman, no Moralist could do without the aid of music, inspiration, and poetry. This will not appear an improbability in those early times, and in a character then held sacred, and respected by all nations. Besides, it will be a full answer to all the Hermit has said, when he dissuaded him from cultivating these pleasing arts; it will shew their use, and make the best panegyric of our favourite and celestial science. And lastly (what weighs most with me), it will throw more of action, pathos, and interest into your design, which already abounds in reflection and sentiment. As to description, I have always thought that it made the most graceful ornament of poetry, but never ought to make the subject. Your ideas are new, and borrowed from a mountainous country, the only one that can furnish truly picturesque scenery. Some trifles in the language or versification you will permit me to remark. . . .

I will not enter at present into the merits of your *Essay on Truth*, because I have not yet given it all the attention it deserves, though I have read it through with pleasure; besides I am partial, for I have always thought David Hume a pernicious writer, and believe he has done as much mischief here as he has in his own country. A turbid and shallow stream often appears to our apprehensions very deep. A professed sceptic can be guided by nothing but his present passions (if he has any) and interests; and to be masters of his philosophy we need not his books or advice, for every child is capable of the same thing, without any study at all. Is not that *naiveté* and good humour, which his admirers celebrate in him, owing to this, that he has continued all his days an infant, but one that has unhappily been taught to read and write? That childish nation, the French, have given him vogue and fashion, and we, as usual, have learned from them to admire him at second hand.

FROISSART, ETC.

[To Norton Nicholls, from Cambridge, January 26, 1771]

. . . I rejoice you have met with Froissart: he is the Herodotus of a barbarous age: had he but had the luck of writing in as good a language, he might have been immortal! His locomotive disposition (for then there was no other way of learning things), his simple curiosity, his religious credulity, were much like those of the old Grecian. Our ancestors used to read the *Mort d' Arthur*, *Amadis de Gaul*, and Froissart, all alike, that is, they no more suspected the good faith of the former than they did of the latter, but took it all for history. When you have tant chevauché as to get to the end of him, there is Monstrelet waits to take you up, and will set you down at

Philip de Comines; but previous to all these, you should have read Villehardouin and Joinville. I do not think myself bound to defend the character of even the best of kings. Pray slash them, and spare not. . . .

THE MINSTREL

[To James Beattie]

Cambridge, March 8, 1771.

The Minstrel came safe to my hands, and I return you my sincere thanks for so acceptable a present. In return, I shall give you my undisguised opinion of him, as he proceeds, without considering to whom he owes his birth, and sometimes without specifying my reasons; either because they would lead me too far, or because I may not always know what they are myself.

I think we should wholly adopt the language of Spenser's time or wholly renounce it. You say, you have done the latter; but, in effect, you retain *fared, forth, meed, wight, ween, gaude, shene, in sooth, aye, eschew*, &c.; obsolete words, at least in these parts of the island, and only known to those that read our ancient authors, or such as imitate them.

St. 2, v. 5. The *obstreperous* trump of fame

hurts my ear, though meant to express a jarring sound.

St. 3, v. 6. *And from his bending*, &c., the grammar seems deficient; yet as the mind easily fills up the ellipsis, perhaps it is an atticism, and not inelegant.

St. 4, and ult. *Pensions, posts, and praise.* I cannot reconcile myself to this, nor to the whole following stanza; especially *the plaister of thy hair*.

Surely the female heart, &c., St. 6. The thought is not just. We cannot justify the sex from the conduct of the Muses, who are only females by the help of Greek mythology; and then, again, how should they bow the knee in the fane of a Hebrew or Philistine devil? Besides, I am the more severe, because it serves to introduce what I most admire.

St. 7. *Rise, sons of harmony*, &c. This is charming; the thought and the expression. I will not be so hypercritical as to add, but it is *lyrical*, and therefore belongs to a different species of poetry. Rules are but chains, good for little, except when one can break through them; and what is fine gives me so much pleasure, that I never regard what place it is in.

St. 8, 9, 10. All this thought is well and freely handled, particularly, *Here peaceful are the vales*, &c. *Know thine own worth*, &c. *Canst thou forego*, &c.

St. 11. *O, how canst thou renounce*, &c. But this, of all others, is my favourite stanza. It is true poetry; it is inspiration; only (to shew it is mortal) there is one blemish; the word *garniture* suggesting an idea of dress, and, what is worse, of French dress.

St. 12. Very well. *Prompting th' ungenerous wish*, &c. But do not say *rambling muse*; *wandering*, or *devious*, if you please.

St. 13. *A nation fam'd*, &c. I like this compliment to your country; the simplicity, too, of the following narrative; only in st. 17 the words *artless* and *simple* are too synonymous to come so near each other.

St. 18. *And yet poor Edwin*, &c. This is all excellent, and comes very near the level of st. 11 in my esteem; only, perhaps, *And some believed him mad*, falls a little too flat, and rather below simplicity.

St. 21. *Ah, no!* By the way, this sort of interjection is rather too frequent with you, and will grow characteristic, if you do not avoid it.

In that part of the poem which you sent me before, you have altered several little particulars much for the better.

St. 34. I believe I took notice before of this

excess of alliteration. *Long, loaded, loud,* lament, *lonely,* lighted, *lingering, listening;* though the verses are otherwise very good, it looks like affectation.

St. 36, 37, 38. Sure you go too far in lengthening a stroke of Edwin's character and disposition into a direct narrative, as of a fact. In the meantime, the poem stands still, and the reader grows impatient. Do you not, in general, indulge a little too much in *description* and *reflection?* This is not my remark only, I have heard it observed by others; and I take notice of it here, because *these* are among the stanzas that might be spared; they are good, nevertheless, and might be laid by, and employed elsewhere to advantage.

St. 42. Spite of what I have just now said, this digression pleases me so well, that I cannot spare it.

St. 46, v. ult. The *infuriate* flood. I would not make new words without great necessity; it is very hazardous at best.

St. 49, 50, 51, 52. All this is very good; but *medium* and *incongruous*, being words of art, lose their dignity in my eyes, and savour too much of prose. I would have read the last line — " Presumptuous child of dust, be humble and be wise." But, on second thoughts, perhaps — "*For thou art but of dust"* — is better and more solemn, from its simplicity.

St. 53. *Where dark*, &c. You return again to the charge. Had you not said enough before?

St. 54. *Nor was this ancient dame*, &c. Consider, she has not been mentioned for these six stanzas backward.

St. 56, v. 5. *The vernal day*. With us it rarely thunders in the spring, but in the summer frequently.

St. 57, 58. Very pleasing, and has much the rhythm and expression of Milton in his youth. The last four lines strike me less by far.

St. 59. The first five lines charming. Might not the mind of your conqueror be checked and softened in the mid-career of his successes by some domestic misfortune (introduced by way of episode, interesting and new, but not too long), that Edwin's music and its triumphs may be a little prepared, and more consistent with probability?

I am happy to hear of your successes in another way, because I think you are serving the cause of human nature, and the true interest of mankind. Your book is read here too, and with just applause.

Notes

Phædo

3, 2. Panætius the stoick: a philosopher of Rhodes (*c.* B.C. 180 — *c.* B.C. III). At Rome, where he lived between 156 and 129, he did much to refine and polish the Stoic teaching.

4, 3. ἀήθη, etc.: "a certain marvelous mixture of pleasure and of pain." *Phædo*, 59 a.

5, 24. Ἐν βιῷ, etc.: "in life is the beginning of death"; the second clause repeats the thought.

5, 28. Τὰ μέν, etc.: "some things I have said of which I am not altogether confident." Trans. Jowett.

6, 8. Dacier: André Dacier (1651–1722), an industrious classical scholar, translator of Horace, Longinus, some of Plato's *Dialogues*, and Plutarch's *Lives*. He entered the French Academy in 1695. Cf. Asse in *La Grande Encyclopédie*. "Dacier has been forced to prove his Plato a very good Christian, before he ventures *to translate him*, and has so far complied with the taste of the age, that his whole book is overrun with texts of Scripture, and the notion of pre-existence supposed to be stolen from two verses *out of the Prophets*." Addison to Charles Montagu, from Paris, Oct. 14, 1699.

Essay on the Philosophy of Lord Bolingbroke

7, 1. Lord Bolingbroke: Henry St. John, Viscount Bolingbroke (1678–1751), was a statesman, orator, and voluminous author. For some years he lived in France, and his thought, that of a pronounced Deist, may have been influenced by Voltaire. He has been censured for a lack of sincerity and honest purpose and for an unscrupulous ambition. His philosophical views can scarcely be called profound.

8, 13. Dr. Clarke: Samuel Clarke (1675–1729), theological writer and controversialist, rector of St. James's, Westminster, and Boyle Lecturer in 1704–5. "His work," says Stephen (*D. N. B.*, x. 443), "is the principal literary result of the speculative movement of which the contemporary English deism was one result.... He was the founder of the so-called 'intellectual' school, of which Wollaston and Price were the chief English followers, which deduced the moral law from a logical necessity."

8, 13. Evid. 26th: this corresponds, apparently, to Proposition VIII. of *A Discourse Concerning the Being and Attributes of God* (*Works*, London, 1738, ii. 543): "That the Self-Existent and Original Cause of all things, must be an Intelligent Being."

10, 24. Mr. Wollaston: William Wollaston (1660–1724), of Sidney-Sussex College, Cambridge (M.A. 1681), who, inheriting a cousin's "noble estate," settled in London in 1689 and never afterward passed a night out of his house. He wrote much on philological and ecclesiastical subjects. *The Religion of Nature Delineated*, his most important work, was privately printed in 1722 and published in 1724; it went through many editions. "Thirty years' profound meditation," says Leslie Stephen, "had convinced Wollaston that the reason why a man should abstain from breaking his wife's head was, that it was a way of denying that she was his wife.... It is a repetition of Clarke's theory of morality." *English Thought in the Eighteenth Century*, i. 130.

11, 22. immovable: G. immoveable.

ESSAY ON NORMAN ARCHITECTURE

13, 1. characteristics: G., like others of his time, spelled this and most other *-ic* words with *k*: *-ick(s)*; so *ethick, topick, Sapphick, politicks*. **Norman**: the earliest instance of the word in this sense in the *New Eng. Dictionary* is dated 1797, in the *Encycl. Brit.*, 3d ed. The style is now, of course, known as the Romanesque, sometimes as the Round-arched Gothic. Cf. Sturgis, *European Architecture*, p. 235, n.

13, 2. Sir Christopher Wren: lived 1632–1723. Besides St. Paul's he designed about fifty churches in London, the Sheldonian Theatre at Oxford, the Greenwich Observatory, the Chelsea Hospital, the Library of Trinity College, Cambridge, the

College of Physicians in Warwick Lane, London, the Chapel of Queen's College, Oxford, etc. His later works show an increasing appreciation of Gothic; but he lived before the days of exact historical knowledge of architecture. **Saxon**: more properly applied to the style in vogue in England before the Conquest. For the characteristics of Saxon architecture proper, see *Encycl. Brit.*, 9th ed., ii. 425.

13, 9. emperors: G. emperours.

13, 22. Normans: settled in France early in the tenth century; acquired Normandy about 911.

14, 15. this kind of architecture: Rickman (*An Attempt to Discriminate the Styles of Architecture in England*, 1817) classified as follows: Anglo-Saxon, to 1066; Norman, 1066–1189; Early English, 1189–1307.

15, 3. aisles: G. here and elsewhere, ailes.

16, 26. old St. Paul's: burnt in the great fire of 1666; rebuilt by Sir Christopher Wren 1675–1710.

19, 1. nebule: the earliest instance of this word in the *New Eng. Dict.* is quoted from Nicholson's *Practical Builder*, 1823. Gray may possibly have coined the word, and does not (cf. *N. E. D.*) misapprehend the meaning of *nebulé*.

19, 26. King Ethelbald: king of the Mercians, d. 757. Visited his kinsman the hermit Guthlac at Crowland. Though of immoral life, he gave much to the Church.

19, 27. King Osric: Gray has apparently here made a slip. He is thinking of the shrine of Osric, king of the Northumbrians (d. 729), erected at Gloucester (on the north side of the presbytery) by Abbot Malvern in the time of Henry VIII. Osric is said to have founded the first religious establishment here. Cf. H. J. Massé, *The Cathedral Church of Gloucester*, London, 1900, pp. 59 f.; J. Britton, *The History and Antiquities of the Abbey, and Cathedral Church of Gloucester*, London, 1836, p. 66. **Robert Courthose**: Duke of Normandy (1054–1134), eldest son of the Conqueror. Called Curthose on account of his short, fat figure. The chest, of the fifteenth century, is of Irish bog-wood; the figure may be of the 12th. The effigy was demolished by the Puritans in 1641, but the pieces were kept by Sir Humphrey Tracy of Stanway and after the Restoration replaced at his expense.

20, 10. five and thirty years: the choir and transepts, as well as the three stages of the central tower and the six central bays of the nave except the clerestory, were probably finished 1155–75. The clerestory of the nave, the west bays of the nave, and the west front were probably built 1177–93. Cf. Bond, *Gothic Architecture in England*, p. 651.

20, 13. surpassed in beauty: G., it thus appears, was one of the earliest admirers of Gothic. On the use of "Gothic" for what was crude and barbaric, cf. G. Lüdtke, *Geschichte des Wortes "Gothisch" im 18. und 19. Jahrhundert*, Strassburg, 1903; *New Eng. Dict.*, s. v. *Gothic*; C. H. Moore, *Development and Character of Gothic Architecture*, 2d ed., 1899, chap. i.

21. Pp. 21–117 have been grouped in previous editions under the head of METRUM, with the following quotation (in Greek) from Longinus' *Fragmenta*, 3, sect. 1, e Cod. Ms. Paris [2881]: "Whether the doctrine of metres is new, or an invention of the ancient Muse, in either case it will be held good. For if it is ancient, it will be venerable for its age; and if it is modern, it will be the more agreeable."

OBSERVATIONS ON ENGLISH METRE

21, 1. Mr. Urry: John Urry (1666–1715), of Christ Church, Oxford, in 1711 began work upon an edition which was published in 1721. As a scholar Urry was much overrated. Cf. Miss Hammond's *Bibliogr. Manual* of Chaucer, pp. 128 ff.; Lounsbury, *Studies in Chaucer*, i. 283 ff.

21, 11. great inequalities: cf. Gray's note on Lydgate's metre, p. 94, n. 1.

21, 25. Francesco [da] Barberino: lived 1264–1348; wrote, among other things, *Il reggimento e costumi di donna* and *I documenti d'Amore*, a moral encyclopedia. **Boccaccio**: G. here and elsewhere, Boccacio.

21, 26. Crescimbeni: Giovan-Maria Crescimbeni (1663–1728) became a well-known Roman poet and savant; wrote several works on literary history. His *Commentarii intorno alla volgar poesia storia*, much used by Gray, appeared at Rome in 1702–11 in 5 volumes, quarto.

22, 2. always prefixed: usually, but not always; cf. Sievers, *O. E. Grammar*, trans. Cook, 3d ed., sec. 366, and Wright, *O. E. Grammar*, sec. 488.

22, 8. Dr. Hickes: George Hickes (1642–1715), titular bishop of Thetford, published his *Anglo-Saxon and Mœso-Gothic Grammar* at Oxford in 1689. A 2d ed. formed part of his celebrated *Linguarum veterum septentrionalium thesaurus grammatico-criticus et archæologicus*, Oxford, 1703–5, folio.

22, 16. Somner's: William Somner (1598–1669), linguist and antiquarian, published his *Dictionarium Saxonico-Latino-Anglicum* at Oxford in 1659, 2 parts, folio; 2d ed., with additions by Thomas Benson, 1701, 8vo.

22, 18. towards the end: *T. and C.*, v. 1793–9.

22, 25. in another place: *House of Fame*, 1096–8.

22, 33. Chronicle of Troy: Dr. Henry Bergen is printing an edition of the *Troy-Book* (E. E. T. S., Extra Series xcvii, ciii, etc.).

23, 9. Cimbrick tongue: Cymric properly, of course, means "Welsh"; in Gray's time there was much confusion between Scandinavian and Celtic. Cf. p. 239. See also Farley, *Scandinavian Influence in the English Romantic Movement*, pp. 202 f.

23, 11. greipan: O. E. *grīpan*, Old Saxon *grīpan*, Gothic *greipan*.

24, 14. wordis: Northern dialect form of O. E. *wordes*.

25, 21. Art of Poetry: published anonymously in 1589, by Richard Field, "dwelling in the black-Friers, neere Ludgate."

25, 23. "Chaucer, Lydgate," etc.: a collation with Arber's reprint shows only slight variants: 23, these *Cesures*; 24, seldome; 27, wordes; **26**, 2, maner; 11, poesie; **27**, 2, should be touched.

25, 26. riding Rhyme: G. Ryme. "This term was applied to '10-syllable couplets' like those of Chaucer's Canterbury Pilgrims, as distinguished from statelier quatrains and stanzas. For long such couplets were considered unfit for serious themes — an idea in Gray's time hardly comprehensible, though he himself wisely preferred quatrains for his famous *Elegy*." T. S. Omond, *English Metrists in the 18th and 19th Centuries*, 1907, p. 20, n. 1.

26, 11. Ryme Dogrell: the obvious connection with *dog*

in the sense of "bastard, dog-rhyme" is suggested by the *New Eng. Dict.*; but the origin of the word is still to be traced.

26, 12. Alderman Fabian: Robert Fabyan (d. 1513); his *Concordance of Histories*, published by Pynson in 1516 as *The New Chronicles of England and France*, began with the arrival of Brutus and extended to his own day. Only a little of it is in verse.

27, 3. Then Puttenham: this quotation really occurs about a page farther back in the same chapter.

27, 5. in the middle: inexactly quoted. Arber: In a verse of twelve sillables the *Cesure* ought to fall right upon the sixt syllable.

27, 24. of pleasure: here Gray omits five and a half lines of Puttenham; cf. Arber, p. 86.

31, 14. Spenser: on his use of the cæsura cf. Schipper, *Engl. Metrik*, 1888, ii. 188 f., 202.

31, 15. Milton: cf. W. Thomas, *De epico apud Joannem Miltonium versu*, Lutetiæ Parisiorum, 1901, pp. 64–71; Schipper, *op. cit.*, ii. 28 ff., 344 ff.; Corson, *A Primer of English Verse*, 1892, pp. 193 ff.; Robert Bridges, *Milton's Prosody*, 2d ed., Oxford, 1893, pp. 23 ff.

32, 1. A monke ther was: Ellesmere Ms., A monk ther was, a fair for the maistrie. *Prol.*, 165.

32, 4. many a: Ellesmere Ms., fful many a.

33, 5. No more of this: *C. T.*, B 2109–12.

34, 8. Bevis: ed. by Kölbing, E. E. T. S., Extra Series, 1885–94. Cf. M. Deutschbein, *Studien zur Sagengeschichte Englands*, i., Halle, 1906, pp. 181–213. **Southampton**: after this Puttenham adds: Guy of Warwicke.

34, 32. the same story: cf. Leo Jordan, *Über Boeve de Hanstone*, Halle, 1908.

35, 1. and historical: Arber's ed., or.

35, 2. on purpose: Arber's ed., purposely for recreation.

35, 4. bride-ales: after this Arber's ed. has and.

The Measures of Verse

39, 17. The Death of Zoroas: by Nicholas Grimald; Arber reprint, pp. 120–3.

39, 19. The Death of Cicero: also by Grimald; Arber repr., pp. 123–5.

40, 12. Man of Honour: now called the Man of Law.

40, 17. Flower and Leaf: ascribed by Skeat (*Athen.*, March 14, 1903, p. 340) to Margaret Neville, daughter of the Earl of Warwick; others have opposed this view. Cf. Miss Hammond, *Chaucer, a Bibliogr. Manual*, pp. 423 f.

40, 17. Assembly of Ladies: determined by internal evidence to be by the author of *The Flower and the Leaf*; cf. Skeat, *Chaucerian and Other Pieces*, 1897, pp. lxii ff.; Miss Hammond, *op. cit.*, pp. 408 f.

40, 18. Complaint of the Black Knight: by John Lydgate.

40, 19. Lamentation of Magdalen: ed. by Bertha M. Skeat as a Zürich diss., Cambridge, 1897. She thinks the author was a young lady, probably a nun.

To this list add Chaucer's *Compleynte unto Pite* and the introduction to his *Compleynt of Mars*.

41, 4. Remedy of Love: formerly printed with Chaucer's works; rejected from the Chaucer canon by Tyrwhitt. Cf. Skeat, *The Chaucer Canon*, p. 113.

41, 8. Epistle to Henry the 4th: often called *The Praise of Peace*.

41, 11. Ballade of our Lady: in MacCracken's list (*The Lydgate Canon*, p. x) entitled *Ballade at the Reverence of Our Lady Qwene of Mercy*; cf. Skeat, *Chaucerian and Other Pieces*, pp. xlvi f.

41, 15. Ballades, &c.: including the *Ballad of Good Counsel* or *Wicked Tongue* (*Chaucerian and Other Pieces*, pp. 285–90), and *Warning Men to Beware of Deceitful Women* (*ib.*, pp. 295 f.), the Lydgatian authorship of which MacCracken rejects. **Assemblé de Dyeus:** *The Assembly of Gods*, ed. by Oscar L. Triggs, *Univ. of Chicago English Studies*, i., 1895. Assigned by Wynkyn de Worde and others to Lydgate. MacCracken rejects Lydgatian authorship, *The Lydgate Canon*, pp. xxxii f.

Gray does not know, for example, of Lydgate's *Horse, Goose, and Sheep* (ed. M. Degenhart, Erlangen, 1900); *Fabula duorum mercatorum* (ed. G. Schleich, Strassburg, 1897); *The Flour of*

Curtesye (*Chaucerian and Other Pieces*, pp. 266–74). Another poem, *To My Soverain Lady* (*ib.*, pp. 281–84), assigned to Lydgate by Skeat, is rejected from the Lydgate canon by MacCracken, p. xlv.

42, 5. To these might be added Henryson's *Testament of Cresseid* (*Chaucerian and Other Pieces*, pp. 327–46), and *The Court of Love* (*ib.*, pp. 409–47).

42, 8. Hymn on the Nativity: the part properly known as the Hymn is not in this metre.

42, 13. in some Envoys: now, I believe, no longer ascribed to Chaucer.

42, 23. Belle Dame sans mercy: trans. from the French by Sir Richard Ros (*Chaucerian and Other Pieces*, pp. 299–326). The first five and the last four stanzas have seven lines each.

42, 25. Add Chaucer's *Former Age*, *Fortune*, *Ballade to Rosemounde*, etc.

43, 3. Some Poems of Chaucer: Gray probably alludes to Hoccleve's *To the Knights of the Garter* (*Chaucerian and Other Pieces*, pp. 233–35), and Scogan's *Moral Balade* (*ib.*, pp. 237–44).

43, 17. Add Chaucer's *Compleynt of Mars*, main part.

44, 8. Cuckoo and Nightingale: probably by Sir Thomas Clanvowe; cf. Miss Hammond's *Chaucer Manual*, pp. 420 f.

47, 11. Chaucer's *Compleynt unto His Lady*, ten lines, aabaabcddc, is not provided for in Gray's scheme.

49, 16. Story of Thebes: in heroic couplets.

49, 19. Romaunce of Merlin: ed. as *Arthour and Merlin* by E. Kölbing, Leipzig, 1890.

49, 20. Welsh: G. here and elsewhere, Welch.

49, 25. wherein he mentions: ll. 85–89. Manning's trans. was ed. by Furnivall in the Rolls Series, No. 87, London, 1887. **different kinds of verse:** on the varieties of rhyme see Schipper, "Fremde Metra," Paul's *Grundriss der germ. Philologie*, 2. Aufl., ii. 224 f.

50, 11. Plowman's Tale: no longer ascribed to Chaucer; cf. Miss Hammond, *Chaucer Manual*, pp. 444 ff.

50, 17. Add Lydgate's *Doubleness* (*Chaucerian and Other Pieces*, pp. 291–94).

50, 26. Couwe: in Manning ryme couwee, "tailed rhyme." Though his etymology is wrong, Gray is right about *Sir Thopas*. There is no connection with *cywydd*; cf. D. S. Evans's *Dictionary*, 1893.

53, 7. The Life of St. Margaret: printed by Hickes, *Thesaurus*, i. 224 ff., from a ms. (since lost) in Trinity College, Cambridge; reprinted by Horstmann, *Ae. Legenden*, N. F., 1881, pp. 489 ff. Dates from the first half of the 13th century. Gray quotes some lines (1–8) on pp. 62 f.

53, 10. Chronicle of Robert of Gloucester: really combines alexandrines with septenaries in what Gascoigne called "poulter's measure"; cf. Gummere, *Handbook of Poetics*, p. 185. **Peter Langtoft's Chronicle:** Manning's translation is in octosyllabic couplets; cf. Oskar Boerner, *Die Sprache Roberd Mannyngs of Brunne*, Halle, 1904, pp. 15 ff.

53, 12. took its name: the origin is still obscure; cf. the *New. Eng. Dict.*

53, 16. Lambert li Cors: should be li Tors, *i. e.*, le Tort. Wrote toward 1170; cf. P. Meyer, *Alexandre le Grand dans la littérature française du moyen age*, Paris, 1886, ii. 214 ff. The *Roman* was edited by Heinrich Michelant (Stuttgart, 1846) **Alexandre de Paris:** Alexandre de Bernay.

53, 24. trest: a better reading is *traist*.

54, 16. Tale of Gamelin: no longer ascribed to Chaucer.

54, 29. thus is written: cf. the note to 53, 10, above.

54, 33. Semi-Saxon moral poem: the *Poema Morale*, which dates from about 1170. Gray obviously meant "*before* Chaucer's time." See p. 63.

55, 23. Gill Morrice: *Childe Maurice*, in Child's *Ballads*, ii. 263. **Glasgerion:** in Child's *Ballads*, ii. 136 ff. **Launcelot du Lake:** in Percy's *Reliques of Antient English Poetry*. An early poem of the same name, in heroic couplets, was ed. by Skeat for the E. E. T. S., No. 6, 1865.

OBSERVATIONS ON THE PSEUDO-RHYTHMUS

57. Pseudo-rhythmus: rhyme.

57, 2. has observed: in his essay *Of Poetry*; *Works*, 1814, iii. 425 f.

57, 8. Taliessin: now regarded as mythical, cf. **61, 10**; formerly reputed to be the author of 77 poems; cf. Skene, *Four Ancient Books of Wales*; *Dict. Nat. Biog.* **Benbeirdh:** properly Benbeirdd, an epithet meaning "chief of bards." The only poets to whom it was applied were Aneurin and Taliesin (cf. T. Stephens, *Literature of the Cymry*, 1849, p. 124). Possibly Gray wrote "Taliesin ben beirdh"; if not, we must understand the second poet of his trio to be Aneurin. For this information I am indebted to H. I. B., *Notes and Queries*, 10th Ser., xi. 236.

57, 9. Lomarkk: Llywarch Hen, "the Aged" (*c.* 496–*c.* 646); cf. Skene, *Four Anc. Books*, i. 569 ff.; *Dict. Nat. Biog.*

57, 11. the Anglo-Saxons: on rhyme in O. E. literature cf. Kluge, "Zur Geschichte des Reimes im Altgermanischen," Paul-Braune, *Beiträge*, ix. 422-50, 1884; O. Hoffmann, *Reimformeln im Westgermanischen*, 1886, pp. 73 ff.

58, 1. any rhyming verses: Gray had of course never seen the O. E. *Rhyming Poem* in the Exeter Book, Grein-Wülker, *Bibliothek der ags. Poesie*, iii. 156–63; cf. Wülker, *Grundriss zur Geschichte der ags. Litteratur*, pp. 215 ff., Kluge in Paul-Braune, *Beiträge*, ix. 440–2, 1884, Ten Brink, *Early Eng. Literature*, trans. Kennedy, pp. 85 f. There are also apparently intentional rhymes in Cynewulf's *Elene*, ll. 114 f., 1237 ff., which dates from the eighth century.

58, 9. Wormius: Ole Worm (1588–1654), professor successively of pedagogy, Greek, physics, and medicine at Copenhagen (1613–54).

58, 15. sometimes strictly: the laws of O. E. metre are now much better understood: cf. Schipper, *Englische Metrik*; E. Sievers, "Altgermanische Metrik," Paul's *Grundriss der germ. Philologie*, 2. Aufl., ii. 1–38.

59, 2. fragment of Cædmon: Cædmon's *Hymn*, Grein-Wülker, *Bibl. der ags. Prosa*, iv. 484.

59, 5. Harmony of the Evangelists: Ms. Cotton Caligula A VII, fol. 11 r.—175 v. Now called *The Heliand*. Hickes printed some extracts in his *Anglo-Saxon and Mœso-Gothic Grammar*, p. 189, and in his *Grammatica Franco-Theotisca*, chap. 22. Dates from 822–40; cf. Paul, *Grundr.*, ii. 93 ff. Ed. by Sievers, 1878.

59, 12. Paraphrase of the Gospels: dedicated about 865 to King Louis the German and to Abp. Liutbert of Mentz. There are now many editions. On Otfrid's metre see Sievers, "Die Entstehung des deutschen Reimverses," Paul-Braune, *Beiträge*, xiii. 121–66, 1888.

60, 18. Franco-Theotische and Anglo-Saxon: not identical, but kindred dialects; cf. Paul's *Grundriss der germ. Philologie*, 2. Aufl., i. 651 f., 785 ff., 928, and the map opp. p. 780.

60, 31. no verses extant: the *Cantilena of St. Eulalia* dates from the end of the ninth century; cf. P. Toynbee, *Specimens of Old French*, pp. 2 ff.

60, 34. Wistace: now generally called Wace. His *Brut* was ed. by Le Roux de Lincy, 2 vols., Rouen, 1836–38. *Brut*, originally from the name of *Brutus*, the great-grandson of Aeneas, came to mean in Welsh a "chronicle, history."

60, 36. the Provençal writers: see Stimming, in Gröber's *Grundriss der romanischen Philologie*, 1897, ii. 2. 1 ff.

62, 2. Gothic: we should now say *Germanic* or *Teutonic*, reserving *Gothic* for the name of one dialect.

62, 27. eches: probably for *e ches* "he chose," O. E. *cēas*.

63, 9 ff. Ic am elder: *Poema Morale*, cf. the note on 54, 33.

63, 24. Rada: O. L. G. *rād*, O. E. *rǣd*.

65, 3. Vision of Peirce Plowman: edited by Skeat, E. E. T. S., 1867–84, and for the Clarendon Press, 1886. On the metre see K. Luick, "Geschichte der heimische Metra," Paul's *Grundriss*, 2. Aufl., ii. 145 ff.

65, 16. the oaths: sworn on Feb. 14, 842; see Brachet-Toynbee, *A Hist. Grammar of the French Language*, Oxford, 1896, pp. 16–17; Toynbee, *Specimens of Old French*, Oxford, 1892, pp. 1 f.

65, 27. The Provençal: see Darmesteter-Hartog, *A Historical French Grammar*, London, 1899, pp. 24 ff.

66, 1. Robert Langland: modern scholars until very recently have spoken of this author as William Langland. Professor Manly has lately (*Modern Philology*, iii. 359–366) combated the theory that *Piers the Plowman* was written by one man; cf. his articles in *The Cambridge History of English Literature*, ii. 1–41,

1908, and *Modern Philology*, vii. 83–144. His view is supported by Theophilus D. Hall in *Mod. Lang. Rev.*, iv. 1 ff. and *Modern Philology*, vii. 327 f. The older view is supported by Jusserand in *Modern Philology*, vi. 271–329, vii. 289–326. Cf. H. Bradley, *Athenæum*, Apr. 21, 1906, and R. W. Chambers, *Mod. Lang. Rev.*, v. 1–32.

66, 3. for instance: the lines quoted correspond to B. ii. 7–13.

66, 7. Worthylich: Mathias and the others print *Worthlyith*.

66, 25. altogether in meter: on Langland's metre see Skeat, ed. of 1886, ii. lviii ff.; F. Rosenthal, *Die alliterierende englische Langzeile im* xiv. *Jahrhundert*, Halle, 1877; Luick, "Die englische Stabreimzeile im xiv., xv., u. xvi. Jahrhundert," *Anglia*, xi. 429–43.

67, 7. Death and Life: this and *Scottish Field* are in the celebrated Percy Folio Ms. ed. by Hales and Furnivall in 1867–68.

67, 12. Thomas Piercy: 1728–82, bishop of Dromore, editor of the *Reliques of Antient English Poetry* and translator of Mallet's *Northern Antiquities*.

68, 6. P. Huet: Pierre-Daniel Huet (1630–1721), bishop of Avranches, member of the French Academy, well reputed as a mathematician, philosopher, theologian, philologist, and writer of Latin and Greek verse. He likewise ascribed the beginnings of romance to the Arabs.

71, 5. De Contemptu Mundi: contains about 3000 lines; translated by J. M. Neale, 1851–62.

71, 6, 14. Bernard: abbot of Cluny 1122–56. G. Benard.

71, 12. Leonine: the *New Eng. Dict.* conjectures that this is derived from some Leo (or Leonius) who wrote in the measure, and refers to Du Cange's attempt to identify him.

72, 9. Ubaldino the Florentine: cf. the quotation **64**, 18 ff.

SOME OBSERVATIONS ON THE USE OF RHYME

73, 3. Tenure of the manor of Cholmer and Dancing: printed in Thomas Blount's *Fragmenta antiquitatis, or Antient Tenures of Land*, new ed., York, 1784, pp. 328 ff. 22 lines.

73, 10. **Cholmer**: Blount has Chelmer. **Dancing**: now called Dengy.

73, 11. **Paperking**: Blount has Peperking.

74, 7. **Ancient Tenures, p. 102**: in the ed. of 1784, pp. 329 f. 21 lines.

74, 12. **about the age of Henry the Third**: Layamon's *Brut* is generally dated 1205. It contains 32,242 lines. Mss. Cotton Caligula A ix and Otho C xiii, British Museum. Ed. by Sir Frederick Madden for the Society of Antiquaries, London, 1847.

74, 17. **Lazamon**: the *z* stands for the pothook, roughly equivalent to *y*.

74, 24. **At Sifforde seten**: from *The Proverbs of Alfred*, ed. by W. W. Skeat, Oxford, 1907. Skeat dates the poem 1205–10. Gray read it, as he indicates, in the Spelman copy of Ms. Cotton Galba A xix.

74, 30. **near Oxford**: rather the Seaford near Newhaven, on the south coast of Sussex; cf. Skeat's note.

75, 28. **the same manuscript volume**: Cotton Caligula A ix. Of this, the *Brut* occupies fol. 3–194; *The Owl and the Nightingale*, fol. 233 r.–246 r.

75, 30. **"The Contention of the Owl and Nightingale"**: the latest edition is that of John E. Wells (Boston, 1907), who dates the poem 1216–25.

75, 31. **seven syllables**: rather eight or nine. The metre is octosyllabic, with or without a final unstressed syllable. Of the 1794 lines, from 195 to 200 lack the initial unstressed syllable.

76, 1. **snwe**: Ms. *supe*, i. e. *swipe*, "very."

76, 3. **I herde**: Ms. *iherde* from O. E. *gehēran*, "hear."

76, 7. **plait**: "debate." **stare**: Gray is right; it should be *starc*.

76, 11. **other agen other**: Ms. Cotton Calig. A ix has aiþer aȝen oþer.

76, 13. **whole mod**: Ms. Cott. wole; Ms. Jesus Coll. vuele, "evil."

76, 15. **cust**: "character."

76, 19. **hure and hure**: "at all events."

76, 23. **On Death, etc.**: this is the poem *Long Life* published from two mss. by Morris in his *Old English Miscellany*, pp. 156 ff.

76, 24. Non: Ms. Jesus Coll. 29 reads *mon* "man."

77, 4. biwench: *bipench* "bethink."

77, 26. told by Ekkehardus: in his *Libri de casibus monasterii Sancti Galli*, cap. 26. This was ed. by G. Meyer von Knonau, St. Gallen, 1877. The author is called Ekkehard IV. He died about 1060.

78, 18. Ethelbert, King of Kent: lived 552–616. His epitaph is:

> Rex Æthelbertus hic clauditur in poliandro;
> Fana pians certus Christo meat absque meandro.

Quoted by Thomas of Elmham, *Historia monasterii S. Augustini Cantuariensis*, ed. Hardwick, 1858, p. 142.

78, 20. Laurentius: d. 619. His epitaph:

> Hic sacra, Laurenti, sunt signa tui monumenti:
> Tu quoque jucundus pater, antistesque secundus,
> Pro populo Christi scapulas dorsumque dedisti;
> Artubus hinc laceris multa vibice mederis.

Quoted by Thomas of Elmham, *op. cit.*, p. 149.

78, 21. by Weever: John Weever (1576–1632) of Queen's College, Cambridge. His *Ancient Funerall Monuments* was published in London in 1631, folio.

ADDITIONAL OBSERVATIONS AND CONJECTURES ON RHYME

80, 10. from *Walen* : *Walen* is now derived from O.E. *wealh*- "foreigner," O.H.G. *walh*-, cf. Low Lat. *Volcæ*.

81, 21. Lewis Morris: lived 1700–65. His *Celtic Remains*, completed in 1760, was published in 1878 in connection with the *Archæologia Cambrensis*, ed. by Silvan Evans. See the *Dict. Nat. Biog.*, xxxix. 101 ff.

83, 16. no rhyme: cf. the note to 58, 1.

83, 19. from their neighbours the Britons: this view is now abandoned.

84, 9. Athelstan's donation: this so-called charter, which

Notes

dates apparently from the time of Edward II., is printed with a translation in the *Memorials of Beverley Minster*, ii. 280–7 (Surtees Society 108, Durham, 1903).

84, 11. granted to Earl Leofric: Gray apparently means *by*. In memory of the act by which Lady Godiva was said to have secured the freedom of Coventry (see Matthew of Westminster, an. 1057, and Tennyson's *Godiva*), pictures of Leofric and Godiva were set up in a south window of Trinity Church, Coventry, about the time of Richard II. The earl held in his right hand a charter on which was written,

> I Luriche for the love of thee
> Doe make Coventre tol-free.

Dugdale, *Monasticon Anglicanum*, iii. 177, n. k. Leofric was Earl of Mercia 1032–57; d. 1057.

85, 13. fragment of Cædmon: cf. 59, 2.

SOME REMARKS ON THE POEMS OF JOHN LYDGATE

87, 17. in 1393: for the evidence cf. Schick's ed. of *The Temple of Glas*, p. lxxxvii.

87, 21. Hatfield-Brodhook: now Hatfield-Broadoak, or Hatfield Regis.

89, 11. King Arthur was not dead: this idea survived even Gray's own time by at least a century. Cf. Sir J. Rhys, *Celtic Folklore, Welsh and Manx*, ii. 458–64. As late as 1800 Arthur was believed in Cornwall to be still living in the form of a chough; cf. Edgar MacCulloch in *Notes and Queries*, Dec. 24, 1853, 1st Ser., viii. 618.

90, 20. Dares Phrygius: a Trojan priest mentioned by Homer (*Iliad*, v. 9) who was said in the Middle Ages to have written a *Historia de excidio Troiae*, which, together with Dictys the Cretan's *Ephemeris belli Troiani*, forms the basis of medieval romances on the fall of Troy.

90, 27. Gowere: cf. Chaucer's dedication of *Troilus and Criseyde* (v. 1856 f.):

> O moral Gower, this book I directe
> To thee, and to the philosophical Strode.

324 Notes

Concerning Ralph Strode, the schoolman and poet, who flourished in the latter part of the fourteenth century, see Gollancz's article in the *Dict. Nat. Biog.* Gollancz's view that Strode wrote *The Pearl* has not found favor.

90, 30. Richard Hermite: Richard Rolle de Hampole (c. 1290–1349), the celebrated Yorkshire mystic. *The Prick of Conscience* (9624 lines) was edited by Morris for the Philological Society in 1863.

91, 15. from the original Latin: on this subject see Emil Koeppel's Munich dissertation, *Laurents de Premierfait und John Lydgates Bearbeitungen von Boccaccios De casibus virorum illustrium*, 1885, pp. 37–46. Koeppel concludes that Lydgate knew the Latin original, but made very little use of it. For a summary of the contents, see Morley, *English Writers*, vi. 110–14.

91, 16. Machabrées Daunce of Death: the *Dance of Death* was probably connected with the name of St. Macarius, the Egyptian anchorite, through his being represented as teaching the emptiness of life and the certainty of death to three youths out hunting; cf. Morley, *English Writers*, vi. 109.

92, 22. "long processes": some of Shakespeare's comic characters, *e. g.*, the Nurse in *Romeo and Juliet* (i. 3. 16–57), reflect this love of leisurely proceeding. Cf. also Edward Biscuit's account of the death of Sir Roger de Coverley, *The Spectator*, Oct. 23, 1712. Professor Raleigh (*The English Novel*, 1894, p. 4) speaks of "the ambling monotony of the chanted recitations concerning Sir Eglamour, Sir Perceval, and Sir Isumbras." Chaucer had his laugh at the dreariness of these stories in *Sir Thopas*.

93, 26. the father of circumstance: for a recent comprehensive criticism of Homer's style see Croiset-Heffelbower, *An Abridged History of Greek Literature*, 1904, pp. 30 ff., 45 ff.

96, 2. our ancient poets so voluminous: MacCracken (*The Lydgate Canon*, London Philological Soc'y, 1908, p. xxvii) concedes to Lydgate the authorship of 145,198 lines, mostly verse. Cf. Schick, Lydgate's *Temple of Glas*, 1891, p. clv. Of Chaucer's works there are extant about 55,150 lines.

98, 8. owe their first formation: this is true, of course, only of the literary speech.

98, 22. the nearest to him: Bale says of Lydgate, in his

Catalogus: "Omnium sui temporis in Anglia poetarum, absit inuidia dicto, facilè primus floruit." Quoted by Schick, Lydgate's *Temple of Glas,* p. xi, n. 1.

101, 29. **the fragment of Simonides**: the *Ode on Danae,* in his *De compositione verborum,* chap. 26.

105, 8. **upon the women**: cf. his *Troy-Book,* iii. 4270–4417.

106, 21. **fellows of colleges**: Gray here hits at the scandal-mongers of his own university.

110, 8. **more frequent in Chaucer**: cf. the portrait of the Monk in the Prologue.

111, 12. **cheerfulness**: G. chearfulness.

111, 29. **Doctor Machabrée**: an amusing mistake of Gray's time; cf. the note on 91, 6.

112, 24 ff. **Like a Midsomer Rose**: also printed by Halliwell-Phillipps, *The Minor Poems of Lydgate,* London, 1840, pp. 22–26, from Ms. Jesus Coll. 56, Cambridge. Cf. MacCracken, *The Lydgate Canon,* p. xix.

115, 1. **eight poets**: besides Sackville other contributors were William Baldwin, George Ferrers, Cavyll, Thomas Phaer, the translator of Virgil, John Skelton, Dolman, Thomas Churchyard, John Higgins, Thomas Blennerhasset, Michael Drayton, Richard Niccols, Francis Segar, and Dingley. Editions appeared in 1559 (ed. by Baldwin), 1563, 1571, 1574 (ed. by Higgins), 1575 (re-issue of Higgins's "First Parte"), 1578 ("The Second Parte," expanded by Blennerhasset), 1587 (ed. by Thomas Newton), 1610 (ed. by Niccols), 1619 (re-issue of the ed. of 1610), and 1815 (ed. by Joseph Haslewood).

115, 7. **Where is now**: on the *ubi sunt?* formula cf. J. W. Bright, *M. L. Notes,* viii. 94, F. Tupper, Jr., same, pp. 253 f.

SAMUEL DANIEL

118, 8. **his youth was passed**: Daniel lived from 1562 till 1619. Besides his prose *History of England* and his masques, he wrote little after 1603.

118, 18. **a pedantic admiration**: this is perhaps as severe an arraignment of the tendency toward classicism as we meet with anywhere in Gray's writings.

118, 23. the expectations Spenser had raised:

> And there is a new shepheard late up sprong,
> The which doth all afore him far surpasse:
> Appearing well in that well tuned song
> Which late he sung unto a scornfull lasse.
> Yet doth his trembling Muse but lowly flie,
> As daring not too rashly mount on hight,
> And doth her tender plumes as yet but trie
> In loves soft laies and looser thoughts delight.
> Then rouze thy feathers quickly, Daniell,
> And to what course thou please thy selfe advance:
> But most, me seemes, thy accent will excell
> In tragick plaints and passionate mischance.
> *Colin Clouts Come Home Again* (1595), ll. 416-27.

The "well tuned song" is *Delia* (1592); the last two lines refer to *The Complaint of Rosamond* (1592).

120, 11. Marino:
Giambattista Marino or Marini (1569-1625). His inflated style became known by the name of *Marinism*.

120, 14. Seneca for a model:
in his *Cleopatra* (1594) and *Philotas* (1605).

SELECTIONS FROM THE LETTERS

122, 1. Richard West:
born in 1716, the son of Richard West, playwright and Lord Justice of Ireland, and grandson of Bishop Burnet. At Eton he was one of the "Quadruple Alliance" with Ashton, Gray, and Walpole, and was called Favonius. He was at Christ Church, Oxford, 1735-8, then began to read law at the Inner Temple, but afterward thought of going into the army; ill health prevented him and he died of consumption on June 1, 1742.

122, 13. Lord Waldegrave's:
James, first Earl Waldegrave (1685-1741), succeeded Sir Horatio Walpole as ambassador and minister-plenipotentiary at Paris in 1730.

122, 15. four acts:
"The French opera has only three acts, but often a prologue on a different subject, which (as Mr. Walpole informs me, who saw it at the same time) was the case in this very representation." Mason.

122, 22. the story of Nireus: the handsomest of the Greeks at Troy; slain by Æneas or Eurypylus (*Iliad*, ii. 671; Diodorus, v. 53).

123, 10. Baucis and Philemon: Ovid, *Metamorphoses*, viii. 611–724.

123, 15. Iphis and Ianthe: Ovid, *Metam.*, ix. 665 ff.

123, 20. Farinelli: "Carlo Broschi (probably took the name Farinelli from his uncle the composer) was in England during the years 1734, 1735, and 1736. Gray had no doubt heard him. He is depicted singing at the lady's *toilette* in the fourth plate of Hogarth's *Marriage à la mode*." Tovey also quotes Burney, *History of Music*, iv. 379, as saying that no other singer of the 18th century was gifted with a voice of such uncommon power, sweetness, extent, and agility.

123, 26. Mahomet Second: by Jean-Baptiste Sauvé, dit de la Noue (1701–60), an actor and dramatist. It had great success.

124, 1. Mademoiselle Gaussin: Jeanne-Catherine Gaussem, called Gaussin (1711–67); her success dates from her appearance in the rôle of Zaire on August 13, 1732. Voltaire was captivated by her acting.

124, 5. Dufrêne: Abraham-Alexis Quinault-Dufresne (1690–1767) made his first appearance on the stage at the Comédie Française in 1712. "He was especially famous in the character of le Glorieux, in the comedy of that name by Destouches." Tovey. On his retirement he received a pension of a thousand livres.

124, 8. the Philosophe marié: by Philippe Néricault Destouches (1680–1754); it was based on an incident in his own life.

124, 9. Mademoiselle Quinault: Jeanne-Françoise Quinault, la cadette (1699–1783), sister of the Dufresne mentioned above. She acted 1718–41. The family produced several celebrated players.

124, 10. Mrs. Clive's way: Catherine Raftor (1711–85), known as Catherine or Kitty Clive. She became famous as a comic actress, but never succeeded in tragic rôles. Of her Johnson said to Boswell, "Clive, sir, is a good thing to sit by; she always understands what you say. In the sprightliness of humour I have never seen her equalled."

124, 11. Monsieur Grandval: Charles-François Racot de Grandval (1710–84), actor and playwright, author of several witty but immoral comic operas. **Wilks**: Robert Wilks (c. 1665–1732), who acted the part of Juba in Addison's *Cato* and who was connected with the management of the Haymarket and Drury Lane Theatres. He was especially celebrated as a comedian.

124, 18. "Gustavus Vasa": a play by Henry Brooke (c. 1703–83), prohibited by the Lord Chamberlain under Sir Robert Walpole's Act for Licensing Plays. In consequence Johnson wrote *A Complete Vindication of the Licensers of the Stage*. As *The Patriot* it was successfully produced in London.

125, 3. Mademoiselle Dumenil: Marie Françoise Marchand, called Dumesnil (1713–1803), who acted at the Comédie Française 1737–76; one of the greatest if not the greatest of French tragic actresses. Her only rival was Mlle. Clairon.

126, 15. a huge heap of littleness: borrowed from Pope's description of Timon's villa, *Moral Essays*, iv. 109. Walpole, writing also to West, speaks of "the great front" as "a lumber of littleness."

127, 13. Latona: Leto, mother of Apollo and Artemis. Homer's *Hymn to Apollo*, 14 ff.

128, 10. in usum Delphini: for the use of the Dauphin.

128, 14. Cambis: Marquis de Cambis-Velleron (1706–72), lieutenant-general of the Pope in France.

128, 16. King, Queen, Dauphin, Mesdames: Louis XV. (1710–74), Queen Maria (Leczinska, of Poland, 1703–68), their son Louis (1729–65), and their daughters, of whom there were eight in all, the seven living at this time ranging in age from eleven to less than two years. See É. de Barthélemy, *Mesdames de France, filles de Louis XV.*, Paris, 1870.

128, 25. Britannicus: Racine's play (1669), on which Gray modeled his *Agrippina*.

128, 27. Phædra and Hippolitus: Racine's *Phèdre et Hippolyte* (1677).

129, 3. Crebillon's Letters: Claude-Prosper Jolyot de Crébillon (1707–77), published in 1732 *Lettres de la marquise de M . . . au comté R.* Gray probably saw the 2d ed. (1738).

129, 4. one Bougeant: Guillaume-Hyacinthe Bougeant

(1690-1743) had just published *L'amusement philosophique sur le langage des bêtes*, which went through a dozen editions and was translated into English, German, and Italian, and which caused Bougeant's banishment to La Flèche.

129, 13. the Grande Chartreuse: fourteen miles north of Grenoble, in the valley of the Guiers, 3205 feet above the sea. Here St. Bruno (1030-1101) in 1084 founded the Order of the Carthusians. The beautiful *Alcaic Ode* written by Gray in 1741, on his second visit, should be compared with Matthew Arnold's *Stanzas from the Grande Chartreuse* as illustrating the similarity of and the difference between the two men in respect to the appeal the place made to them. With this letter cf. Walpole's *Letters*, ed. Mrs. Toynbee, i. 30 f.

130, 3. Abelard and Heloïse: no special reason for remembering them is evident, unless it be their retirement to St. Denis and Argenteuil respectively. Peter Abelard (1079-1142) was born at Palais near Nantes and passed his life in Paris and Northern France. Heloïse, whose tragic story is inseparably linked with that of the great scholastic philosopher, lived *c.* 1101-64, chiefly in Paris and at Argenteuil.

130, 22. Nives cœlo, etc.: Livy, xxi. 32.

131, 2. carries the permission: a phrase borrowed from Madame de Sevigné, who quotes a *bon mot* on Pelisson, "qu'il abusoit de la permission qu'ont les hommes, d'être laids." Mason.

131, 8. can be tedious: West had written (March 25), "His Pannonian sedition in the first book of his annals, which is just as far as I have got, seemed to me a little tedious."

132, 4. Satis constabat, etc.: end of chap. 43.

132, 9. the Dunciad: bk. iv., published in 1742.

133, 13. grave discourses: Mason thought that Gray here had in mind Francis Hutcheson (1694-1746), whose *Inquiry into the Original of Our Ideas of Beauty and Virtue* (1725) had procured him the professorship of moral philosophy at Glasgow. He agreed with Shaftesbury in finding an analogy between the sense of beauty and the moral sense. He emphasized the importance of calm benevolence. "Of all the patrons of this system [which makes virtue consist in benevolence], the late Dr. Hutcheson was undoubtedly beyond all comparison, the most acute, the most distinct, the most philosophical, and what is of the greatest consequence of all, the soberest and most judicious." Adam Smith, *Treatise on the Theory of Moral Sentiments*, 4th ed., 1774, p. 361.

133, 14. paradisiacal pleasures: West's reply was: "I rejoice you found amusement in *Joseph Andrews*. But then I think your conceptions of Paradise a little upon the Bergerac." Tovey, *Gray and His Friends*, p. 162. The reference is to Cyrano de Bergerac.

133, 17. Marivaux: Pierre Carlet de Chamblain de Marivaux (1688–1763). On Nov. 19, 1765, Walpole wrote to Gray from Paris: "Crébillon is entirely out of fashion, and Marivaux a proverb. *Marivauder* and *Marivaudage* are established terms for being prolix and tiresome."

134, 12. museful mopings: *Palamon and Arcite*, i. 541 f.

134, 13. trim of love: *id.*, 540. **pleasant beverage**: *id.*, ii. 15.

134, 14. a roundelay of love: *id.*, ii. 78. **stood silent in his mood**: *id.*, ii. 328.

134, 15. with knots and knares deformed: *id.*, ii. 536. **his ireful mood**: *id.*, ii. 582.

134, 16. in proud array: *id.*, iii. 61. **his boon was granted**: *id.*, iii. 187.

134, 17. and disarray and shameful rout: *id.*, iii. 304. **wayward but wise**: *id.*, iii. 385.

134, 18. furbished for the field: *id.*, iii. 446. **the foiled dodderd oaks**: Gray apparently wrote or intended to write *felled*; *id.*, iii. 905, 907. **disherited**: *id.*, iii. 968.

134, 19. smouldering flames: *id.*, iii. 980. **retchless of laws**: *id.*, iii. 1074.

134, 20. crones old and ugly: *The Wife of Bath's Tale*, 126. **the beldam at his side**: *id.*, 261.

134, 21. the grandam-hag: *id.*, 312. **villanize his Father's fame**: *id.*, 405.

135, 4. But I, that am, etc.: *Richard III*, i. 1. 14–21.

135, 19. silken son of dalliance, etc.: see *Agrippina*, 98, 103 f., 134, 169 f.

136, 15. Davanzati: Bernardo Davanzati (1529–1606), a celebrated Florentine scholar.

136, 21. prayers to the May: refers to West's five stanzas beginning "Dear Gray, that still within my heart Possessest far the better part!" printed by Tovey in *Gray and His Friends*, pp. 165 f.

137, 14. Broukhusius: Jean van Broekhuizen (1649–1707), soldier, Latin poet, and editor of the works of Propertius, his favorite author (1702). On May 5 West had written, "I am only sorry you follow the blunders of Broukhusius, all whose insertions are nonsense." **Scaliger**: Julius Cæsar Scaliger (1484–1558), in his *Poetics*, vi. 7.

137, 16. in sad condition: after these words Mason omitted some criticism of West's elegy.

137, 22. the Peloponnesian war: in Thucydides.

138, 3. three lines in Anacreon: *Odes*, i. 29, on the portrait of Bathyllus. "Make his locks to curl without restraint and let them lie as they will."

138, 10. Sigilla in mento, etc.: from Varro's *Papiapapae*, iv. Riese reads *Laculla* (for *Sigilla*) and *demonstrat*. Quoted by Nonius Marcellus in his *De honestis veterum dictis, s. v. mollitudinem*.

138, 12. John Chute: lived 1701–76. He was educated at Eton. Between 1722 and 1754 he lived chiefly on the Continent. He met Gray and Walpole at Casa Ambrosio, Horace Mann's house in Florence, in 1740. Tovey says, "He was a man of taste and culture, — there is a quiet and graceful pleasantry in his recorded *bons mots*."

138, 13. Mr. Mann: Horace Mann (1701–86), then British minister at Florence; an intimate friend of Horace Walpole, with whom he corresponded (for publication) for forty-four years. In 1755 he was created a baronet.

138, 21. Middleton: Dr. Conyers Middleton (1683–1750) in 1741 published a *Life of Cicero*, a part of which he is said to have plagiarized from William Bellenden.

138, 22. the Sofa: *Le Sopha, conte moral* (1742), by the younger Crébillon, "which does not strictly justify its subtitle."

139, 1. Mr. Garrick: Walpole likewise "opposed" Garrick; see his letter to Mann, May 26, 1742.

139, 5. Pergolesi's songs: Giovanni Battista Pergolese

(1710–36) was an eminent composer of the Neapolitan school, in his own day something of a failure, but more highly valued afterward. Gray was an eager student of his music and made collections of it with the works of Palestrina, Leo, Marcello, and others.

139, 7. Galuppi's: Baldassare Galuppi (1706–85), called "the father of Italian comic opera." Cf. Browning, *A Toccata of Galuppi's*.

139, 11. Pescetti's: Giambattista Pescetti, a prolific Venetian composer, d. 1758. He lived in London three years.

139, 13. My Lady of Queensbury: Catherine Douglas, wife of the third Duke of Queensberry (d. 1777), celebrated for her beauty and eccentricity, the friend of many literary men.

139, 14. my Lady of Marlborough: Sarah Churchill, Duchess of Marlborough (1660–1744), whose *Memoirs* appeared in 1742.

139, 19. Mr. Glover's: Richard Glover (1712–85), a first cousin of Gray's friend West, and a poet, merchant, and M. P. (1761–68); besides much trash he wrote one ballad, *Hosier's Ghost*, which is still remembered. *Boadicea* was performed at Drury Lane for nine nights in December, 1753.

140, 4. Ἀζομενος, etc.: "Reverencing the sacred grove, abounding in game, of the far-darting Queen, leave, O hunter, the groves of the fearful goddess. Then the baying of the divine hounds alone resounds there; thou sounding in answer to the music of the wild Nymphs." For κλαγγεῦσιν cf. Theocritus, Ep. vi. 5, κλαγγεῦντι.

140, 9. an Heroic Epistle: *Sophonisba ad Massinissam*, which Gray appended.

141, 17. young friend: Dr. Mark Akenside (1721–70), whose poem, *The Pleasures of the Imagination*, begun in 1738, was accepted by Dodsley on Pope's recommendation and published in January, 1744. It was highly praised in general, though both Gray and Warburton saw defects.

142, 9. Hutchinson-Jargon: see the note on **133,** 13.

142, 12. à la Mode du Temple: an example of the critical methods of the lawyers of the Temple is related by Walpole in his letter to Mann, March 11, 1748: "There has been a new comedy, called *The Foundling* [by Edward Moore]; Lord Hobart and some more young men made a party to damn it, merely for the love of damnation. The Templars espoused the play, and went armed with Syringes charged with stinking oil, and with sticking plaisters; but it did not come to action."

142, 16. the Enthusiast: *The Enthusiast, or The Lover of Nature*, which Joseph Warton wrote in 1740. Cf. **144**, 3, and the note.

142, 18. Health: *The Art of Preserving Health*, 1744, by John Armstrong (1709–79), a Scotch physician and poet. Mr. Bullen says of it, "No writer of the eighteenth century had so masterful a grasp of blank verse as is shown in parts of this poem" (*Dict. Nat. Biog.*, ii. 95).

142, 23. Mr. Fraigneau: William Fraigneau (1717–88) became M.A. of Trinity College in 1743 and was professor of Greek 1744–50, succeeding Walter Taylor, who died Feb. 25, 1744. Alsager Vian (*D. N. B.*, xx. 158) gives the date of Fraigneau's election as 1743; this is O. S.

143, 3. the twentieth Year of the War: Thucydides, bk. vii.

143, 6. Xenophon, or Plutarch: "Meaning, I think, how do you relish Xenophon (his account of the Retreat of the Ten Thousand), or Plutarch (*e. g.*, his *Nicias*), after Thucydides?" Tovey.

144, 3. Mr. Warton: Joseph Warton (1722–1800), elder brother of Thomas Warton, and headmaster of Winchester College 1766–93. His *Odes on Various Subjects* were published in December, 1746, by Dodsley, and reached a second edition. **Mr. Collins:** William Collins (1721–59) was a schoolmate of Warton at Cambridge. His *Odes* (dated 1747) were published in December, 1746, by Millar. He and Warton intended a joint publication, but apparently could not find a publisher. Collins is said by Langhorne to have burnt the unsold copies of his *Odes*. Posterity has not sustained Gray's opinion of Collins.

144, 14. Cibber's book: *The Character and Conduct of Cicero Considered from the History of His Life by the Rev. Dr. Middleton*, London, 1747, by the dramatist Colley Cibber (1671–1757).

144, 17. Mrs. Letitia Pilkington's: this adventuress

(1712–50) seems to have charmed Cibber, and wrote a poem to him about the *Cicero*; cf. her *Memoirs*, 3d ed., 1754, iii. 82.

145, 3. Dr. Waterland: Daniel Waterland (1683–1740), a learned and trenchant champion of orthodoxy. From 1730 until his death he was archdeacon of Middlesex and vicar of Twickenham.

145, 10. the Doctor's recommendation: Middleton's book was highly laudatory. Cibber justified his treatment of Cicero's weaknesses by observing that "David, the very man after God's own heart, has not the least veil thrown over his sins or frailties, but that they are as copiously laid open as his piety and virtues."

145, 23. Mr. Spence's pretty book: *Polymetis, or An Enquiry concerning the Agreement between the Works of the Roman Poets and the Remains of the Antient Artists, being an Attempt to Illustrate Them Mutually from one another*, London, 1747, folio. The author, Joseph Spence (1699–1768), succeeded Thomas Warton as professor of poetry at Oxford (1728–38). *Polymetis* paid him £1500.

148, 9. a little conversant: our idiom requires, (but) little conversant.

148, 27. our Laurel: The laurel was imported into Europe by the botanist Clusius, about the year 1590, from Trebizond. The orange was certainly unknown to Virgil, having been brought from Ispahan at a much later period. Whitaker's ms. note, quoted by Mitford.

149, 24. Mr. Lyttleton's elegy: the *Monody* on the death of his wife (formerly Miss Lucy Fortescue) published by Lord Lyttelton (1709–73) in 1747. Walpole's criticism has apparently not been preserved. **kids and fawns:** stanza vi begins:

> Sweet babes, who, like the little playful Fawns,
> Were wont to trip along these verdant lawns.

150, 11. Your epistle: *An Epistle from Florence to T[homas] A[shton], Esq.* In Walpole's *Works*, i. 4. A poem of about 375 lines, written in 1740.

150, 25. Nugent: Robert Craggs, Earl Nugent (1702–88), a wealthy politician and poet, later patron of Goldsmith.

Notes

150, 26. G. West: Gilbert West (1703–56), who was to translate Pindar's *Odes* (1749), which his father had edited (1697).

151, 2. one of Mr. West's: *A Monody on the Death of Queen Caroline*, printed also by Tovey in *Gray and His Friends*, pp. 110–114.

151, 5. Archibald Bower: lived 1686–1766; twice joined and withdrew from the Jesuit order; had a very shady career. The *History* appeared in seven volumes, beginning in 1751; the earlier part at least was a mere translation of Tillemont. **Professor.** G. Professour.

151, 21. the account of the Gold-Mines: bk. iii., chaps. 12 f.

151, 24. Gresset: Jean Baptiste Louis Gresset (1709–77); educated by the Jesuits, he became a celebrated poet, and in 1748 entered the Academy. *Le Méchant* appeared in 1747; *Vert-Vert*, in 1734; *Sidnei*, in 1745.

152, 9. the Castle of Indolence: published in May, 1748.

152, 10. Mr. Mason: William Mason (1724–97), who became Gray's devoted friend and biographer. A voluminous poet, he also composed church music, and invented the celestina. Gray here refers to the *Ode to a Water-Nymph*, published about this time in Dodsley's *Miscellany*.

152, 20. Mr. Dodsley's book: *A Collection of Poems by Several Hands, in Three Volumes*, 1748. Commonly called the *Miscellany*.

153, 6. a state-poem: *On the Prospect of Peace*, praised by Addison in *The Spectator*, No. 523, Oct. 30, 1712; written by Thomas Tickell (1686–1740).

153, 17. his ballad: *Colin and Lucy*, beginning, "Of Leinster fam'd for maidens fair," also in the *Collection*.

153, 19. M. Green: Matthew Green "of the Custom House" (1696–1737), a poet whom Gray consistently admired, wrote *The Grotto*, 1732, and *The Spleen*, 1737. He was a charming writer of octosyllabic verse, dealing with homely themes in a Dutch spirit of neatness. Gosse. This letter concludes with a transcript of one of his poems.

153, 24. The "School Mistress": by William Shenstone (1714-63), said to have been "written at college, 1736"; first published in 1742. An imitation of Spenser.

153, 26. "London": by Johnson; reprinted from the ed. of 1738.

154, 1. Mr. Dyer: John Dyer (c. 1700-1758), author of *Grongar Hill* and *The Ruins of Rome*.

154, 5. Mr. Bramston: Rev. James Bramston (c. 1694-1744) wrote *The Art of Politicks*, *The Man of Taste*, etc.

154, 9. Mr. Nugent: Earl Nugent was suspected of paying Mallet to write his best Ode, that addressed to [William] Pulteney, his later and obviously unaided efforts being contemptible. Gosse.

154, 11. Mr. Whitehead's: William Whitehead (1715-85), poet laureate from 1757 on.

154, 27. your Epistle: see 150, 11, and the note.

155, 12. the beauties: *The Beauties, an Epistle to Mr. Eckardt, the Painter*, written by Walpole in July, 1746.

155, 14. Mr. Lowth: probably Robert Lowth (1710-87), professor of poetry at Oxford 1741-50 and in 1777 created bishop of London. **Mr. Ridley**: probably Glocester Ridley (1702-74), fellow of New College, Oxford, 1724-34, a miscellaneous writer. **Mr. Rolle**: unidentified; in the 5th ed. (1758) at least, his name is not attached to any poem; and this is true also of Lowth, Ridley, and Seward.

155, 15. the Reverend Mr. Brown: Tovey thinks this is the John Brown (1715-66) whose *Estimate of the Manners and Principles of the Times* appeared in 1757; see p. 185. He committed suicide; see Gray to Mason, Oct. 5, 1766. **Seward**: Thomas Seward (1708-90), a clergyman, editor of Beaumont and Fletcher; of him Coleridge, in his *Lectures on Shakespeare*, exclaimed, "Mr. Seward! Mr. Seward! you may be, and I trust you are, an angel, but you were an ass!"

155, 18. the sickly Peer: Lord Hervey, in his *Epistle to Mr. Fox from Hampton Court*, 1731.

155, 24. Mr. S. Jenyns: in *An Essay on Virtue*. Soame Jenyns (1704-87) was a voluminous but generally superficial writer.

155, 28. an Ode: *To a Water-Nymph*.

156, 7. Lady Mary: Lady Mary Wortley Montagu.

156, 11. Sir T. Fitz-Osborne's Letters: written by William Melmoth (1710–99) and published in 1742 under the pen-name of Sir Thomas Fitz-Osborne. Melmoth was a popular translator of Cicero and Pliny.

156, 16. Edward: Gresset's *Edouard III*.

157, 13. the President Montesquieu's: Montesquieu (1689–1755) was president of the Parlement of Bordeaux from 1716 till 1726. Gray's criticism in every way stands the test of time.

158, 17. Catilina: played Dec. 10, 1748. Prosper Jolyot de Crébillon, the elder, lived 1674–1762, and was the bitter rival of Voltaire.

159, 4. Travels in Egypt: *Voyage d'Égypte et de Nubie*, written by the Danish artist-traveller Friderik Ludvig Norden (1708–42), captain in the Danish Royal Navy; translated into French partly by the author, partly, it is said, by Des Roches de Parthenay (Copenhagen, 1755, 2 volumes, folio, 159 plates), and into English by Dr. Peter Templeman (London, 1757, folio).

159, 12. Mr. Birch: Rev. Thomas Birch (1705–66), a voluminous antiquary, historian, and biographer. Gray refers to his *Historical View of Negotiations between the Courts of England, France, and Brussels, 1592–1617*, published in 1749, 8vo, pp. xxiv, 529. Carew's account occupies pp. 413–528.

160, 2. Mason's Ode: *Ode performed in the Senate House in Cambridge, July 1st, 1749, at the Installation of His Grace Thomas Holles, Duke of Newcastle, Chancellor of the University*. It was set to music by William Boyce, composer to the King.

160, 23. a book: *A Dissertation on 2 Peter i. 19, in which it is shown that the Interpretation of this Passage . . . as it is proposed by the Author of the Grounds and Reasons of the Christian Religion* [Anthony Collins] *is not probably the Sense of the Author*, etc., 8vo, London, 1750. The book completed the rupture between Walpole, a partisan of Middleton's, and Ashton.

161, 11 ff. Οἱ τόποι: " Distances do not destroy friendship absolutely, they only destroy its active exercise. Still, if the absence be prolonged, it is supposed to work oblivion of the friendship itself;

whence the saying, 'Many a friendship is dissolved by lack of converse.'" Trans. Welldon.

162, 8. Dr. Middleton: see the note on **138, 21**; and L. Stephen, *English Thought in the Eighteenth Century*.

162, 16. a good writer: Mr. Gray used to say, that good writing not only required great parts, but the very best of those parts. Mason.

162, 19. by Montesquieu himself: unmistakably by Montesquieu, although he neither gave his name to it nor wrote in the first person. It was a small pamphlet published at Geneva, "chez Barillot et Fils," 1750, and sold at thirty sous. It was written in answer to two successive articles in some journal (October 9th and 16th, 1749). Montesquieu was therein accused of Spinozism and Deism. One objection urged against Montesquieu is that in his first chapter he says nothing about original sin! The reply is exactly in the brief concise manner of *L'Esprit des Lois*. Tovey.

162, 23. Histoire de Cabinet du Roi: *Histoire naturelle, générale et particulière, avec la description du Cabinet du Roi*, 44 volumes, 4to, 1749–1804. The first part, the joint work of Buffon and Daubenton, was completed in 15 volumes in 1767. Daubenton supplied the anatomical descriptions. **Buffons**: George Louis Leclerc, Comte de Buffon (1707–88).

163, 3. vivacity of imagination: one cannot therefore help lamenting that Mr. Gray let his imagination lie dormant so frequently, in order to apply himself to this very science. Mason.

163, 21. the Abbé de Mongon: Charles Alexandre Montgon (1690–1770) was secretly employed by Philip V. of Spain in 1726 in studying the means of securing the French crown for Philip in case of the death of Louis XV., and helped to bring about reconciliation between France and Spain in 1727. His *Mémoires de ses différentes négociations dans les cours de France, d'Espagne et de Portugal de 1725 à 1731* were published at La Haye in 1745–53 in eight volumes.

163, 25. Presid. Henault's: Charles Jean François Hénault (1685–1770) became in 1710 president of the first chamber of inquests of the parliament of Paris. He achieved success as a poet and a historian. The *Abrégé* (1744) extended to the death of Louis XIV. Eight editions appeared before the author's death.

165, 2. Gil Blas: a comedy by Edward Moore which appeared in 1751. *The Lying Valet* (1741) was by Garrick.

165, 3. The Fine Lady: *The Female Rake, or The Modern Fine Lady* (1750), a poem by Soame Jenyns, who had written *The Modern Fine Gentleman* in 1746.

165, 5. Mr. Coventry: Francis Coventry (died c. 1759), M.A. of Magdalene College, Cambridge, wrote anonymously *The History of Pompey the Little, or The Adventures of a Lapdog* (1751). **to him you knew:** Henry Coventry (d. 1752), also of Magdalene (M.A. 1733); author of *Philemon to Hydaspes, relating a Conversation with Hortensius upon the Subject of False Religion* (1736–44).

165, 10. Lady Vane: the beautiful but notorious daughter of Francis Hawes, a South Sea director; lived 1713–88; married Viscount Vane, her second husband, in 1735. In 1751 she paid Smollett to insert her *Memoirs of a Lady of Quality* as chap. 81 of *Peregrine Pickle*.

165, 14. "Gosling Scrag": this and the Monody were afterward omitted.

165. Remarks on the Letters, etc.: Mr. Tovey, after comparing these remarks with the letters to which they refer, concludes "that Mason's original correspondent was other than Gray, and possibly a man of straw." I agree with him, but not for the reasons set down in his note (*Letters*, ii. 293, n. 2). The unknown correspondent, X, is represented as approving the method Mason has "taken of softening the rigour of the old [Greek] drama," but as advising him to modify the Chorus parts and as proposing a scheme for the alteration. Gray, on the other hand, while fully aware that the chorus was a "clog," expressly urged the retention of the choruses in *Elfrida* (cf. **168**, 8 ff.) as the best part, which, had the play been changed, would have been lost. I am inclined to believe that X was an imaginary person; that there were originally four of the letters (I agree again with Mr. Tovey); that Gray read them in ms. (they *may* have been especially intended for his eye) and that his comments and quotations refer to this ms. draft. Before publication (1752) they were thoroughly revised in the light of Gray's criticism and increased in number to five. They bear the date "Pemb. Hall. 1751." That X was hypothetical cannot of course be proved; it is inferred from the lack of names and dates, the fact that Gray apparently takes it for granted that *X* was invented, and the fact that Mason published the remarks as five Letters instead of four as originally planned. The Letters were summarized in *The Monthly Review*, May, 1752, vi. 387-393.

165, 18. Dear Sir . . . I am yours: omitted by Mason in the revision of his letters. Mason had presumably said: "I meant only to pursue the antient method, so far as it is probable a Greek poet, were he alive, would now do, in order to adapt himself to the genius of our times, and the character of our Tragedy. According to this notion, every thing was to be allowed to modern caprice, which nature and Aristotle could possibly dispense with." "Modern caprice" was later changed to "the present taste."

166, 6. Love and tenderness: Mason had said: "A story was chosen, in which the tender rather than the noble passions were predominant."

166, 26. more intrigue: Mason had said (Letter III): "Hence it is [because of the lack of restraint imposed on the poet by a chorus], that secret intrigues become (as Mr. Dryden gravely calls them) *the beauties of our modern Stage*."

167, 20. the verisimilitude or the regularities: Mason (end of Letter II) had said: "In France, the excellence of their several poets is chiefly measured by this standard [*i. e.*, the artificial or regular construction of the fable]. And amongst our own writers, if you except Shakespeare (who indeed ought, for his other virtues, to be exempt from common rules), you will find, that the most regular of their compositions is generally reckon'd their *Chef d'œuvre*; witness the *All for Love* of Dryden, the *Venice preserv'd* of Otway, and the *Jane Shore* of Rowe." See Tovey's note.

168, 8. Modern Melpomene: Mason expunged this before printing, probably substituting "these playmakers." He printed this: "But whatever these Play-makers may have gain'd by rejecting the Chorus, the true Poet has lost considerably by it. For he has lost a graceful and natural resource to the embellishments of Picturesque Description, sublime allegory, and whatever else comes under the denomination of *pure Poetry*. Shakespear, indeed, had the power of introducing this naturally, and, what is most strange, of joining it with *pure Passion*. But I make no doubt, if we had a Tragedy of his form'd on the Greek model, we should find in it more frequent, if not nobler, instances of his high Poetical capacity, than in any single composition he has left us."

169, 14. young girls: an obvious allusion to Racine's *Esther* and *Athalie*, originally written for the girls of Saint Cyr. Tovey.

169, 18. Jane Shore's reflections: Rowe, *Jane Shore*, i. 2. 181–193. Mason's statement which this apparently contradicts was expunged.

169, 22. the ——: perhaps referred to *Elfrida* as Gray read it, in ms.; but there is no situation corresponding to this in the ed. of 1752.

169, 27. Maffei's Merope: Scipione Maffei (1675–1755); his *Merope*, first played June 12, 1713, was published at Venice in 1714 and "helped to enfranchise Italian tragedy."

170, 6. express poetry: Mason had remarked (Letter V) that the stage omission of the chorus from *Athalie* and *Esther* was due to the refinement of modern music, "which makes it utterly incapable of being an adjunct to Poetry." Tovey adds that the error of this view was demonstrated in 1762 by Gluck's *Orfeo*, in which "the music is everywhere made to minister to characterization."

171, 3. bishop Burnet: Gilbert Burnet (1643–1715), bishop of Salisbury from 1689 on. "For I do solemnly say this to the world, and make my humble appeal upon it to the great God of truth, that I tell the truth on all occasions, as fully and freely as I upon my best inquiry have been able to find it out." Preface to *A History of My Own Time*, 1723–24.

171, 10. a man here: apparently Christopher Smart (1722–71), the mad poet, whose first confinement in Bethlehem Hospital occurred in the year 1751.

171, 15. Dr. Middleton's: see **138**, 21, and the note. The first collective edition of his works (except the *Life of Cicero*) appeared in 1752, in 4to. It does not include this work, which probably remained unpublished.

171, 17. Dr. Waterland: see **145**, 3, and the note.

172, 12. The second: also apparently unpublished; has no connection with his *Vindication of the Free Inquiry into the Miraculous Powers, which are Supposed to have Subsisted in the Christian Church, &c., from the Objections of Dr. Dodwell and Dr. Church*, London, 1751.

173, 11. His Prussian Majesty: Friedrich II (1712–86), called "the Great," third king of Prussia.

173, 24. History of Crusades: Voltaire's *Histoire des croisades* now forms chapters liii. to lviii. of his *Essay sur l'histoire générale et sur les mœurs et l'esprit des nations*; it originally appeared in *Le Mercure historique*, September, 1750, to February, 1751.

174, 2. Voix du Sage et du Peuple: this was Voltaire's *La voix du sage et du peuple à Amsterdam chez Le Sincère* (Paris), of which Bengesco (*Voltaire: Bibliographie de ses œuvres*, ii. No. 1609) notes four editions published in 1750. "It laughs," says Tovey, "at the distinction between spiritual and temporal power, and affirms that a philosophic prince would abolish celibate orders, encourage religion, but suppress dogmatic disputes." It was promptly condemned (January 25, 1751) by the Roman Church.

174, 7. the Speculum of Archimedes: so called because of the legend that Archimedes invented a burning-glass that set fire to the Roman ships when within bow-shot of the wall. Neither Livy, Plutarch, nor Polybius mentions the story. A. is also said to have written a treatise, now lost, on the burning-glass.

174, 10. de Maintenon's letters: Françoise d'Aubigné, Marquise de Maintenon (1635–1719), privately married to Louis XIV. in 1684. She became governess to Madame de Montespan's sons in 1669. Gray's view of her is now generally held.

175, 15. Bishop Hall's Satires: Joseph Hall (1574–1656), bishop of Norwich; his satires were written at Emanuel College, Cambridge, and first published in 1597–98.

175, 17. Dr. Donne: John Donne (1573–1631), dean of St. Paul's. His satires were versified by Pope and published in 1735.

176, 11. Lord Radnor's Vagaries: Lord Radnor's landscape gardening was ridiculed by both Gray and Walpole. The latter wrote to Conway, November 8, 1752: "Have you any Lord Radnor that plants trees to intercept his own prospect, that he may cut them down again to make an alteration?" Lord Radnor lived at Twickenham, near Strawberry Hill.

176, 16. Dr. Akenside: see 141, 17, and the note. Akenside was at this time writing for and editing Dodsley's *Museum*.

176, 20. Dr. Pococke: Richard Pococke (1704-65), bishop of Meath and celebrated as a traveler. He visited Egypt in 1737-38.

176, 24. Diodorus: bk. i., chap. xlvi.

177, 7. Dr. Shaw's book: *Travels or Observations Relating to Several Parts of Barbary and the Levant*, Oxford, 1738, by Thomas Shaw (1694-1751), principal of St. Edmund Hall and Regius professor of Greek at Oxford; celebrated as an African traveler.

177, 25. Strophe and Antistrophe: he often made the same remark to me in conversation, which led me to form the last Ode of *Caractacus* in shorter stanzas: But we must not imagine that he thought the regular Pindaric method without its use; though, as he justly says, when formed in long stanzas, it does not fully succeed in point of effect on the ear: for there was nothing which he more disliked than that chain of irregular stanzas which Cowley introduced, and falsely called Pindaric; and which, from the extreme facility of execution, produced a number of miserable imitators. Had the regular return of Strophe, Antistrophe, and Epode no other merit than that of extreme difficulty, it ought on this very account, to be valued; because we well know that "Easy writing is no easy reading." It is also to be remarked, that Mr. Congreve, who first introduced the regular Pindaric form into the English language, made use of the short stanzas which Mr. Gray here recommends. Mason.

178, 6. nine lines each at the most: see the end of the last note.

178, 11. Monsignor Baiardi's book: Ottavio Antonio Bajardi (c. 1690-c. 1765), archbishop of Tyre and antiquarian, was employed by the King of Naples to describe the antiquities of Herculaneum. His *Prodromo delle antichità di Ercolano*, Naples, 1752-56, 5 volumes, 4to, was the introduction to this work, which was eventually performed by the Herculanean Academy.

179, 9. Voltaire's performance: *An Epistle of Mr.*

de Voltaire, upon His Arrival at His Estate near the Lake of Geneva, in March, 1755. From the French, 4to. Dodsley. Cf. *The Monthly Review,* October, 1755, pp. 285-287.

180, 26. hover'd in thy noontide ray: I follow Tovey in italicizing in this poem whatever Gray strikes through.

183, 19. Sully's Memoirs: *Mémoires des sages et royales œconomies d'estat, domestiques, politiques, et militaires, de Henry le Grand,* etc., 4 vols., folio, 1634 and 1662. The eccentric author, Maximilien de Béthune (1560-1641), became Duke of Sully in 1606. Written by his secretaries, by order, as an address to himself, the book was rewritten in 1745 in third person narrative form by the Abbé de l'Écluse.

184, 12. Mémoires de Monsieur de la Porte: Pierre de la Porte (1603-80), valet de chambre of Louis XIV. His *Mémoires* were printed at Geneva in 1756, 12mo; they relate to the years 1624-66 and are to be accepted with caution.

184, 17. Madame Staal: Marguerite Jeanne Cordier, baroness of Staal de Launay (1684-1750). Her *Mémoires* were published at Paris in 1755, 4 vols., 12mo.

185, 2. Dr. Brown's book: see the note on **155, 15.** Mitford notes that the book "occupied for a time a very large share of public attention and applause; several editions were called for in the course of a year, and a second volume followed the first."

185, 9. the little wicked book: *The Origin of Evil,* by Soame Jenyns. Dr. Johnson exposed the absurdity of this book by his famous review in *The Literary Magazine.* Gosse. Cf. the note on **155, 24.**

185, 18. the chicken: probably *The Bard.*

186, 4. Neville: Thomas Neville (d. 1781), of Jesus College, Cambridge, published imitations of Horace (1758) and of Juvenal and Persius (1759), and a translation of Virgil's *Georgics* (1767).

187, 18. the old Scotch ballad: *Child Maurice,* Child, *English and Scottish Popular Ballads,* ii. 263-75.

188, 16. this thing: *The Bard.*

188, 28. your first Chorus: in *Caractacus.* Gray now deals with the ode beginning "Mona on Snowdon calls."

188, 31. "the sober sisters," etc.: ed. of 1759:

> King of mountains, bend thine ear:
> Send thy spirits, send them soon,
> Now, when Midnight and the Moon
> Meet upon thy front of snow:
> See, their gold and ebon rod,
> Where the sober sisters nod,
> And greet in whispers sage and slow.

190, 5. with emotion: on the drama which excited *emotion in Gray*, Walpole writes [to George Montagu, June 2, 1759], "Mr. Mason has published another drama called *Caractacus*. There are some incantations poetical enough, and odes so Greek as to have very little meaning. But the whole is laboured, uninteresting, and no more resembling the manners of Britons than of the Japanese," &c. — *Misc. Lett.*, iii. p. 455. Mitford. Mrs. Toynbee reads, "of Japanese." Walpole adds, "It is introduced by a piping elegy, for Mason, in imitation of Gray, *will cry and roar all night without the least provocation*."

The plot of *Caractacus*, adapted from Mason's argument, is as follows: Caractacus, king of the Silures, having been defeated by Ostorius, the Roman prefect, his queen Guideria taken prisoner, and his son Arviragus (as it is supposed) either being slain or having fled, retired with his only daughter Evelina and took sanctuary among the Druids in Mona. Ostorius, after the battle, marched into northern Britain, to the frontiers of the Brigantes. Their queen, Cartismandua, made with him a truce, one condition being that she should help him secure Caractacus to grace the triumph of Claudius at Rome. She gave her sons Elidurus and Vellinus as hostages, to be sent themselves to Rome in case they failed to capture Caractacus. On the expedition they were accompanied by Aulus Didius and a sufficient force. The drama opens with their arrival in the sacred grove, a little before midnight, while the chorus of Druids are preparing to admit Caractacus to their order. Elidurus, the elder brother, is loath to betray Caractacus; but the less honorable Vellinus argues that it will give them freedom. They are seized as spies. Vellinus reports that Guideria is safe with Cartismandua. The Druids insist on testing the spies by bringing them to a huge monolith which a pure man can sway but which a traitor cannot move. Meanwhile Arviragus, who was merely wounded, has collected his father's scattered forces and now comes upon the scene. He and Elidurus become allies, but Vellinus flees and leads the Romans back to the grove. Arviragus, bravely fighting, is killed; and Caractacus is captured, though not till after he has slain Vellinus.

191, 7. the abstract idea personified: ed. of 1759:

> Patience, here,
> Her meek hands folded on her modest breast,
> In mute submission lifts th' adoring eye,
> Ev'n to the storm that wrecks her.

192, 24. Caractacus: ed. of 1759, p. 16; ed. of 1811, pp. 97 f.

197, 4. writing an Ode: Mason had written (Jan. 5): "I send you two odes, one so very ancient that all the Æolian lyres that ever sounded are mere things of yesterday in comparison. If you have a mind to trace my imagery, you will find it all huddled together by Keysler, in his 'Antiquitates Selectæ Septentrionales et Celticæ' [Hanover, 1728]. The book I do not doubt is to be met with at Cambridge; and if you have not seen it you need only read his second chapter. But tell me, may this sort of imagery be employed? will its being Celtic make it Druidical? If it will not, burn it; if it will, why scratch it *ad libitum*. . . . The other Ode is as modern as can be wished," etc.

The first of these Odes, which Gray now criticizes, was the Druid's song on Death (*Caractacus*, ed. of 1759, pp. 68 ff.; Mason's *Works*, 1811, ii. 153–55). The second was Mason's *Ode to Mr. Joliffe*, printed by Mitford (*Correspondence of Gray and Mason*, pp. 123 f.) and by Tovey (*Letters*, ii. 8–11).

198, 28. Mallet's Introduction: Paul Henri Mallet (1730–1807), b. at Geneva and professor of history there, published in 1755–6 his *Introduction à l' histoire du Danemark*, prefatory to the history of Denmark which Frederick V, king of Denmark, commissioned him to write. Part of the *Introduction* was translated by Bishop Percy in 1770 as *Northern Antiquities*.

199, 6. pure, perspicuous, and musical: Tovey thinks

this is phrased after Milton's description of good poetry as "simple, sensuous, and passionate" (*Tractate of Education*).

200, 9. this Elegy: *Written in the Garden of a Friend.*

201, 2. "A mountain hoar," etc.: Tovey thinks Mason had written:

A mountain hoar, the savage peak surrounds.

Gray objects to the omission of the relative; see Tovey's note, *Letters*, ii. 20, n. 4.

202, 5. Pelloutier: Mason had asked if Pelloutier had published vol. iii. of his *Histoire des Celtes* (1750). Pelloutier had followed Cluverius (1616) and Keysler in the error of confusing Celt and Teuton.

202, 13. Elegy I: *To a Young Nobleman Leaving the University.* Addressed to Lord John Cavendish, in 1753.

202, 15. "choir": Mason spelled *quire*.

202, 20. "Fervid": cf. **224, 27**, and the note.

203, 5. Elegy II: *Written in the Garden of a Friend*, 1758. In the 2d ed. of the *Elegies*, 1763, this was Elegy II; it is now No. III.

203, 23. Elegy III: *On the Death of a Lady*, 1760; on Lady Coventry. Second ed., Elegy III; now No. V.

205, 13. Agis: by John Home (1722–1808); it was played at Drury Lane Feb. 21, 1758, Garrick playing a leading part. *Douglas* had appeared in Edinburgh Dec. 14, 1756, and in London March 14, 1757.

205, 18. the Miscellany: cf. Gray's previous criticism, **152 ff.**

206, 3. Dr. Swift: *History of the Last Four Years of the Queen*, published by Charles Lucas, M.D., 1758.

206, 12. M. de Torcy: Jean Baptiste Colbert, Marquis de Torcy (1665–1746), secretary of state under Louis XIV. His *Mémoires* were published in 1756 and an English translation appeared in 1757.

207, 4. Monsieur Freret: Nicholas Freret (1688–1749), a celebrated savant, whose bold *L'histoire de l'origine des Français* caused him to be imprisoned for three months in the Bastille. His works were collected in 1796–99 in twenty volumes.

208, 9. Hodges: Gray alludes to the two additional volumes to Dodsley's *Collection of Poems* which came out in the year 1758, and contained his two Odes, and some Poems by Mason, Shenstone, Akenside, &c. From Mitford, who adds, quoting from Norton Nicholls, that Gray disliked Akenside, and in general all poetry in blank verse, except Milton.

208, 12. the tragic poet: perhaps Arthur Murphy (1727–1805), author of *The Orphan of China*, who quarrelled with Garrick over this play. See Garrick's *Private Correspondence*, 1831, i. pp. xxx ff., 81 ff.

208, 15. Dr. Stukeley's: William Stukeley (1687–1765), physician, clergyman, and antiquary, sometimes called "the Arch-Druid." He wrote much on Stonehenge. *Stonehenge and Abury* appeared in 1740.

210, 3. the Greek Sophist: Hegesias the Cyrenaic, nicknamed, from his encouragement to suicide, Peisithanatos; cf. Cicero, *Tusc. Disp.*, i. xxxiv. Tovey.

211, 4. William Palgrave: c. 1735–1799, of Pembroke College; became LL.B. in 1760. He was in Scotland at this time. Cf. Tovey's note, *Letters*, ii. 49 f.

212, 24. your second packet: contained the practically completed *Caractacus*, except the ode, "Hark, heard ye not yon footsteps dread?" Tovey.

214, 10. the six last lines: they are addressed to the harp of the minstrel Camber:

> Sublime upon the burnish'd prow,
> He bad thy manly modes to flow;
> Britain heard the descant bold,
> She flung her white arms o'er the sea;
> Proud in her leafy bosom to enfold [ed. 1759 unfold]
> The freight of harmony.

214, 20. the four last lines: these read in the edition of 1759:

> Dismal notes, and answer'd soon
> By savage howl the heaths among,
> What time the wolf doth bay the trembling moon,
> And thin the bleating throng.

Notes

214, 27. "The Fairy Fancy": the ed. of 1759 reads:

Fancy, the fairy, with thee came.

215, 3. "Beat on," etc.: ed. of 1759:

Pants thro' the pathless desart of the air.
'Tis not the flight of her.

215, 13. Dr. Long: Roger Long (1680-1770), the celebrated astronomer; became master of Pembroke Hall, Cambridge, in 1733, and Lowndean professor of astronomy and geometry in 1750. See the Introduction, p. xxxviii.

216, 3. Cleone: by Dodsley; acted at Covent Garden Dec. 2, 1758. Garrick had condemned it as "cruel, bloody, and unnatural." It ran sixteen nights.

216, 8. Merope: a translation by Aaron Hill (1685-1750) of Voltaire; first acted in 1749.

216, 9. The Guardian: adapted by Garrick from Fagan's *Pupille*.

216, 10. Cocchi's: Gioacchino Cocchi (before 1720-*c.* 1804); lived in England 1757-72 and composed there eleven operas, acquiring a considerable reputation.

216, 11. the Cyrus: *Il Ciro riconosciuto* is the title of an opera composed by Cocchi, produced at the King's Theatre in 1759, and said by Dr. Burney to be the best of Cocchi's productions during his residence in England. Mitford.

216, 14. II. 2.—These are, etc.: a criticism of the revised ode beginning, "Hail, thou harp of Phrygian fame!" This criticism, extending as far as *execution*, **217**, 3, was printed by Mitford as a part of Gray's letter dated Dec. 19, 1756, while the detailed criticisms beginning "I liked the opening" were appended to the same letter. Mitford was followed by Gosse and Tovey, in vol. i. Tovey, however, afterward rightly concluded (see *Letters*, ii. 61, n. 3, 63, n. 1, 65, n. 1, 70, n. 1) that these criticisms belong here. Tovey's Letter CLXXX, it will be observed, is the end of his No. CXXXVI (i. 317), set off and redated; but he does not reprint the matter that went with it. **my favorite stanzas:** the poet is speaking of Inspiration; ed. of 1759:

High her port; her waving hand
A pencil bears; the days, the years,

>   Arise at her command,
>   And each obedient colouring wears.
>   So [ed. 1811, Lo], where Time's pictur'd band
>   In hues æthereal glide along;
>   O mark the transitory throng;
>   Now they dazzle, now they die,
>   Instant they flit from light to shade,
>   Mark the blue forms of faint futurity,
>   O mark them ere they fade.

217, 1. tout-ensembles: Mason had written, in the latter part of November, 1758: "I will attempt a new Mador's song to please you, but, in my own mind, I would not have him sing there at all on account of the *tout ensemble*, for he sings all the second Ode, and also all the fourth, so I am afraid he will be hoarse."

217, 6. blank: Mason changed it to *stern*.

217, 17. "trickling runlet": this was cut out.

218, 2. "philosophy": ed. of 1759:

>   On the left
>   Reside the Sages skill'd in Nature's lore:
>   The changeful universe, it's numbers, powers,
>   Studious they measure, save when meditation
>   Give place to holy rites: etc.

218, 16. Cæsar and Fate: ed. of 1759:

>   Cæsar and Fate demand him at your hands.

218, 29. "modest mounds": Tovey thinks *mounds* is a misprint for *bounds*. Mason changed it to "the level course of right and justice."

219, 14. this ceremony: in the ed. of 1759 the Semi-chorus says:

>   Circle, sons, this holy ground;
>   Circle close, in triple row;
>   And, if mask'd in vapors drear,
>   Any earth-born Spirit dare
>   To hover round this sacred space,
>   Haste with light spells the murky foe to chace.
>   Lift your boughs of vervain blue,

Notes

> Dipt in cold September dew;
> And dash the moisture chaste, and clear,
> O'er the ground, and through the air
> Now the place is purg'd and pure.

It then asks if the steers are ready for the sacrifice.

219, 20. aske: a newt or lizard; a common word in northern England, cf. Wright, *Eng. Dial. Dict.*

219, 25. "Gender'd by," etc.: ed. of 1759:

> And the potent adder-stone,
> Gender'd 'fore th' autumnal moon?

220, 2. an old British fancy: that the adder-stone, or druid's egg (a bead of glass used as a charm) was produced "by snakes joining their heads together and hissing, which forms a kind of bubble like a ring about the head of one of them, which the rest by continual hissing blow on till it comes off at the tail, when it immediately hardens and resembles a glass ring." See Brand-Hazlitt, *Faiths and Folklore*, i. 194 f.

220, 13. Its nodding walls, etc.: Mason accepted the lines except this one.

220, 26. "pestilent glare": ed. of 1759:

> . . . and Heav'n, who bade these warrior oaks
> Lift their green shields against the fiery sun,
> To fence their subject plain, did mean, that I
> Should, with as firm an arm, protect my people,
> Against the pestilent glare of Rome's ambition.

221, 1. "I know it, rev'rend Fathers": ed. of 1759:

> I know it, reverend fathers!
> 'Tis heav'n's high will, that these poor aged eyes
> Shall never more behold that virtuous woman,
> To whom my youth was constant, 'twas heav'n's will
> To take her from me at that very hour,
> When best her love might soothe me; that black hour,
> [May memory ever raze it from her records]
> When all my squadrons fled, and left their king
> Old and defenceless: him, who nine whole years

> Had stemm'd all Rome with their firm phallanx: yes,
> For nine whole years, my friends, I bravely led
> The valiant veterans, oft to victory,
> Never 'till then to shame.

222, 16. **Mingotti**: Regina Valentini Mingotti (1728–1807), born at Naples, sang with great success in many European capitals. Cf. *Letters*, ed. Tovey, i. 297, n. 4.

222, 18. **Metastasio**: Pietro Bonaventura Metastasio (1698–1782), a Roman, especially famed as a lyric poet.

222, 24. **hares**: Tovey suspects that Gray punned on *hairs*.

223, 18. **Money**: cf. Gray's letter to Wharton, June 5, 1748.

224, 20. **the end of the scene**: ed. of 1759, pp. 46–48; ed. of 1811, pp. 129–31.

224, 22. **"Thou, gallant boy"**: changed by Mason to "Thou best of brothers."

224, 27. **"Fervid"**: Tovey notes that Shakespeare does not use the word, but Milton uses it twice [*P. L.*, v. 301, vii. 224]. Pope does not use the word. Cf. **202**, 20.

225, 3. **the joint criticism**: by Dr. Warburton, owner of Prior Park, and Mr Hurd, who was frequently there.

225, 12. **the chorus of the rocking-stone**: the ode beginning, "Thou Spirit pure, that spread'st unseen," ed. of 1759, pp. 40 f., Mason, *Works*, 1811, ii. 122 ff.

226, 14. **Whitehead's two Odes**: *Ode for His Majesty's Birthday* and *Ode for the New Year*, 1759.

228, 4. **Froissard**: Tovey here reminds us of Sainte-Beuve's comment on Froissart (*Causeries du lundi*, ix. 63–96, October 24, 31, 1853), in which (p. 74) he quotes this letter of Gray, and adds: "Combien cela semble plus vrai encore lorsque l'on parcourt un de ces beaux Froissart manuscrits comme en possède notre grande Bibliothèque [Nationale] et comme l'Angleterre en a sans doute aussi, tout ornés de vignettes du temps, admirablement coloriées, d'une vivacité et d'une minutie naïve qui commente à chaque page le texte et le fait parler aux yeux, avec une entière et fidèle représentation des villes et châteaux, des cérémonies, des sièges, des combats sur terre et sur mer, des costumes, vêtements et armures ! Toutes ces choses y sont peintes comme d'hier ; la poésie de Gray elle-même n'est pas plus nette ni plus fraîche, et ne reluit pas mieux." See also Sir J. F. Stephen, *Horae sabbaticae*, i. 22–54.

228, 13. the succeeding century: the fifteenth. Jean Froissart lived *c.* 1338–*c.* 1410; his Chronicle ends at 1400.

228, 16. King Arthur: supposed to have lived in the fourth and fifth centuries. His story became celebrated through the fabulous account in Geoffrey of Monmouth's *Historia regum Britanniae* (*c.* 1139), which formed in part the ultimate source of the French romancers of the twelfth, thirteenth, and fourteenth centuries. Sir Thomas Malory's romance *Le Morte d'Arthur* (1469, printed by Caxton in 1485) was compiled and translated from English and French sources. **Sir Tristram:** at first the hero of an independent legend, but very early associated with Arthur. The story of Arthur and Guinevere was probably influenced by that of Tristram. See Malory, books viii., x.

228, 17. Archbishop Turpin: died *c.* 800; figured as one of the peers of Charlemagne; his name was connected with the twelfth-century half-legendary chronicle which recounted Charlemagne's expeditions to Spain, including the treason of Ganelon and the battle of Roncesvalles.

228, 22. the four Irish kings: bk. iv., chap. 64.

228, 24. who informed Froissard: bk. iv., chap. 62.

229, 3. specimens of Erse poetry: translations from the Gaelic by the notorious James Macpherson (1736–96). At Moffat in the previous autumn he had shown sixteen pieces to John Horne and Dr. Alexander Carlyle. Two of these, apparently, were sent by Sir David Dalrymple to Horace Walpole in January, 1760, and passed on by Walpole to Gray. Macpherson's *Fragments of Ancient Poetry Collected in the Highlands* appeared in July. On the present state of the vexed Ossianic question, see the introduction to P. Christian's *Ossian, barde du IIIe siècle*, Paris, 1905.

229, 13. Hardycanute: printed by Percy, *Reliques of Ancient English Poetry*, ed. Schröer, i. 328–338, 992–994. According to Percy, written by Sir John Bruce of Kinross. First published at Edinburgh in 1719.

230, 3. the K. of Prussia's poetry: *Œuvres du philosophe de Sans Souci*, Potsdam [Paris], January, 1760, an unauthorized edition published (by whom is not known) to make trouble between Frederick and his uncle George III. of England, then his ally. Cf. Walpole's letter to Mann, May 7, 1760.

230, 5. the scum of Voltaire: Gray retained this prejudice; he wrote to Walpole, March 17, 1771: "He must have a very good stomach that can digest the *Crambe recocta* of Voltaire. Atheism is a vile dish, though all the cooks of France combine to make new sauces to it. As to the Soul, perhaps they have none on the Continent; but I do think we have such things in England. Shakespeare, for example, I believe had several to his own share. As to the Jews (though they do not eat pork) I like them because they are better christians than Voltaire."

230, 6. Crambe recocta: cf. Occidit miseros crambe repetita magistros. Juv., vii. 154. Tovey.

230, 8. Tristram Shandy: vols. i. and ii. appeared January 1, 1760.

231, 8. Musæus: Mason's monody on Pope, written in 1744 and published in 1747; Gray had just revised it.

231, 10. a bloody satire: *Two Odes*, to Obscurity and Oblivion, by George Colman the elder (1732–94) and Robert Lloyd (1733–64), written to ridicule Gray and Mason respectively. According to Joseph Warton they afterward repented of the satire. Cf. Boswell's *Johnson*, ed. Hill, ii. 334 f.

231, 12. Mr. Pottinger: Richard Pottinger, who in 1754 became under-secretary of state.

233, 21. Mr. Evans: Evan Evans (1731–89), who in 1764 published *Some Specimens of the Poetry of the Antient Welsh Bards*; it included the Latin discourse *De bardis dissertatio* which Gray saw in manuscript.

235, 2. M. D'Alembert: Jean le Rond d'Alembert (1717–83), one of the greatest figures in eighteenth-century France; he especially distinguished himself in mathematics and philosophy. With Diderot he was engaged from 1751 till 1758 in editing the *Encyclopédie*.

235, 3. his Elements: *Éléments de philosophie*, 1759.

235, 6. the letter to Rousseau: the "polished, cool, ironical answer" to Rousseau's *Lettre à M. d'Alembert sur les spectacles*. In the art. "Genève" in the *Encyclopédie*, vol. vii.,

D'Alembert had expressed the wish that comedy might be tolerated by the Genevan clergy, while he praised their exemplary morals and perfect Socinianism. Rousseau's letter rebuked D'Alembert for praising the clergy to the injury of their reputation, and denounced comedies in general.

235, 7. "Discourses on Elocution": *Reflexions sur l'élocution oratoire, et sur le style en général,* in his *Mélanges de littérature, d'histoire, et de philosophie,* Amsterdam, 1767, ii. 314–56.

235, 8. "Liberty of Music": *De la liberté de la musique,* also a reply to Rousseau; in the *Mélanges,* iv. 381–462.

236, 7. while rocking winds: *Il Penseroso,* l. 126.

236, 14. has described it gloriously: I agree with Tovey that Gray probably had in mind ll. 191–94.

236, 21. "The waves are tumbling," etc.: since published in a note to "Croma," Ossian, vol. i. Tovey.

238, 3. a letter from Mr. David Hume: printed in *The European Magazine,* March, 1784, v. 327.

240, 20. the nave of York Minster: now dated 1291–1324; F. Bond, *Gothic Architecture in England,* p. 657.

240, 21. the choir: Bond dates *c.* 1380–*c.* 1400.

240, 25. The Lady Chapel: begun in 1321.

241, 1. the Chapel of Bishop West: Bond, p. 643, dates 1534.

242, 2. Lady M. C.: Lady Mary Coke, daughter of the Duke of Argyll, who married Viscount Coke in 1747; became known for her eccentricities.

242, 13. lightning: Mason changed it to *lustre.* The Prince of Wales had written *brightness.*

243, 12. this line: Tovey thus restores:
That led her hence; though soon, the steps were slow.
Mason revised it thus:
That led her hence, though soon, by steps so slow.

243, 23. a less metaphorical line: ll. 73–76 now read (2d ed., 1763):
Yet will I praise you, triflers as ye are,
   More than those Preachers of your fav'rite creed,
Who proudly swell the brazen throat of War,
   Who form the Phalanx, bid the battle bleed;

that is, while shallow persons and soldiers (*e. g.*, Frederick the Great) both deny immortality, the latter are the more reprehensible.

243, 25. a good line: it now reads:

> The breeze of bliss, that fills your silken sail.

244, 14. "Truth ne'er can sanctify": the stanza now reads:

> And why must murder'd myriads lose their all,
>   (If life be all), why desolation lour,
> With famish'd frown, on this affrighted ball,
>   That thou may'st flame the meteor of an hour?

245, 4. the Nouvelle Heloise: Rousseau's *Julie, ou La nouvelle Héloïse* was published in 1760.

245, 12. Amadis de Gaul: mentioned in 1379 as a book much read in Spain; immensely popular on the Continent in the 15th and 16th centuries. Probably originated in Spain, though some defend the claims of France. Gray presumably read it in French. Southey, who translated it into English from the Spanish, ascribed it to Vasco Lobeira, a Portuguese knight who died in 1403.

245, 24. mistake his own talents: Mitford here quotes Landor, *De cultu Latini sermonis*, p. 197: "*Rossæo* nec in sententiis ipse suavior est (qui parum profecto præter suavitatem habet) Isocrates, nec in verbis uberior aut amplioris in dicendo dignitatis Plato, nec Sophronisci filius melior sophista. Nemo animi affectus profundius introspexit, delicatius tetigit, solertius explicavit. Odium vero hominum quos insinceros *Graius* aut pravos existimabat, aut religionis Christianorum inimicos, transversum egit et præceps judicium." For the different effect which the book had upon Kant and others, see Lord Morley's *Rousseau*, 2d ed., ii. 31-33.

246, 2. Elisi: a man of great reputation and abilities; performed at the opera in London 1760 and 1761. A great singer and eminent actor. See Burney's *History of Music*, iv. 473 f. Mitford.

246, 20. The Mattei: Colomba Mattei; she "was both a charming singer and a spirited and intelligent actress." Burney, iv. 464 f. In 1759 she won distinction in Cocchi's *Ciro riconosciuto*.

246, 22. the Paganina: Signora Paganini, who sang with her husband in *Il mondo della luna*; the airs, says Burney, "ex-

Notes

cellent in themselves, by the captivating manner in which they were sung and acted by the Paganini, became doubly interesting."

246, 28. the Spiletta: the part of Spiletta in Cocchi's *Gli amanti gelosi*, taken by the eldest sister of the Giordani family with such skill that it gave the name to the company. Burney, iv. 365, n., year 1755.

247, 3. Mr. Richardson: probably Jonathan Richardson the younger (1694–1771), son of the painter (of the same name, 1665–1745) to whom Gray sat about 1729 for the portrait now in the Fitzwilliam Museum.

248, 5. Hollar: Wenceslaus Hollar (1607–77), a Bohemian engraver brought to England by the Earl of Arundel; appointed by Charles II. "His Majesty's designer." He produced over 2700 prints.

248, 6. Mr. Halfpenny: William Halfpenny, a London architect, had just published a work on *Useful Architecture*.

249, 6. his new play: Whitehead's *School for Lovers* was acted at Drury Lane Feb. 10, 1762.

249, 10. "Elegy against Friendship": the poem *On Friendship, written about 1751*; the sentiment to which Gray objected being doubtless that friendships may die from natural causes for which neither person is to be greatly blamed; ll. 73 ff. According to Mason, Gray "disapproved of the general sentiment which it conveyed, for he said it would furnish the unfeeling and capricious with apologies for their defects, and that it ought to be entitled *A Satire on Friendship*."

249, 17. a very serious compliment: the praise of Gray occurs in Lloyd's "Epistle to Churchill"—

> What muse like Gray's shall pleasing, pensive, flow,
> Attempered sweetly to the rustic woe;
> Or who like him shall sweep the Theban lyre,
> And, as his master, pour forth thoughts of fire?   Mitford.

250, 7. Dr. Lowth's Grammar: Robert Lowth's *Short Introduction to English Grammar* (1762) was much used and influenced Lindley Murray. Cf. the note on 155, 14.

250, 11. the bishop: Warburton, bishop of Gloucester.

251, 15. the chapel of St. Sepulchre: originally "a

stately chapel founded in the 12th century and dedicated to St. Mary and the Holy Angels, but generally called St. Sepulchre's chapel, probably because the Easter-Sepulchre of the minster found a temporary home in it." Quoted from James Raine's *York*, 1893, p. 158, which see further. A cut of it is given in Drake's and Burton's histories of York.

251, 16. Archbishop Roger: Roger of Pont l'Evêque, archbishop of York, d. 1181.

254, 4. a rude draught: the accuracy of Gray's drawing has been questioned; see Mitford's note, *Correspondence of Gray and Mason*, 2d ed., p. 518.

255, 7. Johnny Ludlam: there were two persons well known in literature and science, the Rev. William and the Rev. Thomas Ludlam, both Fellows of St. John's College. William was M.A. 1742, and died 1788; Thomas was M.A. 1752, and died 1811. . . . My friend Mr. Nichols agrees with me in thinking that one of these brothers was alluded to: the familiar name Johnny being given to him from his residence at St. John's College. Mitford.

255, 19. the individual chapel: "The chapel was restored, if not rebuilt, by Archbishop Thoresby, and was removed at the Reformation." Raine.

255, 25. the south transept: dates from 1230–c. 1241; the north transept dates from 1241–60.

256, 9. the chapter-house: not easily dated; Bond puts it c. 1300, but thinks it may belong to the preceding period.

257, 8. Roger's own tomb: cf. Murray's Yorkshire *Handbook*, 1867, p. 32; A. Clutton-Brock, *The Cathedral Church of York*, London, 1902, p. 125.

257, 17. Mr. Howe: William Taylor Howe, of Standon Place, near Ongar, Essex, an honorary Fellow of Pembroke College. Mitford.

257, 21. Count Algarotti's: Count Francesco Algarotti (1712–64), a learned dilettante, who corresponded on matters of taste with Frederick the Great, with Voltaire, and with Augustus III., king of Poland. Gosse. Cf. Carlyle, *Frederick*, iii. 327.

259, 3. Émile: published in 1762.

260, 18. one Prince in Europe: Frederick the Great;

cf. Carlyle's *Life*, iii. 287. On Algarotti's relations with Frederick, cf. the same, v. 319, 380.

261, 28. Cocchi: the first of Cocchi's productions mentioned by Burney, *History of Music*, iv. 465, as produced in England, is *Gli amanti gelosi*, c. 1755.

263, 14. Inigo Jones: lived 1573–1652; designed the banqueting-hall of Whitehall, the façade of St. Paul's, the Physicians' College, etc.; the chief architect of his time.

265, 2. Count Algarotti's books: three small treatises on Painting, the Opera, and the French Academy for Painters in Italy; they have been since collected in the Leghorn edition of his works. Mason.

265, 21. the Jesuits' Letters: *Lettres édifiantes et curieuses, écrites des missions étrangères par quelques missionaires de la Compagnie de Jésus*, Paris, 1707–73. A partial translation by Lockman, *Travels of the Jesuits into Various Parts of the World*, appeared in London in 1743, in 2 vols.

265, 22. Chambers's little discourse: *A Treatise of Civil Architecture*, 1759, by Sir William Chambers (1726–96). He had a weakness for Chinese architecture; see his work in Kew Gardens.

267, 7. your Sonnet: *Sonnet to the Earl of Holdernesse*, beginning, "D'Arcy, to thee, whate'er of happier vein"; prefixed to the first volume of Mason's *Works*, and printed by Mitford, *Correspondence of Gray and Mason*, pp. 310 f.

267, 19. a mass of Pergolesi: on Gray's musical library see the opening chapter of Henry E. Krehbiel's *Music and Manners in the Classical Period*, 2d ed., New York, 1898.

269, 17. the Epigram: "I possess several of Mason's political and personal epigrams, which Walpole used to insert for him in *The Evening Post*, but do not recognize the one here alluded to. Those against the King are written in the bitterest feeling of personal animosity." Mitford.

269, 23. Mr. Churchill: Charles Churchill died Nov. 4, 1764.

270, 7. Mr. Langhorne's: John Langhorne (1735–79) was at this time curate and lecturer at St. John's, Clerkenwell. He had been publishing verse for five years.

270, 10. comes from Voltaire: one of the best modern estimates of Voltaire is that of Sir J. F. Stephen, *Horae sabbaticae*, ii. 211-79.

272, 6. Rousseau's Letters: *Lettres écrites de la montagne*, 1764.

274, 5. at Modena: Mason adds the following (I print his own words in italics): *When our Author was himself in Italy, he studied with much attention the different manners of the old masters. I find a paper written at the time in which he has set down several subjects proper for painting, which he had never seen executed, and has affixed the names of different masters to each piece, to shew which of their pencils he thought would have been most proper to treat it. As I doubt not that this paper will be an acceptable present to the Reynoldses and Wests of the age, I shall here insert it.*

An Altar Piece. — Guido.

The top, a Heaven; in the middle, at a distance, the Padre-Eterno indistinctly seen, and lost, as it were, in glory. On either hand, Angels of all degrees in attitudes of adoration and wonder. A little lower, and next the eye, supported on the wings of Seraphs, Christ (the principal figure) with an air of calm and serene majesty, his hand extended, as commanding the elements to their several places: near him an Angel of superior rank bearing the golden compasses (that Milton describes); beneath the Chaos, like a dark and turbulent ocean, only illumined by the Spirit, who is brooding over it.

A small Picture. — Correggio.

Eve newly created, admiring her own shadow in the lake.

The famous Venus of this master, now in the possession of Sir William Hamilton, proves how judiciously Mr. Gray fixed upon his pencil for the execution of this charming subject.

Another. — Domenichino.

Medea in a pensive posture, with revenge and maternal affection striving in her visage; her two children at play, sporting with one another before her. On one side a bust of Jason, to which they bear some resemblance.

A Statue. — Michael Angelo.

Agave in the moment she returns to her senses; the head of her Son, fallen on the ground from her hand.

A Picture. — Salvator Rosa.

Æneas and the Sybil sacrificing to Pluto by torch light in the wood, the assistants in a fright. The Day beginning to break, so as dimly to shew the mouth of the cavern.

Sigismonda with the heart of Guiscardo before her. I have seen a small print on this subject, where the expression is admirable, said to be graven from a picture of Correggio.

Afterwards, when he had seen the original in the possession of the late Sir Luke Schaub, he always expressed the highest admiration of it; though we see, by his here giving it to Salvator Rosa, he thought the subject too horrid to be treated by Correggio; and indeed I believe it is agreed that the capital picture in question is not of his hand.

Another. — Albano, or the Parmeggiano.

Iphigenia asleep by the fountain side, her maids about her; Cymon gazing and laughing.

Another. — Domenichino, or the Carracci.

Electra with the urn, in which she imagined were her Brother's ashes, lamenting over them; Orestes smothering his concern.

Another. — Correggio.

Ithuriel and Zephon entering the bower of Adam and Eve; they sleeping. The light to proceed from the Angels.

Another. — Nicholas Poussin.

Alcestis dying; her children weeping, and hanging upon her robe; the youngest of them, a little boy, crying too, but appearing rather to do so, because the others are afflicted, than from any sense of the reason of their sorrow: her right arm should be round this, her left extended towards the rest, as recommending them to her Lord's care; he fainting, and supported by the attendants.

Salvator Rosa.

Hannibal passing the Alps; the mountaineers rolling down rocks upon his army; elephants tumbling down the precipices.

Another. — Domenichino.

Arria giving Claudius's order to Pætus, and stabbing herself at the same time.

N. Poussin, or Le Seur.

Virginius murdering his daughter; Appius at a distance, starting up from his tribunal; the people amazed, but few of them seeing the action itself.

275, 15. the dedicatorial sonnet: see 267, 7, and the note.

275, 19. "his ghastly smile": a jocose allusion to what Gray, in another place, calls Lord Holdernesse's *ugly face*. Mitford. The line reads "his wonted smile."

276, 3. Mr. Bentham: James Bentham (1708–94), prebendary of Ely. The "Historical Remarks on the Saxon Churches," which Gray here reviews, formed the introduction to his *History of Ely Cathedral*. It was afterward erroneously attributed to Gray (*The Gentleman's Magazine*, May, 1783, liii. 1. 376, July, 1784, liv. 2. 505).

280, 19. the epitaph: the *Epitaph on Miss Drummond*, Mason's *Works*, i. 138. The draft (16 lines) which Gray criticized is printed in the *Correspondence of Gray and Mason*, pp. 394 f. The Archbishop of York, Robert Hay Drummond (1711–76), was translated from Salisbury in 1761. His daughter died in 1766, aged 16.

283, 13. My only objection is . . . : the erasure here was made by Mason in compliment to Beattie. Gosse. A like erasure occurs at 284, 10.

283, 19. Mr. Ferguson's: Adam Ferguson (1723–1816), professor of philosophy at Edinburgh 1759–85.

283, 22. the fault you mention: Beattie had written (March 30): "A Professor at Edinburgh has published an *Essay on the History of Civil Society*, but I have not seen it. It is a fault common to almost all our Scotch authors, that they are too metaphysical."

287, 12. the book: *Historic Doubts on Richard the Third*, 1768. For other contemporary opinions concerning Walpole's ingenious work, see the articles by Dr. Milles and Robert Masters in *Archæologia*, i. 361-83, ii. 198-215 (1770, 1771), both adverse to Walpole.

292, 17. Speed: John Speed (c. 1552-1629), whose *History of Great Britaine* appeared in 1611. **Leslie:** John Leslie (1527-96), bishop of Ross; his *History of Scotland*, Latin version, was first published at Rome in 1578.

293, 17. Mr. Boswell's Book: *An Account of Corsica, the Journal of a Tour to that Island, and a Memoir of P. Paoli*, 1768.

294, 2. Sir William Cornwallis: ambassador to Spain under James I.; d. c. 1631.

295, 21. Guthrie: William Guthrie (1708-70), who published in 1767 *A General History of Scotland* in ten volumes.

301, 15. Some trifles: Here followed some verbal suggestions, the exact form of which has not been preserved, but the tenor of Gray's criticism, in detail, may be found in Forbes's *Life of Beattie*, i. 197, and the appendix to the same. Gosse.

302, 23. Monstrelet: Euguerrand de Monstrelet (1390-1453); his *Chronique* covers the years 1400-44.

303, 1. Philip de Comines: 1445-1509. His *Mémoires*, 4 vols., edited by Lenglet-Dufresnoy, had been published in London in 1747. See Sir J. F. Stephen, *Horae sabbaticae*, i. 55-123.

303, 2. Villehardouin: Geoffroi de Villehardouin (c. 1160-c. 1213) wrote a history of the Fourth Crusade, covering the years 1198-1207. **Joinville:** Jean, Sire de Joinville (1225-1317), whose *Histoire de Saint Louis* gives a vivid picture of the reign of Louis IX. (1226-70). See Sir J. F. Stephen, *Horae sabbaticae*, i. 1-21.

303, 23. such as imitate them: *To fare*, i. e., to go, is used in Pope's *Odyssey*, and so is *meed*; *wight* (in a serious sense) is used by Milton and Dryden. *Ween* is used by Milton; *gaude* by Dryden; *shene* by Milton; *eschew* by Atterbury; *aye* by Milton. The poetical style in every nation (where there is a poetical style) abounds in old words. Beattie.

304, 10. the plaister of thy hair: I did not intend a poem uniformly epical and solemn; but one rather that might be lyrical, or even satirical, upon occasion. Beattie.

304, 18. I most admire: I meant here an ironical argument. Perhaps, however, the irony is wrong [sic] placed. Mammon has now come to signify *wealth* or *riches*, without any regard to its original meaning. Beattie.

305, 6. garniture: I have often wished to alter this same word, but have not yet been able to hit upon a better. Beattie.

305, 11. wandering: *wandering* happens to be in the last line of the next stanza save one, otherwise it would certainly have been here. Beattie.

305, 25. that part: I had sent Mr. Gray from st. 23 to st. 39 by way of specimen. Beattie.

306, 4. like affectation: it does so, and yet it is not affected. I have endeavoured once and again to clear this passage of those obnoxious letters, but I never could please myself. Alliteration has great authorities on its side, but I would never seek for it; nay, except on some very particular occasions, I would rather avoid it. When Mr. Gray, once before, told me of my propensity to alliteration, I repeated to him one of his own lines, which is indeed one of the finest in poetry —

Nor cast one longing lingering look behind.

Beattie.

306, 16. to advantage: this remark is perfectly just. All I can say is, that I meant, from the beginning, to take some latitude in the composition of this poem, and not confine myself to the epical rules for narrative. In an epic poem these digressions and reflections, etc., would be unpardonable. Beattie.

306, 22. hazardous at best: I would as soon make new coin, as knowingly make a new word, except I were to invent any art or science where they would be necessary. *Infuriate* is used by Thomson, *Summer*, 1096 [and *Autumn*, 39]; and, which is much better authority, by Milton, *Par. Lost*, book vi. v. 487. Beattie; to which Mrs. Thrale added: "By twenty people; Gray was a merciless critic." The "twenty" would not include Shakespeare or Pope. Burns used it once (*Sent to a Gentleman Offended*).

307, 4. enough before: what I said before referred only to sophists perverting the truth; this alludes to the method by which they pervert it. Beattie.

307, 9. rarely thunders: it sometimes thunders in the latter part of spring. *Sultry day* would be an improvement perhaps. Beattie.

307, 21. with probability: this is an excellent hint; it refers to something I had been saying in my last letter to Mr. Gray, respecting the plan of what remains of *The Minstrel*. Beattie.

Index

Abelard and Héloïse, 130, 329.
Adam Bell, 34, 54.
Addison, J., xxviii–xxxi, 110, 134, 153, 324, 328, 335.
Adrian IV., Pope, 49, 69, 77.
Æsop, 128.
Akenside, M., 141 f., 176, 205, 208, 332, 343, 348.
Alamanni, L., 39.
Albani, F., 361.
Alembert, J. le R. d', 235, 354 f.
Alexandre, Roman d', 53, 317.
Alexandrine, 27 f., 47 f., 53 ff., 317.
Alfred, Proverbs of, 74 f., 321.
Algarotti, Count F., 257 ff., 265 ff., 284 ff., 291, 358 f.
Alliteration, 58, 364.
Alps, The, xiii, xxxi f., 129 ff.
Amadis de Gaul, 245, 302, 356.
Amici, The, 262.
Anacreon, 137 f., 331.
Angelo, Michael, 361.
Anno, Life of, 59.
Appian, 141.
Arabs, Rhyme among the, xlvi, 68.
Archimedes, Speculum of, 174, 342.
Architecture, xlii ff., Egyptian, 176; English, xvii, 263;
Gothic, 175 ff., 227, 240 f., 256 f., 273, 276 ff.; Grecian, 176 f.; Moorish, 176 f.; Norman, xlii, 13 ff., 310 ff.; Persian, 176. See also Gothic design.
Ariosto, 43, 108.
Aristophanes, xiv, xxxix, lii.
Aristotle, xiv, xxix f., xxxiii, 3, 143, 161, 165, 187, 337 f., 340.
Armstrong, John, 142, 333.
Arnold, Matthew, xxii f., xxxiv, liii.
Arthur, 89, 228, 323, 353; *Arthour and Merlin*, 49, 316; *Morte d'Arthur*, 302, 353.
Ashton, T., xi, 124, 160 f., 334, 337.
Assembly of Gods, The, 41, 315.
Assembly of Ladies, The, 40, 315.
Atterbury, Bp. F., 363.
Augustine, St., 57.

Bach, Carlo, 267.
Baiardi, O. A., 178 f., 343.
Baif, J. A. de, 38.
Baldwin, W., 48, 54, 117, 325.
Ballads, xxx. See also *Chevy*

Chase, Child Maurice, Childe Waters, Glasgerion, The Nut-brown Maid.
Ballet de la paix, 122.
Barberina, The, 260.
Barberino, F. da, 21, 312.
Barclay, A., 32.
Baucis and Philemon, 123, 327.
Beattie, J., 282 ff., 299 f., 303 ff., 362 ff.
Bel Inconnu, Le, 51.
Belle dame sans mercy. See Ros, Sir R.
Benbeirdh, 57, 318.
Bentham, James, 276 ff., 362.
Bentley, R. (1662–1742), xxxiv.
Bentley's *Designs*, xvi.
Bernard of Cluny, 71, 320.
Beryn, Tale of, 35, 54.
Bevis of Southampton, 34 f., 51, 314.
Bible, The, xxx.
Birch, T., 159, 337.
Boccaccio, G., 21, 43, 91 f., 101, 105, 108, 112, 119, 324.
Boileau Despréaux, N., xxx.
Bolingbroke, Lord, xl, 7 ff., 230, 309.
Bonfoy, Mr., 186.
Bonstetten, C. V. de, xx, xxvi, li, 296.
Boswell, J., xx, 293, 354, 363.
Bougeant, G. H., 129, 328 f.
Bower, A., 151, 335.
Bramston, J., 154, 336.
Britain's Ida, 47.

Broekhuisen, Jean, 137, 331.
Brooke, Henry, 124, 328.
Brooke, Lord, 120.
Brown, James, xxii, xxiv, xxxviii, xlix, 208, 244, 251, 257, 284, 286.
Brown, John, 155, 185, 336, 344.
Buckhurst, Lord, 116, 120, 325.
Buffon, Comte de, 162 f., 174, 231, 269, 338.
Burnet, G., 171, 326, 341.
Burns, R., 364
Bury Abbey, 277.
Butler, S., 55.
Bysshe, E., xxx.

Cædmon's *Hymn*, 59, 85, 318.
Cæsar, J., 197, 206, 218, 350.
Cæsura, 25 ff., 314.
Cambis-Velleron, Marquis de, 128, 328.
Cambridge University, xi, xxiv, xxxvii.
Canterbury Cathedral, 278.
Canzoni, 47.
Carew, Sir G., 159, 184, 337.
Carlisle, The Earl of, 52.
Carracci, The, 274, 361.
Catullus, xlvi.
Cavalcanti, G., 70.
Caxton, W., 41.
Celtic literature, xiii, xviii, xxxv, xlvii. See also Ossian, Welsh literature.
Cephalo and Procri, 139.
Chambers, Sir W., 265, 359.

Champneys, B., xliv.
Charles I. of England, 263.
Chaucer, G., xxxiii, xxxv, xlvii f., 21 f., 24 f., 31 ff., 36, 39-44, 49 ff., 53 f., 63, 90 f., 98, 103, 105, 109 f., 312 ff., 324 f.
Chevy Chase, 55.
Child Maurice, 55, 187 f., 317, 344.
Childe Waters, 54.
China, Gardening in, 265.
Cholmer and Dancing, Tenure of, 73, 84, 320.
Chorus, l, 166 ff., 190, 339 ff.
Christina, Life of St., 70.
Churchill, C., 269 f., 357, 359.
Chute, J., xxiv, xxxviii, xlix, 138, 154, 331.
Cibber, C., xvii, 144 f., 333 f.
Cicero, xxix, 144 f., 158, 333 f., 337, 341, 348.
Cignani, Carlo, 274.
Ciullo del Camo, 64.
Clanvowe, Sir T., 44, 316.
Clarke, Dr., 239.
Clarke, S., xli f., 8, 309 f.
Clive, Mrs., 124, 327.
Clough, A. H., xxiii.
Clymme of the Clough, 34.
Cocchi, G., 216, 246, 261, 349, 357, 359.
Coke, Lady Mary, 242, 355.
Collins, W., 144, 333.
Colman, G., 231, 233 f., 237, 249, 354.
Comedy, 167.
Comines, P. de, 296, 303, 363.

Congreve, xxi.
Cornwallis, Sir W., 294, 363.
Correggio, F., 360 f.
Coventry, F. and H., 165, 339.
Crébillon, C. P. J. de (*fils*), 129, 133, 138, 328, 330 f.
Crébillon, P. J. de (*père*), 158, 337.
Crescimbeni, G. M., 21, 23, 30, 33 f., 38, 40, 43 ff., 47, 56, 61, 64, 68 ff., 82, 312.
Criticism in Gray's time, xxvii ff.

Dacier, A., 6, 309.
Dance of Death, The, 91, 111, 324.
Daniel, A., 30, 46.
Daniel, S., xlix, 46, 118 ff., 325 f.
Dante, xxxv, 23, 30, 44, 48, 61, 63 f., 72.
Dante da Majano, 70.
Dares Phrygius, 90, 323.
Darwin, C., xxv.
Daubenton, L. J. M., 162 f., 338.
Davanzati Bostichi, B., 136, 330.
Death. See *Long Life*.
Death and Life, 67, 320.
Degree, Sir, 52.
Delap, J., 249 f.
Dennis, J., xxviii f.
Destouches, P. N., 124, 327.
Diodorus, 151, 176, 327, 335, 343.
Dionysius of Halicarnassus, 101, 147.

Dodsley, J., *Collection of Poems*, 1, 150 ff., 170 f., 185, 205, 230, 332, 335, 347 f.
Dodsley, R., 216, 349.
Doggerel, xlv f., 26, 33 ff., 55, 313 f.
Domenichino. See Zampieri, D.
Donne, J., 37, 48, 175, 342.
Douglas, G., xxxiii, 38–44, 49.
Drant, T., 38.
Drayton, M., 35, 53, 119, 325.
Druids, 83, 86, 206. See also Mythology, Celtic.
Dryden, J., xx, xxviii, xxxii, xxxv, 28, 40, 94, 98, 109, 134, 154, 219, 330, 340, 363.
Dufresne, A. A. Q., 124, 327.
Dugdale, Sir W., 251, 323.
Dumenil, Mlle., 125, 328.
Durham Cathedral, 16 f., 278.
Durham Field, 54.
Dyer, Sir E., 38.
Dyer, J., 154, 336.

Edda, The, 207.
Eger and Grime, 52.
Eglamour, Sir, 51, 324.
Ekkehard IV., monk of St. Gall, 62, 77 f., 322.
Elegy, Requirements for, 121.
Elisi, 246, 356.
Elizabeth, Queen, 27, 54.
Ely Cathedral, 14, 16 ff., 240 f., 277, 280, 355, 362.
England, Arts in, 259 ff., 265.
Ethelbert, Epitaph on, 78, 322.
Eton College, xi.

Eustace. See Wace.
Evans, Dr., 154.
Evans, E., 233, 354.

Fabyan, R., 26, 41, 314.
Farinelli, C. B., 123, 246, 327.
Federigo, Imperador, 64.
Fénel, Abbé, 206.
Ferguson, A., 283, 362.
Fides, Life of St., 65.
Fielding, H., 132, 330.
Fitz-Osborne, Sir T. See Melmoth, W.
Fleury, A. H. de, 174.
Flodden Field, 54, 67, 320.
Flower and the Leaf, The, 40, 315.
Folcacchio de' Folcacchieri, 47.
Fontaine. See La Fontaine.
Fontenelle, B. le B. de, 268.
Fortune, 149.
Fraigneau, W., 142, 333.
France, Gray traveling in, xii, 122–129; sights in, 272 f.
Francis, St., 40.
Frederick the Great, 173, 230, 260, 288, 342, 353 f., 356, 358 f.
Frere and the Boy, The, 51.
Freret, N., 207, 347.
Froissart, J., 228, 302, 352 f.

Galuppi, B., 139, 332.
Gamelyn, Tale of, 35, 54, 317.
Garrick, D., 139, 154, 165, 208, 216, 231, 234, 331, 339, 347 ff.
Gascoyne, G., 40, 42, 50 f., 54.

Index

Gaussin, Mlle., 124, 327.
Gautier de Châtillon, 53.
Gaveston, P., 119.
Gawayne, Sir, and the Green Knight, 51.
George III. of England, 263.
German literature, Gray's knowledge of, xxxvi.
Gil Blas. See Moore, E.
Gill Morrice. See *Child Maurice*.
Girard de Borneil, 47.
Glasgerion, 55, 317.
Glass, Stained, 226 f.
Glover, R., 139, 332.
Godiva, Lady, 323.
Goldynge, A., 55.
Gosling Scrag, 165, 339.
Gothic design, 247. See also Architecture, Gothic.
Gower, J., xlvii, 41, 49, 90, 98, 315, 323.
Grande Chartreuse, xiii, 129, 272 f., 329.
Grandval, C. F. R. de, 124, 328.
Gray, Dorothy, xi, xvi, xlix.
Gray, Philip, xi, xiv.
Gray, Thomas, *Agrippina*, xiii, 135, 330; *Alcaic Ode*, xiii; *The Alliance of Education and Government*, xiv, xxxiii; *The Bard*, xvi f., 179 ff., 185 ff., 249, 344; *De principiis cogitandi*, xiii; *Elegy Written in a Country Churchyard*, xiii–xv, 249; *Essay on Norman Architecture*, xvi, xlii ff., 13 ff., 310 ff.; *Essay on the Philosophy of Lord Bolingbroke*, xl ff., 7 ff., 309 f.; *History of English Poetry*, proposed, xviii, xlv, xlix; *Hymn to Adversity*, xiii; *Inscription for a Wood*, 140, 332; *Journal in the Lakes*, xix, xxv, xlix–lii, 122 ff., 326 ff.; *A Long Story*, xv; *Metrum*, xliv ff., lii, 21 ff., 312 ff.; minor poems, xxxiii; *Notes on Aristophanes*, xxxix; *Notes on Plato*, xxxix, 3 ff., 309 f.; *Ode for Music*, xx; *Ode on a Distant Prospect of Eton College*, xiii; *Ode on Vicissitude*, xvi; *Ode to Spring*, xiii; *The Progress of Poesy*, xvi f., 249; *Sonnet on the Death of West*, xiii; *Sophonisba ad Massinissam*, 140, 332.
Grecian republics, 183.
Greek, Gray a student of, xii, xiv, xxv, xxxiv, xxxix.
Greek Anthology, The, xiv.
Green, M., 153, 335.
Gresset, J. B. L., 151, 156 f., 335, 337.
Grimald, N., 39, 314 f.
Guido delle Colonne, 64.
Guittone d' Arezzo, 45.
Gustavus Vasa. See Brooke, H.
Guthrie, W., 295, 363.

Halfpenny, W., 248, 357.

372 Index

Hall, Mr., 230 f.
Hall, J., 175, 342.
Hardycanute, 229, 353.
Hardynge, J., 41.
Harvey, G., 38.
Hecuba. See Delap, J.
Hegesias the Cyrenaic, 210, 348.
Heliand, The, 59, 318.
Helinand, 63.
Hénault, C. J. F., 163, 338.
Henry IV. of France, 183 f.
Henryson, R., 316.
Herculaneum, 178 f., 194, 343.
Hereford Cathedral, 18, 278.
Herodotus, 302.
Hervey, A., 154.
Hervey, Lord, 154, 336.
Hickes, G., 22, 58 ff., 63, 313.
Hill, A., 216, 349.
Hoccleve, T., xlvii, 41, 98.
Hodges, 208, 348.
Hogarth, W., xiv.
Holbein, H., 291.
Hollar, W., 248, 357.
Home, J., 187, 205, 347.
Homer, xii, xxxv, 90 f., 93, 122, 324, 327.
Horace, xii, xxix f., xxxiii, xlvi, 309, 344.
Howe, W. T., 257 f., 264, 268, 284, 358.
Hudibras. See Butler, S.
Huet, P., 68, 320.
Hume, D., xviii, 238, 240 f., 289, 295, 301 f., 355.
Huon de Mari, 34.

Hurd, R., 186, 225, 248, 250, 352.
Hutcheson, F., 133, 142, 329 f.

Iphis and Ianthe, 123, 327.
Isocrates, 299, 356.
Isola, A., xx.
Italian republics, 183.
Italy, Arts in, 260 ff., 360 ff.; Gray traveling in, xiii; sights in, 273 f., 360 ff.

Jacopo da Lentino, 64.
Jean li Nevelois, 53.
Jenyns, S., 154, 165, 185, 336, 339, 344.
Jesuits' Letters, The, 265, 359.
Jews, The, 354.
Jodelle, Étienne, 38.
Johnson, S., xxi, xxxv f., 153, 336, 344, 354.
Joinville, J., Sire de, 303, 363.
Jones, I., 263, 359.
Juvenal, 344, 354.

Kant, I., 356.
Keysler, J. G., 197, 346 f.
King, Dr., 154.

Lady Jane Grey. See Rowe, N.
La Fontaine, J. de, 108.
Lambwell, Sir, 52.
Lamentation of Mary Magdalen, 40, 315.
Landor, W. S., 356.
Landscape gardening in England, 265.
Langhorne, J., 270, 359.

Langland, W., xlvi, 65 f., 319 f.
Latini, Brunetto, 44.
Latona, 127, 328.
Launcelot du Lake, 55, 317.
Laurel, 148 f., 334.
Laurence de Premierfait, trans. of Boccaccio, 92, 324.
Laurentius, Epitaph on, 78, 322.
Layamon, 74, 321.
Leo II. (?), Pope, 71.
Leofric, Earl of Mercia, 84, 323.
Leonius, 69, 71, 320.
Leslie, J., 292 f., 363.
Le Sueur, E., 272, 362.
Livy, xii, 130, 141, 329.
Lloyd, R., 231 f., 233 f., 249, 354, 357.
Llywark. See Lomarkk.
Lodge, T., 42, 53.
Lomarkk, 57, 61, 80, 318.
Long, Roger, xxxviii, 215, 349.
Long Life, 76, 321 f.
Longinus, 309, 312.
Lorris, G. de, 63.
Lowth, R., 154, 250, 336, 357.
Lucian, 148.
Lucretius, xii, xlvi.
Ludlam, W. and T., 255, 358.
Lybius Disconius. See *Bel Inconnu, Le*.
Lydgate, J., xxxiii, xxxv, xlvii ff., 22, 24 f., 39–43, 49 f., 87 ff., 119, 315 f., 323 ff.
Lyndesay, Sir D., 41, 43, 49, 119.
Lyttelton, G., Baron, 149 f., 154, 165, 334, 339.

Machiavelli, N., 105, 108, 286.
Macpherson, J., xviii, 232 f., 237 ff., 241, 353.
Maffei, S., 169, 341.
Mahomet Second. See Sauvé, J. B.
Maintenon, Mme. de, 174 f., 342.
Mallet, P. H., 198 f., 206 f., 346.
Mann, Sir H., xxv, 138, 331 f., 354.
Manning, R., of Brunn, 49, 53, 316 f.
Marcello, B., 260, 332.
Margaret, Life of St., 53, 62, 317.
Marino, G., 120, 326.
Marivaux, P. C. de C. de, 133, 330.
Marlborough, Lady, 139, 332.
Marlowe, C., 168.
Martial, 137.
Mason, W., xvii, xxi, xxiv, xxxi, xxxviii, xlv, xlix–lii, 152, 155 f., 160, 164 ff., 185, 188 ff., 197, 200, 205–208, 212–226, 231, 237, 241–245, 248–251, 255, 258, 266 f., 269, 275, 280 ff., 291, 335–340, 344–352, 354 f., 357, 359–362.
Massinissa, 140 f.
Materialism, 208 ff.
Mattei, C., 246, 356.
Mazzola, F., 361.
Melmoth, W., 156, 337.

Menander, 167.
Merlin, 90.
Merlin, Romance of. See *Arthour and Merlin.*
Merveille, Arnauld de, 30.
Metastasio, P. B., 222, 352.
Meun, J. de, 63.
Middleton, C., xxiv, 138, 154, 161 f., 171, 331, 333 f., 337 f., 341 f.
Milton, J., xx, xxvii, xxix, xxxii, xxxv, 28 f., 31, 37, 39, 42, 44 f., 47, 51, 134, 137, 201, 221, 236, 260, 275, 307, 314, 347 f., 352, 355, 363 f.
Mingotti, R. V., 222, 352.
Mirror for Magistrates, The, 40, 54, 117, 119, 325.
Monstrelet, E. de, 302, 363.
Montagu, Lady M. W., 156, 337.
Montesquieu, C. de Secondat, Baron de, xv, 157 f., 162, 174, 283, 337 f.
Montgon, C. A., 163, 338.
Moore, E., 165, 332 f., 339.
Morris, L., 81, 322.
Murphy, A., 208, 348.
Music in England, 262.
Mythology, Celtic, 189, 197 f., 206 f., 215; Germanic, 197 ff., 206; Grecian, 127, 189, 304; Italian, 147, 149.

Neville, T., 186, 267, 344.
Nicholls, N., xviii, xx, l, liii, 299, 302, 348.

Norden, F. L., 159, 337.
Norwich Cathedral, 277.
Nugent, Earl, 150, 154, 334, 336.
Nut-brown Maid, The, 54.

Oaths of Strasburgh, The, 65, 319.
Observation and memory, 211 f.
Occleve. See Hoccleve.
Odo delle Colonne, 64.
Olympiade, L', 139.
Orphan, The. See Otway, T.
Osric, Shrine of King, 19, 311.
Ossian, xviii, 229, 232, 235 ff., 241, 248, 250, 258, 353, 355.
Otfrid, 59, 318 f.
Ottava rima, 43.
Otway, T., 168, 340.
Ovid, xii, 90, 101, 122, 327.
Owl and the Nightingale, The, 49, 75 f., 321.

Paganini, The, 262; Signora, 246, 356 f.
Painting in England, 263; in Italy, 360 ff.
Palgrave, W., 211, 272, 348.
Paris, The Judgment of, 123.
Parmigiano. See Mazzola, F.
Parrott, T. M., xxiii f., xxvi, liii.
Pasquier, É., 38 ff., 53, 70.
Passerat, J., 38.
Patrick's Purgatory, St., 228.
Pelloutier, S., 202, 347.
Percy, T., 67, 320.

Pergolese, G. B., 139, 262, 267, 331 f., 359.
Persepolis, 176.
Peru, Natural History of, 159.
Pescetti, G., 139, 332.
Peter of Blois, 89.
Peterborough Cathedral, 14, 16–20, 278, 312.
Petrarch, 21, 23, 30, 44 ff., 48, 63, 91, 137 f.
Phaer, T., 55, 325.
Phelps, W. L., xxiii f., xxxii, lii.
Philosophe marié, Le. See Destouches, P. N.
Philosophy, Study of, 297 f.
Pierre de St. Cloit, 53.
Pilgrimage of the Soul, 91.
Pilkington, Letitia, 144, 333 f.
Plato, xiv, xxxix, li, 3 ff., 298, 309, 356.
Pliny, 137, 149, 337.
Ploughman's Tale, The, 50, 316.
Plumptre, Dr., xxxviii.
Plutarch, 143, 309, 333.
Pococke, R., 176, 343.
Poems morale, 54, 63, 317, 319.
Poetry, Epic, xxix, xxxi, 222, 364; language of, xxxii, l, 133 ff., 363; lyric, xxvi, xxxi, 199, 221 f.; subjects for, 193 f.
Pope, A., xiv, xxviii, xxx, xlv, 28, 97 f., 109, 132, 134, 153, 328 f., 332, 352, 354, 363 f.
Porson, R., xxxiv.

Porte, P. de la, 184, 344.
Poseidippus, xii.
Pottinger, R., 231, 354.
Poussin, N., 361 f.
Propertius, 137.
Psalter, Poetical, 77.
Pseudo-rhythmus. See Rhyme.
Puttenham, R. or G., xlv, 25 ff., 41, 54, 313 f.

Queensberry, Lady, 139, 332.
Quinault, Mlle., 124, 327.
Quintilian, xxx.

Racine, J., 125, 128, 175, 328, 341.
Radnor, Lord, 176, 342 f.
Rambald de Vachères, 72.
Rapin, N., 38.
Religion. See Mythology.
Remedy of Love, The, 41, 315.
Reni, Guido, 360.
Rhyme, xliv ff., 39 ff., 57 ff., 73 ff., 80 ff., 96 ff., 317 ff., 322 ff.; doggerel, xlv f., 26, 33 ff., 55, 313 f.; leonine, 70 f., 320; octave, 43; riding, 25, 32, 35, 313. See also Rime.
Rhys, D. ap, 50, 82.
Richard III., 135, 287 ff., 294 ff.
Richardson, J., the elder, 357; the younger, 247, 357.
Ridley, G., 154, 336.
Rima alla Provenzale, 70.
Rime couée, 50, 317; riche, 70.
Rinaldo d' Aquino, 70.

Robert Courthose, 19, 311.
Robert of Gloucester, 53 f., 77, 89, 317.
Robin Hood, 54.
Robin of Portingale, 54.
Roger, abp. of York, 251 ff., 358.
Rolle, Mr., 154, 336.
Rolle, R., of Hampole, 90, 324.
Ronsard, P. de, 28, 39.
Ros, Sir R., 42, 316.
Rosa, Salvator, 361 f.
Rousseau, J. J., 235, 245, 248, 259, 270 ff., 354 ff., 358, 360.
Rowe, N., 134, 168 f., 340 f.
Rucellai, G., 39.

Sackville, T. See Buckhurst, Lord.
St. Paul's, London, 16, 18, 311.
Sainte-Beuve, C. A., 352 f.
Salisbury, Dean of, 188.
Sallé, The, 260.
Sauvé, J. B., 123, 327.
Scalds, 86, 197.
Scaliger, J. C., xxxvi, 61, 70, 137, 331.
Scandinavian studies, xviii, xxxv.
Scogan, H., 42.
Scottish Field. See *Flodden Field*.
Sculpture in England, 263.
Seneca, L. A., 120, 326.
Sepulchre, St., York, 251 ff., 357 f.

Sequentiæ, 82.
Sestine, 46.
Seward, T., 154, 336.
Shaftesbury, A. A. Cooper, 3d Earl of, xxviii, 208 ff.
Shakespeare, W., xxix, xxxii, xxxv f., 134 f., 164, 166 ff., 175, 244, 324, 330, 340, 352, 354, 364.
Shaw, T., 177, 343.
Shenstone, W., 153, 205, 208, 336, 348.
Sidney, Sir P., 38.
Simonides, 101, 325.
Smart, C., 171, 216, 341.
Smith, A., xviii, 238, 240.
Smollett, T., 165.
Socrates, 4 ff., 142, (Sophronisci filius) 356.
Sonnet, 45.
Speed, Miss H., xv, xviii.
Speed, J., 292, 295 f., 363.
Spence, J., 145 ff., 334.
Spenser, E., 27, 31, 35–43, 45–48, 51 ff., 118, 120, 303, 314, 326.
Staal de Launay, Baroness de, 184, 344.
Statius, xii.
Steele, Sir R., xxviii, xxx.
Sterne, L., 230, 234, 354.
Stonehewer, R., xxiv, xxxviii, 178, 208, 232, 235, 248.
Stowe, J., 74, 295.
Strabo, xiv.
Strawberry Hill, 176, 227.
Stricher, The, 59.
Strode, R., 90, 324.

Strophe, 177 f., 343.
Stukeley, W., 208, 348.
Sully, Duke of, 183 f., 344.
Surrey, H. Howard, Earl of, 27, 29 ff., 40 ff., 44 ff., 50–54.
Swift, Dr., 206, 347.
Swift, J., xxix.

Tacitus, 131, 135 f., 158, 196 f., 206 f., 235, 283, 329.
Taliesin, 57, 61, 80, 318.
Tasso, T., xx, 39, 43.
Taylor, Jeremy, 247.
Temple, Sir W., 57.
Temple, W. J., xx ff.
Tennyson, A., Lord, xv.
Terence, 167.
Terza rima, 44.
Theocritus, 137.
Theodulus, 57.
Theology, 171. See also Materialism.
Theophrastus, 149.
Thibaut, King of Navarre, 43, 63.
Thomson, J., 152, 236, 335, 364.
Thrale, Mrs., 364.
Thucydides, 136 f., 143, 331, 333.
Tibullus, xlvi.
Tickell, T., 153, 335.
Tolomei, C., 38.
Torcy, Marquis de, 206, 347.
Tragedy, Greek, xxix, 168, 340 f. See also Chorus.
Triamore, Sir, 51.

Trissino, 39.
Tristram, 228, 353.
Tully. See Cicero.
Turpin, Abp., 228, 353.

Ubaldini, U., 64, 72, 320.
Ubi sunt? etc., 115, 325.
Urry, J., 21, 312.

Vane, Lady, 165, 339.
Varro, 138, 331.
Venus de' Medici, 213.
Versailles, xxxi, 125 ff., 328.
Verse, Alexandrine, 27 f., 47 f., 53 ff., 317; blank, 333, 348; heroic, 28, 30, 94; leonine, 70 f.; ottava rima, 43; sestine, 46; sonnet, 45; strophe, 177 f., 343; terza rima, 44. See also Cæsura, Rhyme.
Versi sciolti, 39.
Vida, xxx.
Viginelle, B., 39.
Villehardouin, G. de, 303, 363.
Villeneuve, H. de, 34.
Virgil, xii, xlvi, 90 f., 148 f., 263, 344.
Voltaire, xxi, xxxvi, 124, 173 f., 179, 230, 269 f., 342 ff., 349, 354, 358, 360.

Wace, 60, 319.
Walafrid Strabo, 62.
Waller, E., 96.
Walpole, H., xi–xiv, xxiii, xxv, xxxvi, xlix, 144, 146, 149 f., 154 f., 160, 164 f., 170,

227, 229, 239, 271, 287 ff., 294 ff., 331 f., 334, 336 f., 342 f., 345, 353 f., 359, 363.
Warburton, W., 198, 225, 332, 352, 357.
Warton, J., 142, 144, 333, 354.
Warton, T., xlv, 35, 333 f.
Waterland, D., 145, 171, 334.
Welsh literature, Gray studying, xviii; W. poetry, 233.
West, G., 150, 335.
West, R., xi f., xxiii, xxxii, xlix f., 122, 125, 129, 131 f., 136 f., 139, 151, 156, 326, 329, 331 f., 335.
Wharton, T., xiv, xix, xxiv, xxxviii, xlix, 141, 143 f., 150 f., 156 ff., 160 f., 173 ff., 177, 179, 183 f., 196, 204, 226, 228, 230, 232, 247 f., 259, 269, 352.
Whitehead, W., 154, 216, 226, 249, 336, 352, 357.
Wilks, R., 124, 328.
Wistace. See Wace.
Wollaston, W., xli f., 10 f., 310.
Wordsworth, W., xix.
Wormius, O., 58, 318.
Wren, Sir C., 13, 177, 276, 310 f.
Wyatt, Sir T., the elder, 27, 30, 40 ff., 44–47, 50 ff., 54.

Xenophon, 143, 333.

York Minster, 240 f., 279, 355; St. Sepulchre, 251 ff., 357 f.

Zampieri, D., 149, 273, 360 ff.

Advertisement

The Belles-Lettres Series

The following volumes are now ready:

SECTION I

The Gospel of Saint Matthew in West-Saxon. Edited from the manuscripts by Professor J. W. Bright. 40 cents.

The Gospel of Saint John in West-Saxon. Edited from the manuscripts by Professor J. W. Bright. With notes and glossary. 60 cents.

Judith. With notes and glossary by Professor A. S. Cook. 40 cents.

The Battle of Maldon and short poems from the Saxon Chronicle. With notes and glossary by Professor W. J. Sedgefield. 40 cents.

Juliana. With notes and glossary by Professor W. Strunk, Jr. 40 cents.

SECTION III

Chapman's Bussy D'Ambois (both parts). Edited by Professor F. S. Boas. 60 cents.

Jonson's Eastward Hoe and **The Alchemist.** Edited by Professor F. E. Schelling. 60 cents.

Webster's White Devil and **Duchess of Malfy.** Edited by Professor M. W. Sampson. 60 cents.

Goldsmith's Good-Natur'd Man and **She Stoops to Conquer.** Edited by Austin Dobson. 60 cents.

Browning's A Blot in the 'Scutcheon, Colombe's Birthday, A Soul's Tragedy, and **In a Balcony.** Edited by Professor Arlo Bates. 60 cents.

Robertson's Society and **Caste.** Edited by T. E. Pemberton. 60 cents.

SECTION VI

Select Poems of Coleridge. Edited by A. J. George. 60 cents.

Select Poems of Swinburne. Edited by W. M. Payne. *Nearly ready.*

---

200 volumes in preparation

D. C. HEATH & CO., PUBLISHERS

Boston   New York   Chicago   London